American English

Personal Best

Student's Book

A2
Elementary

Series Editor
Jim Scrivener

Author
Louis Rogers

CONTENTS

		LANGUAGE			SKILLS	
		GRAMMAR	PRONUNCIATION	VOCABULARY		
1 **You and me**		■ the verb *be* ■ possessive adjectives ■ *'s* for possession	■ contractions of *be* ■ sentence stress	■ countries and nationalities ■ numbers 1 – 1,000 ■ personal objects	**READING** ■ a blog about a summer vacation ■ approaching a text ■ simple statements with *be*	**SPEAKING** ■ asking for and giving personal information ■ asking for clarification **PERSONAL BEST** ■ a conversation in Lost and Found
1A Meeting and greeting	p4					
1B My summer blog	p6					
1C Is that a "man bag"?	p8					
1D Where's my wallet?	p10					
2 **Work and play**		■ simple present: affirmative and negative ■ simple present: questions	■ *-s* and *-es* endings ■ auxiliary verbs *do/does* in questions	■ jobs and job verbs ■ activities (1)	**LISTENING** ■ a video looking at work and free-time activities ■ listening for names, places, days, and times ■ introduction to the sound /ə/	**WRITING** ■ opening and closing an informal e-mail ■ connectors: *and, but,* and *or* **PERSONAL BEST** ■ an e-mail to a friend
2A What I do	p12					
2B Weekdays, weekends	p14					
2C Find a roommate	p16					
2D A new city	p18					
1 and **2** REVIEW and PRACTICE	p20					
3 **People in my life**		■ frequency adverbs and expressions ■ *love, like, hate, enjoy, don't mind* + noun/-*ing* form	■ sentence stress ■ *-ing* forms	■ family ■ activities (2)	**READING** ■ a website about local clubs you can join ■ scanning a text ■ *also* and *too*	**SPEAKING** ■ making plans ■ accepting or declining an invitation **PERSONAL BEST** ■ making plans with a friend to do an activity
3A Time together	p22					
3B A new group	p24					
3C Opposites attract	p26					
3D A night out	p28					
4 **Home and away**		■ prepositions of time ■ present continuous	■ sentence stress ■ linking consonants and vowels	■ daily routine verbs ■ the weather and the seasons	**LISTENING** ■ a video about the weather in different parts of the world ■ listening for the main idea ■ sentence stress	**WRITING** ■ describing a photo ■ using personal pronouns **PERSONAL BEST** ■ an e-mail describing a vacation
4A 24 hours in the dark	p30					
4B Weather around the world	p32					
4C A long weekend	p34					
4D A vacation with friends	p36					
3 and **4** REVIEW and PRACTICE	p38					
5 **What are you wearing?**		■ simple present and present continuous ■ *can* and *can't*	■ dates ■ *can* and *can't*	■ clothes ■ ordinal numbers ■ hobbies	**READING** ■ an article about uniforms and if we like wearing them ■ identifying facts and opinions ■ adjectives	**SPEAKING** ■ shopping for clothes ■ offering help **PERSONAL BEST** ■ a conversation in a clothing store
5A Party time	p40					
5B Don't tell me what to wear	p42					
5C Do the things you love	p44					
5D Can I try it on?	p46					
6 **Homes and cities**		■ *there is/there are, some/any* ■ prepositions of place ■ modifiers	■ *there's/there are* ■ sentence stress	■ rooms and furniture ■ common adjectives ■ places in a city	**LISTENING** ■ a video about unusual homes ■ identifying key points ■ contractions	**WRITING** ■ topic sentences ■ describing places **PERSONAL BEST** ■ a description of your town or city
6A A small space	p48					
6B Amazing homes	p50					
6C The Big Apple	p52					
6D Beautiful places	p54					
5 and **6** REVIEW and PRACTICE	p56					

Language App, unit-by-unit grammar and vocabulary games

CONTENTS

		LANGUAGE			SKILLS	
		GRAMMAR	PRONUNCIATION	VOCABULARY		

7 Food and drink

7A	Food to your door	p58
7B	Stopping for lunch	p60
7C	Are you hungry?	p62
7D	Out for dinner	p64

- countable and uncountable nouns + *some/any*
- quantifiers: *(how) much/many*, *a lot of*, *a few*, *a little*

- *some/any*
- weak form of *of*

- food and drink
- containers and portions

READING
- an article about what people eat for lunch around the world
- skimming a text
- pronouns and possessive adjectives

SPEAKING
- in a restaurant
- asking politely for something

PERSONAL BEST
- ordering food in a restaurant

8 In the past

8A	Technology through the ages	p66
8B	Life stories	p68
8C	Life in the 1980s	p70
8D	What happened to you?	p72

- past of *be*, *there was/there were*
- simple past: irregular verbs
- simple past: regular verbs and past time expressions

- *was* and *were*
- *-ed* endings

- inventions
- life stages
- irregular verbs

LISTENING
- a video about our favorite inventions and inspirations
- listening for numbers, dates, and prices
- phrases

WRITING
- planning and making notes
- sequencers

PERSONAL BEST
- a story about an experience you had

7 and 8 — REVIEW and PRACTICE p74

9 Education, education!

9A	School days	p76
9B	Lifelong learning	p78
9C	Change your life	p80
9D	What's the problem?	p82

- simple past: questions
- verb patterns: verb + *to* infinitive

- intonation in questions
- *'d like* and *like*

- school subjects and education
- resolutions

READING
- an article about different education experiences
- understanding words that you don't know
- *because* and *so*

SPEAKING
- making suggestions
- sounding sympathetic

PERSONAL BEST
- describing and responding to problems

10 People

10A	First dates	p84
10B	You look so different!	p86
10C	The yearbook	p88
10D	Someone that I admire	p90

- comparative adjectives
- superlative adjectives

- *-er* endings
- superlative adjectives

- adjectives to describe places
- describing appearance
- personality adjectives

LISTENING
- a video about changing our appearance
- listening for detailed information (1)
- weak forms

WRITING
- writing a description of a person
- clauses with *when*

PERSONAL BEST
- a description of someone you admire

9 and 10 — REVIEW and PRACTICE p92

11 On the move

11A	Getting to work	p94
11B	Looking for Elizabeth Gallagher	p96
11C	Road trip	p98
11D	In a hotel	p100

- *have to/don't have to*
- *be going to*, future time expressions

- *have to/has to*
- sentence stress

- travel and transportation
- vacation activities

READING
- an article about the unusual way Jordan Axani found a travel partner
- reading for detail
- adverbs of probability

SPEAKING
- arriving at a hotel
- checking information

PERSONAL BEST
- a conversation at a hotel reception

12 Enjoy yourself!

12A	Going out	p102
12B	The book was better!	p104
12C	A famous voice	p106
12D	Would you like to come?	p108

- present perfect with *ever* and *never*
- present perfect and simple past

- sentence stress
- vowels

- entertainment
- opinion adjectives

LISTENING
- a video about books that have become movies
- listening for detailed information (2)
- linking consonants and vowels

WRITING
- writing and replying to an invitation
- articles: *a/an*, *the*, or no article

PERSONAL BEST
- an invitation to a party and a reply

11 and 12 — REVIEW and PRACTICE p110

Grammar practice p112   Vocabulary practice p136   Communication practice p158   Irregular verbs p176

 Language App, unit-by-unit grammar and vocabulary games

UNIT 1

You and me

LANGUAGE — the verb *be* ■ countries and nationalities ■ numbers 1–1,000

1A Meeting and greeting

1 What country are you from? Name three more countries near your country.

2 A Match the countries in the box with maps 1–6.

Colombia   Germany   Turkey   the U.S.   Brazil   Japan

 1 _____
 2 _____
 3 _____
 4 _____
 5 _____
 6 _____

B ▶ 1.1 Listen. Write the letter of each speaker next to the correct map.

3 ▶ 1.1 Listen again. Write the nationality of each country in exercise 2.

the U.S. – American

Go to Vocabulary practice: countries and nationalities, page 136

4 A In pairs, look at the pictures. Where do you think the people are from?

B Read the conversations in exercise 5 and match them with pictures a–c.

a _____

b _____

c _____

5 ▶ 1.3 Listen and complete the conversations.

1
Emilia Hello. My name's Emilia and this is Sara.
Sabine Hi, ¹_____ Sabine. Nice to meet you.
Emilia You, too. Where ²_____ from?
Sabine I'm from Germany. And you?
Emilia ³_____ from Colombia, from Bogotá.
Sara I'm not! I'm from Cali.

2
Sam Oscar, this is Meiko. ⁴_____ from Japan. And Meiko, this is Oscar. ⁵_____ from Brazil.
Oscar Nice to meet you, Meiko.
Meiko You, too, Oscar.
Oscar How do you spell your name?
Meiko ⁶_____ M-E-I-K-O.

3
Jo Hi, Ali. How are you?
Ali Good, thanks. And you?
Jo I'm fine. Where are Jean and Paola?
Ali They're not here. ⁷_____ at the conference center.
Jo What about Andreas?
Ali ⁸_____ here. His train's late.

4

the verb *be* ■ countries and nationalities ■ numbers 1–1,000   **LANGUAGE**   **1A**

6 Choose the correct forms of *be*. Use the conversations in exercise 5 to help you. Then read the Grammar box.

'm not   's   're not   'm   're   's not

1 I am = _____
2 You / We / They are = _____
3 He / She is = _____

4 I am not = _____
5 You / We / They are not = _____
6 He / She is not = _____

📖 **Grammar**   the verb *be*

Affirmative:
I**'m** from Italy.   She**'s** Japanese.   We**'re** German.

Negative:
I**'m not** from Spain.   He**'s not**/He **isn't** here.   They**'re not**/They **aren't** American.

Questions and short answers:
Are you from Spain? Yes, I **am**. No, I**'m not**. **Is** Andreas here? Yes, he **is**. No, he**'s not**/ he **isn't**.

Go to Grammar practice: the verb *be*, page 112

7 A ▶1.5 **Pronunciation:** contractions of *be* Listen and repeat the contractions.

I'm   you're   he's   she's   it's   we're   they're

B ▶1.6 Say the sentences. Listen, check, and repeat.

1 I'm American and they're Brazilian.
2 He's Irish.
3 You're Peruvian and we're Turkish.
4 She's from Russia.

8 Complete the sentences with the correct form of *be*. Use contractions if possible.

1 Pedro _____ Brazilian. He _____ from Recife.
2 My parents _____ from Poland.
3 Dublin _____ in the UK. It _____ in the Republic of Ireland.
4 "_____ your name Carlos?" "No, it _____ Carlo."
5 "_____ you from Mexico?" "No, I _____. I _____ from Peru."

9 In pairs, look at the pictures. What countries are the people from? What nationality are they?

A *This is …   He's American.*   **B** *No, he's not. He's Canadian!*

a   b   c   d   e

Go to Communication practice: Student A page 158, Student B page 167

10 Write the words or numbers.

1 ____   twenty-five
2 36   _____
3 ____   a hundred and forty-three
4 364   _____
5 ____   seventy-seven

6 634   _____
7 ____   two hundred and eight
8 908   _____
9 ____   a thousand
10 894   _____

Go to Vocabulary practice: numbers 1–1,000, page 136

11 In pairs, introduce yourselves to each other. Say your age if you want to.

Hello. My name's …   You, too.   I'm …   I'm … years old.
Nice to meet you.   Where are you from?   How old are you?

Imagine that you meet a famous person. Write the conversation. Introduce yourself and ask him/her about himself/herself.

5

1 SKILLS READING approaching a text ■ simple statements with *be*

1B My summer blog

1 Do you like sports? What's your national sport? What sports do people usually do in the summer?

> **Skill** approaching a text
>
> **Before you read a text, predict as much information as you can.**
> - Read the title of the text. Can you guess what it means?
> - Are there any pictures? What people, places, and things can you see?
> - Are there any headings for the different sections? What are the sections about?

2 Read the Skill box. In pairs, look at the title, headings, and pictures in the text. Answer the questions.
   1 What type of text is it?
   2 Who is the text about?
   3 Where is she right now?
   4 What is she doing there?

3 Read the text. Choose a title for each post.
   1 Week 1   a Time to go home
   2 Week 2   b Learning English
   3 Week 3   c My host family
   4 Week 4   d Enjoying the tournament

4 Read the text again and answer the questions.
   1 What is María's nationality?
   2 Where are Helen and Alex from?
   3 What are María's favorite places in London?
   4 Who is Hitoshi?
   5 Where is María's English teacher from?
   6 Where are the teams in the tournament from?
   7 When are the games?

5 Find words in the text to match to the pictures.

1 h_____ f_____   2 c_____   3 t_____

4 g_____   5 c_____

> **Text builder** simple statements with *be*
>
> Simple statements with *be* have this pattern: **subject** + **verb** + **complement** :
> This is my blog.
> The teams are from Spain, Brazil, Portugal, Poland, Russia, England, Mexico, and Japan.

6 Read the Text builder and look at the Week 1 post in the text again. Draw a box around the subjects, circle the forms of *be*, and underline the complements.

7 In pairs, think of a sport you love. Tell your partner about it.
   I love ...   It's really ...

approaching a text ■ simple statements with be   READING   SKILLS   1B

María Gómez
My month in London

Hello! I'm María Gómez. I'm 21 years old, and I'm from Cádiz in Spain. I'm a student, and I love soccer! Right now, I'm in the U.K. I'm at a language school to learn English, but I'm also here for an international soccer tournament for students! This is my blog about my month in London.

Week 1

This is my host family. They're very nice. Helen's English and Alex is Scottish, and their children are named Jenny and Jacob. Jenny's fourteen and Jacob's twelve. Sometimes I play soccer in the park with Jenny and Jacob, and sometimes we all go for a walk in the center of London. It's a really interesting city. My favorite places are Big Ben, Buckingham Palace, and Tower Bridge.

Week 2

This is my language school. There are lots of students from different countries, and we all speak English together. My classmates are really friendly. I always sit with Hitoshi. He's Japanese. Our English lessons are fun! Our teacher's name is Kerry, and she's from Australia.

Week 3

I'm at the soccer tournament now. The teams are from Spain, Brazil, Portugal, Poland, Russia, England, Scotland, and Japan. We train every morning. I think we're a good team because we're very fast. The games are in the evening. They're really exciting!

Week 4

We're the champions! 😊 I'm happy, but I'm also sad because it's the end of my month here. Goodbye, London! Until next time!

Personal Best How many examples of the verb *be* can you find in the text?

7

1 LANGUAGE — possessive adjectives • 's for possession • personal objects

1C Is that a "man bag"?

1 In pairs, look at the pictures in the text below. Can you name the objects?

2 A Read the text. Do you think the objects in the list are from a handbag, a "man bag", or both?

   B 🔊 1.8 Listen to a radio program. Check (✓) the objects that you hear.

His bag or her bag?

Where do you put your things when you go out? If you're a woman, your things are probably in your handbag, but what about men? Today, 50% of men also have a bag – a "man bag." Is a "man bag" the same as a handbag? And what do men and women carry in their bags?

	HANDBAG	MAN BAG
keys	☐	☐
chewing gum	☐	☐
hairbrush	☐	☐
gloves	☐	☐
candy	☐	☐
tablet	☐	☐
umbrella	☐	☐
phone	☐	☐
wallet	☐	☐
change purse	☐	☐

Go to Vocabulary practice: personal objects, page 137

3 🔊 1.11 Listen to the start of the radio program again and choose the correct options.

> **Host** Zoe's here with ¹ *she / her* handbag, and Harry's here with ² *he / his* "man bag." What's in ³ *their / they* bags? Zoe, you first. What's in ⁴ *you / your* handbag?
> **Zoe** Let's take a look. Here are ⁵ *I / my* keys and ⁶ *my / me* hairbrush.

4 A Look at exercise 3 again. Then read the Grammar box. Which possessive adjective is for things that belong to:

1 a man? _____   2 a woman? _____   3 more than one person? _____

B Are possessive adjectives the same or different with singular and plural nouns?

📖 Grammar — possessive adjectives

I	my	*my* bag/bags
you	your	*your* umbrella/umbrellas
he	his	*his* pen/pens
she	her	*her* glove/gloves
it	its	*its* photo/photos
we	our	*our* key/keys
they	their	*their* tablet/tablets

Go to Grammar practice: possessive adjectives, page 113

8

possessive adjectives ■ 's for possession ■ personal objects   LANGUAGE 1C

5 A ▶ 1.13 **Pronunciation:** sentence stress   Listen and repeat the sentences. <u>Underline</u> the stressed words in each sentence.

1 What's in your handbag?
2 Here are my keys.
3 His sunglasses are on the table.
4 What's their phone number?

B ▶ 1.14   Practice saying the sentences. Listen, check, and repeat.

1 Your tablet's new.
2 Where's my umbrella?
3 Here are our photos.
4 Her gloves are blue.

6 Complete the sentences with a subject pronoun or a possessive adjective.

1 My friends are Brazilian. _____'re from Rio de Janeiro.
2 A Where are _____ sunglasses?
    B On your head!
3 _____'m Spanish. Here's _____ identity card.
4 _____ name's Ahmed. He's 32 years old.
5 They're from Italy. _____ names are Francesca and Marco.
6 This is George. _____'s from San Diego.
7 We're in the baggage area at the airport, but are _____ bags here?

7 Look at the sentences. Complete the rules about possession. Then read the Grammar box.

1 It's Carl's bag.
2 It's my sister's phone.
3 They're my friends' umbrellas.

After a singular name (e.g., *Mary*), we add ____.
After a singular noun (e.g., *girl*), we add ____.
After a regular plural noun (e.g., *boys*), we add ____.

📖 Grammar   's for possession

For a singular noun or name:
Mary**'s** glasses are in her bag.

For a plural noun:
My paren**ts'** car is red.

Irregular plural nouns:
The children**'s** toys are everywhere!

Go to Grammar practice: 's for possession, page 113

8 ▶ 1.15   Look at the picture and listen to John and Mary. Match the possessions with the people in the box.

John   Mary   John's friends   Mary's sister   Carl

9 Choose the correct options to complete the sentences.

1 It's *Lucy's bag / Lucy bag*.
2 They're *Harry's / Harrys'* glasses.
3 I'm an English teacher. Here are all my *student's / students'* books.
4 It's my *friends' / friend's* phone. Look, this is his photo.
5 Here are the *mens' / men's* umbrellas.

Go to Communication practice:
Student A page 158, Student B page 167

10 A In groups of three to five, follow the instructions.

Student A: Close your eyes.
Other students: Put one of your possessions on the table.
Student A: Open your eyes. Guess whose things are on the table.

Is it Manuel's watch?   *Are they Maria's glasses?*

B Repeat the activity. Take turns being Student A.

Personal Best   Think of a person that you know well. Imagine what he/she has in his/her "man bag" or handbag. Say the objects.

SKILLS **SPEAKING** asking for and giving personal information ■ asking for clarification

1D Where's my wallet?

1 Answer the questions below.
1 Look at the picture of a lost property office (Lost and Found) in London. What can you see?
2 What other things can you find in a Lost and Found?
3 What things do you often lose?
4 What buildings usually have a Lost and Found?

2 A ▶ 1.16 Watch or listen to the first part of a webshow called *Learning Curve*. What object is missing?

B ▶ 1.16 Watch or listen again. Check (✔) the things that are in Kate's backpack.

keys ☐	sunglasses ☐	cookies ☐
wallet ☐	mirror ☐	tissues ☐
stamps ☐	tablet ☐	chewing gum ☐

3 ▶ 1.17 Watch or listen to the second part of the show. Are the sentences true (T) or false (F)?
1 The assistant in the Lost and Found is named Harry. ___
2 Kate's personal information is already in the computer. ___
3 Kate loves James Bond. ___
4 Kate's phone is in the assistant's box. ___
5 Simon's phone is different from Kate's. ___

4 A In pairs, complete the questions in the conversation with the words in the box.

| address   mobile number   e-mail address   postcode   number   first name   spell |

Assistant Here's the lost property form. Time to fill it out. I'm ready. What's your ¹_____?
Kate It's Kate.
Assistant K-A-T-E. What's your surname?
Kate Oh ... it's McRea.
Assistant How do you ²_____ that, please?
Kate M-C-R-E-A.
Assistant Thanks. And what's your ³_____?
Kate It's missing.
Assistant Could you say that again, please?
Kate My cell phone is lost.

Assistant OK. Lost mobile. What's your ⁴_____, please?
Kate It's 02079 46007.
Simon Isn't that your home phone number?
Kate Yes, he can call me at home!
Assistant Could you say that again, please?
Kate Yes, it's 02079 46007.
Assistant And what's your ⁵_____, please?
Kate 222 Baker Street, Marylebone, London.
Assistant OK. What's your ⁶_____?
Kate NW1 5RT.
Assistant Do you have an ⁷_____?
Kate Yes, it's k.mcrea_007@gmail.com.

B ▶ 1.17 Watch or listen again to check.

asking for and giving personal information ■ asking for clarification **SPEAKING** **SKILLS** **1D**

Conversation builder — asking for and giving personal information

Asking for information:
What's your first name/last name (surname)/address/cell-phone number/home phone number/postal code?
Do you have an e-mail address?
How do you spell that, please?

Saying your phone number:
02079 46007 – oh two oh seven nine four six oh oh seven

Saying your email address:
k.mcrea_007@gmail.com – k dot mcrea underscore oh oh seven at g mail dot com

5 Read the Conversation builder. Answer the questions in pairs.
1 How do you say "0" and "44" in a phone number?
2 How do you say "@," "_," and ".com" in an e-mail address?

6 ▶ 1.17 Read the sentences. Then watch or listen again. Choose the correct options to complete the sentences.
1 The assistant asks Kate to spell her *first name* / *last name* / *address*.
2 He asks her to say her *cell-phone number* / *e-mail address* / *home phone number* again.

Skill — asking for clarification

When you don't understand something, ask the speaker for help:
- Ask him/her to say the sentence again or to spell the word.
- Use **Sorry, could you ...** and **please** to be polite:
  Sorry, could you say that again, please? How do you spell that, please?
- Use polite intonation: Sorry, could you say that again, please?

7 ▶ 1.18 Read the Skill box. Listen and repeat the questions when you hear the beeps. Copy the intonation.

8 ▶ 1.19 Listen to three conversations in a school Lost and Found. For what information does the assistant ask for clarification?

Conversation 1   address / postal code / e-mail address
Conversation 2   home phone number / cell-phone number / postal code
Conversation 3   first name / last name / first name and last name

Go to Communication practice: Student A page 158, Student B page 167

9 A **PREPARE** You lose an important personal object. Look at the Conversation builder again. Think about your answers to the questions.

B **PRACTICE** You are at the Lost and Found. In pairs, take turns asking and answering questions and complete the form for your partner. Ask for clarification to check the information is correct.

First name	E-mail address
Last name	Cell-phone number
Address	Home phone number
Postal code	

C **PERSONAL BEST** Exchange with your partner. Read his/her work and correct any mistakes. How could you improve it?

Personal Best — Write the e-mail addresses and phone numbers of five people you know. Practice saying them in English.

UNIT 2

Work and play

LANGUAGE simple present: affirmative and negative ■ jobs and job verbs

2A What I do

1 Look at the pictures. What jobs can you see?

2 A Read the text. Check your answers to exercise 1.

   B Label the pictures with the names of the people. What other jobs are mentioned in the text?

a   b   c   d

My other job

Lots of people around the world have two jobs. Sometimes it's because they need the money, and sometimes they want to learn something new. Let's meet some people who each have two jobs.

1 I'm Luisa. I'm from Brazil, but I live in Lisbon with my parents and my sister. I work as a receptionist for an IT company at an office downtown, but I also help my parents at our family restaurant in the evening and on the weekend. It's a traditional Brazilian restaurant. My sister helps, too. My parents cook the food, and we serve it! I like my two jobs, but I don't have a lot of free time.

2 Michal lives in Prague. He's a mechanic, and he works at a garage. He likes his job because he loves cars, but he doesn't work there on the weekend. On Saturdays, he has a second job – he's a tour guide for tourists. He knows a lot about his city.

3 Zoe's 26 years old and lives in Toronto in Canada. She's a receptionist for a TV company. She works from 9 a.m. to 5 p.m. during the week. Zoe has another job three evenings a week – she teaches Zumba at a gym. She doesn't work on the weekend.

4 Isaac's from Jamaica, but he lives in New York. He's a taxi driver, and he works every day. Isaac likes his job, and he loves New York. He often goes back to Jamaica for his other job. He doesn't drive a taxi in Jamaica – he's a singer, and he sings at festivals!

3 Read the text again. Write the names of the people.
   1 They work with cars. _____, _____
   2 He/She works with food. _____
   3 They have office jobs. _____, _____
   4 They come from one country and work in another country. _____, _____
   5 They work on the weekend. _____, _____, _____

4 Complete the sentences with verbs from the text.
   1 I _____ in Lisbon.
   2 My sister _____, too.
   3 My parents _____ the food.
   4 I _____ a lot of free time.
   5 She _____ Zumba at a gym.
   6 He _____ a taxi in Jamaica.

Go to Vocabulary practice: jobs and job verbs, page 138

12

simple present: affirmative and negative ■ jobs and job verbs | LANGUAGE | **2A**

5 Complete the rules for the simple present. Use the text to help you. Then read the Grammar box.

1 For the *he/she/it* form, we add _____ or _____ to the base form of the verb.

2 For the negative form, we use _____ and _____.

📖 **Grammar** **simple present: affirmative and negative**

Affirmative:

I **work** for an IT company.   He **loves** New York.   She **teaches** Zumba.   My parents **cook** the food.

Negative:

I **don't have** a lot of free time.   He **doesn't drive** a taxi.

Go to Grammar practice: simple present: affirmative and negative, page 114

6 Complete the text with the correct form of the verbs in parentheses in the simple present.

My parents ¹_____ (have) a hotel in a small town in Spain. I ²_____ (go) to college every day, but I ³_____ (help) my parents in the evening. My dad ⁴_____ (cook) the food, but he ⁵_____ (not serve) it – that's my job. I have two sisters, but they ⁶_____ (not work) in the restaurant. One sister ⁷_____ (live) in Germany, and my other sister ⁸_____ (work) in a hospital.

7 **A** ▶2.4 **Pronunciation:** *-s* and *-es* endings Listen and repeat the sounds and verbs in the chart.

/s/	/z/	/ɪz/
likes	goes	finishes

B ▶2.5 Add the verbs to the chart. Listen and check.

teaches lives helps works drives watches makes sells

8 ▶2.6 In pairs, say the sentences. Listen, check, and repeat.

1 He teaches English.

2 He lives in New York.

3 She helps her parents.

4 He works from 2 p.m. to 10 p.m. every day.

5 He drives a taxi.

6 She watches TV after work.

7 She makes clothes in a factory.

8 She sells books in a store.

9 **A** Think of three people you know. Write about their jobs, but don't say what the jobs are.

My friend Ana works in the city. She doesn't work on the weekend. She likes her job because she works with people. She cuts people's hair.

B In pairs, tell each other about your people. Guess the jobs.

A *Is Ana a hairdresser?*   **B** *Yes, she is. Your turn.*

Go to Communication practice: Student A page 159, Student B page 168

10 **A** Write about your job. Use the prompts to help you.

I'm a …   I work in/for a …   In my job, I …   I work during the week/on the weekend.   I work/don't work in the evening.   I like/don't like my job because …

B Work in groups of five or six. Exchange your descriptions with another student. Take turns talking about the person whose description you have. The other students guess who it is.

A *This person's a teacher. She works in a language school. She teaches Spanish. She likes her job. She works in the evening, but she doesn't work on the weekend.*

B *I think Carla's a teacher. Carla, is it you?*

Personal Best Write sentences about a dream job.

13

2 **SKILLS** **LISTENING** listening for names, places, days, and times ■ activities (1)

2B Weekdays, weekends

1 Match the activities in the box with pictures a–h.

> play tennis   read a book   go to the movies   watch TV
> go for a walk   listen to music   study   meet friends

2 In pairs, talk about the activities in exercise 1. What activities do you do?

I listen to music in the car. I don't go to the movies.

Go to Vocabulary practice: activities (1), page 139

3 ▶ 2.8 Watch or listen to the first part of *Learning Curve*. What do they talk about? Check (✓) the two correct answers.

a free-time activities ☐
b people who enjoy their jobs ☐
c people who don't have any free time ☐

Skill listening for names, places, days, and times

Names, places, days, and times are important pieces of information when you listen.
- Important words like names, places, days, and times are usually stressed. Listen for stressed words.
- We often use prepositions with places, days, and times: *in France*, *on Monday*, *at 6:30*, etc. Listen for the prepositions *in*, *on*, and *at*.
- Remember to use capital letters for names, places, and days when you write them down.

4 **A** ▶ 2.8 Read the Skill box. Watch or listen again. Complete the chart with words from the box.

> lawyer   Argentinian   dance teacher   Puerto Rican
> Marcus   English   Maggie   Pablo   tennis coach

Name	Nationality	Job

B In pairs, talk about people you know. Do they love their jobs? Why?/Why not?

My friend Justyna's Polish. She's a receptionist. She likes her job, but she doesn't love it.

listening for names, places, days, and times ■ activities (1)   LISTENING   SKILLS   2B

5 ▶ 2.9 Watch or listen to the second part of the show. Complete the sentences with the names and cities in the box.

Toronto   Chip   New York   Gillian   Khan   London

1 This is _____.
  She's from _____.

2 This is _____.
  He lives in _____.

3 This is _____.
  He's from _____.

6 ▶ 2.9 Watch or listen again. Are the sentences true (T) or false (F)?

1 Gillian meets friends on Saturday. ____
2 She goes running on Monday mornings. ____
3 Khan watches football on Saturday evenings. ____
4 He studies Italian and Spanish. ____
5 Chip starts work at 9 a.m. every day. ____
6 He finishes work at 4 p.m. ____

7 In pairs, talk about the people in the video. Answer the questions.

1 Where do they work?
2 What activities do they do in their free time?
3 What do you think of their jobs?
4 Do you do the same activities in your free time?

Listening builder   introduction to the sound /ə/

The unstressed vowel sound /ə/ is also called "schwa." It is very common in English. We use it in almost every sentence. It is underlined in these phrases:

Marcus isn't a famous tennis player.   What do you do in your free time?   We want to know!

8 ▶ 2.10 Read the Listening builder. Read the sentences and underline the letters that you think have the sound /ə/. Then listen and check.

1 My sister's a doctor.
2 When do you play tennis?
3 I go to the movies on the weekend.
4 John's a police officer.
5 I want to go out for dinner.

9 A Think of three people that you know. Make notes about the following questions:

• Where do they live? What's their job?
• What activities do they do in their free time? When do they do them?

my friend Victoria – Boston – studies French – Wednesday evenings

B Take turns telling your partner about the people. Listen and complete the chart about your partner's people.

Name	Place	Activity	Day(s)/Time

Personal Best   What do you remember about the people in the video? Write a sentence about each person.

2 LANGUAGE — simple present: questions

2C Find a roommate

1 Look at the pictures in the text. What do you think "speed-roommating" is?

2 A Read the text and check your answer to exercise 1.

B Look at the questions. Who asks them: people who need a roommate or people who need a room in an apartment, or both?

How to find the perfect roommate

You have a great apartment, and you need a new roommate. How do you find one? Why not try speed-roommating? It's a great way to find the perfect roommate.

The idea for speed-roommating comes from speed-dating. Speed-dating events are for single people who want to find a boyfriend or girlfriend. Speed-roommating is the same idea, but it's for people who need a roommate or a room. You meet new people, talk, and ask questions.

What questions do you ask?

1 Where do you live now?
2 Where's your apartment?
3 What do you do?
4 Are you a neat person?
5 Do you have a boyfriend/girlfriend?
6 Does your boyfriend/girlfriend live near here?
7 Does your apartment have a balcony?
8 What do you do in your free time?

3 A ▶ 2.11 Bruce is at a speed-roommating event. He is looking for a roommate. Listen and decide who is the best roommate for Bruce – Mike, Phil, or Andrea. Why?

B ▶ 2.11 Listen again. Are the sentences true (T) or false (F)?

1 Mike and Bruce work on the weekend. ____
2 Bruce is a DJ at a club. ____
3 Phil doesn't work near Bruce's apartment. ____
4 Phil doesn't like his job. ____
5 Andrea doesn't live with her parents. ____
6 Bruce has a girlfriend. ____

4 Match questions 1–5 with answers a–e.

1 Where do you work?
2 What do you do?
3 Do you work in the evening?
4 Where does your boyfriend live?
5 Do you have a boyfriend/girlfriend?

a He lives in another city.
b I work at a local restaurant.
c No, I don't. Not at the moment.
d I'm an accountant.
e Yes, I do. I finish at about 11:30.

5 A Look at the questions in exercise 4. Which questions have a *yes/no* answer?

B Complete the rule. Then read the Grammar box.
We use the auxiliary verbs ¹_____ and ²_____ to make questions in the simple present.

Grammar — simple present: questions

yes/no questions and short answers:
Do you **work** long hours? Yes, I do. No, I don't.
Does she **go** out? Yes, she does. No, she doesn't.

Wh- questions:
What **do** you **do** in your free time?
Where **do** you **work**?
When **does** he **finish**?

Look! We don't use *do* and *don't* in questions with the verb *be*:
Do you **live** in San Francisco? **Are** you from San Francisco?

Go to Grammar practice: simple present: questions, page 115

simple present: questions   LANGUAGE 2C

6 A ▶ 2.13 **Pronunciation:** auxiliary verbs *do* and *does* in questions Listen to the questions. How do we pronounce *do* and *does*?

1 Do you listen to music?
2 Does Phil have a cat?
3 When do you finish work?
4 What does Bruce do after work?
5 Where do they live?
6 Do they play tennis?

B ▶ 2.13 Listen again and <u>underline</u> the stressed words. Repeat the questions.

7 A Complete the questions asked by different people at a speed-roommating event.

1 _____ you like music?
2 _____ your apartment have two bathrooms?
3 What kinds of TV programs _____ you watch?
4 Where _____ you work?
5 Who _____ you live with?
6 _____ you go out in the evening?

B Ask and answer the questions in pairs.

8 A Do the quiz in pairs. Write down your partner's answers.

B Are you and your partner similar?

What type of roommate are you?

1 What time / you / go to bed?
   a 9:00-11:00   b 11:00-01:00   c after 1:00

2 What / you / have for dinner?
   a I cook a healthy meal.   b I have a pizza on the sofa.   c I go out for dinner.

3 What / do / on the weekend?
   a I relax at home.   b I spend time with friends.   c I go to parties.

4 How many friends / you / have?
   a 4 or 5 good friends   b about 50   c more than 500 on Facebook

5 What / be / your perfect job?
   a a writer   b a fashion designer   c a rock singer

9 A What do you do in your free time? Ask and answer questions in pairs.

A *What do you do in your free time?*   B *I meet friends, I go out for coffee, and I spend time with my family.*

B Work with a new partner. Ask and answer questions about your first partner.

What does Gabriela do in her free time?

Go to Communication practice: Student A page 159, Student B page 168

10 A Imagine that you want to find a roommate. Write six questions to ask people.

B Go speed-roommating with your classmates. Talk to lots of people. Ask and answer questions. Choose three good roommates.

A *Who do you live with right now?*
B *I live in an apartment with three other people.*

Personal Best   Imagine you meet someone at speed-roommating who is a terrible roommate. Write the conversation you have with him/her.

2 SKILLS WRITING opening and closing an informal e-mail ■ connectors: *and*, *but*, and *or*

2D A new city

1 Think about a town or city that you know well. What do you do there? In pairs, say three sentences to describe the place.

I like Rio de Janeiro. It's a great city. I eat out with my family, I go to the beach, and I go to clubs with my friends.

2 Lucas is in a new city. Read his e-mail to Hayley. Why is he writing? Choose the correct answer.
  a to tell her about his new life
  b to tell her about his new girlfriend
  c to invite her to visit

Hi Hayley,

How are things back home in Australia?

I'm fine here in Singapore. I love life here – it's a fantastic city for students! I share an apartment with two more students near my college. My roommates are named Steve and Susie, and they're great!

I have a part-time job. I work at an Italian restaurant as a waiter. Susie has a job there, too, but I don't work with her because she works on different days. Steve doesn't have a job right now because he goes to college every day.

In the evenings, I study, or I relax and watch TV. I don't have much free time, but sometimes I go to the movies with Steve and Susie. On weekends, I play sports or I go out with my friends. I love the clubs in Singapore!

Write soon.
Lucas

3 Read the e-mail again and answer the questions.
  1 Where is Lucas from?
  2 Who does he live with?
  3 What does he do in Singapore in his free time?
  4 What do Lucas and his friends do when they go out?
  5 Where does Susie work?
  6 Why doesn't Steve work?

Skill opening and closing an informal e-mail

We write informal e-mails to people we know well, like friends and family.
Opening: Closing:
Hi/Hello (+ name)   *Hey!*   *Hello!*   *Write soon.*   *Take care.*   *See you soon.*
For very close friends and family, we often close with *Love* + (your name) + the letters *xx*.

4 Read the Skill box. Which opening and closing words or phrases does Lucas use?

opening and closing an informal e-mail ■ connectors: *and*, *but*, and *or* **WRITING** | **SKILLS** | **2D**

5 Complete the e-mails with opening and closing phrases.

---

¹ _____ John,

How are you? I hope you're OK.
Are you free on the weekend? Do you want to play tennis on Saturday? I usually play with Victor, but he's in Chicago this weekend.

² _____

Tom

---

³ _____ Sara!

How are you? How's your new job?
I'm in a new apartment, and I have two new roommates! The apartment's lovely, and my roommates are really nice.
Do you want to see a movie or go out for coffee on the weekend? I want to hear your news!

⁴ _____

Nikki xx

Text builder | connectors: *and*, *but*, and *or*

We use *and* to add information:
*My roommates are named Steve and Susie, **and** they're great!*

We use *but* to introduce a different idea:
*I don't have much free time, **but** sometimes I go to the movies.*

We use *or* to add another possibility:
*In the evenings, I study, **or** I relax and watch TV.*

6 Read the Text builder. Find other examples of connectors in Lucas' e-mail.

7 Complete the sentences with *and*, *but*, and *or*.

1 Eduardo's my roommate _____ he's 22 years old.
2 I like my job, _____ I don't like my boss.
3 On the weekend, I meet my parents at a restaurant, _____ I go to their house for lunch.
4 I play the guitar, _____ I'm not in a band.
5 I have two jobs. I work at a café _____ I drive a taxi.
6 Does your girlfriend have a job, _____ is she a student?

8 Complete the sentences with your own ideas.

1 Elena's from Colombia, and she ...
2 Stefan's from Germany, but he ...
3 We often go out on the weekend, and we ...
4 In the evenings, we go to the movies, or we ...
5 I watch soccer on TV, but I don't watch ...
6 In the evening, I ..., or I ...

9 A PREPARE Plan an e-mail about your life for a friend in another city. Answer the questions.

• Where do you live?
• Who do you live with? Do you like him/her/them?
• Do you have a job? What do you do?
• What do you do in your free time at home? What do you do when you go out?

B PRACTICE Write the e-mail. Use different paragraphs to write about your home, your job, and your free time. Use *and*, *but*, and *or* to connect your ideas.

• Open your e-mail.
• Paragraph 1: Say where you live and who you live with.
• Paragraph 2: Say if you have a job and describe what you do.
• Paragraph 3: Describe what you do in your free time.
• Close your e-mail.

C PERSONAL BEST Exchange e-mails with a partner. Underline three sentences with connectors that you think are interesting.

Personal Best Describe a city in a different country. Ask your partner to guess the city.

19

1 and 2 REVIEW and PRACTICE

Grammar

1 Choose the correct options to complete the sentences.

1 _____ in Mexico City.
   a My brother works
   b My brother work
   c My brother has

2 My sister _____ .
   a lives with his parents
   b lives with our parents
   c lives with their parents

3 _____ on the weekend?
   a What does you do
   b What you do
   c What do you do

4 Jack _____ . He's an electrician.
   a 's not construction worker
   b 's not a construction worker
   c no builds

5 How old are you? _____ 25.
   a I
   b I've
   c I'm

6 My hairdresser's Italian. _____ .
   a She comes from Rome
   b They come from Rome
   c She come from Rome

7 _____ American?
   a Your wife's
   b Has your wife
   c Is your wife

8 Who _____ ?
   a do work for
   b do you work for
   c does he works for

2 Put the words in the correct order.

1 apartment New York Harry in Tim and live an in
   _____
2 Canada from 's Harry
   _____
3 a British Tim in 's and bank works
   _____
4 nine He at starts work
   _____
5 restaurant works Harry a in
   _____
6 watch after TV work They
   _____
7 with out On friends the they go weekend
   _____
8 listen and computer games play They music to
   _____

3 Complete the text with the correct form of the verbs in parentheses.

Charles ¹_____ (live) in France, but he works in Switzerland. His wife's German, and they ²_____ (have) three children. He ³_____ (be) a lawyer, and she ⁴_____ (teach) music. In the evening, she ⁵_____ (play) the guitar, and he ⁶_____ (fix) watches. On the weekend, they ⁷_____ (meet) friends, or ⁸_____ (relax) with the family.

Vocabulary

1 Circle the word that is different. Explain your answer.

1 guitar	newspaper	tennis	games
2 doctor	dentist	teach	lawyer
3 Mexico	Irish	Brazil	Peru
4 police officer	Colombian	nurse	teacher
5 Mexican	French	Japan	Italian
6 handbag	keys	gloves	phone
7 sixty	nineteen	seventy	eighty
8 chef	wear	fix	serve

REVIEW and PRACTICE 1 and 2

2 Match definitions 1–8 with objects a–h.

1 They help you see better.
2 They keep your hands warm.
3 It helps you see at night.
4 You keep your money in it.
5 It tells you the time.
6 You use it to send a letter.
7 You use them to open and close a door.
8 You use this on your hair.

a flashlight
b stamp
c glasses
d wallet
e watch
f comb
g keys
h gloves

3 Complete the sentences with the jobs in the box.

chef   dentist   flight attendant   nurse
waiter   mechanic   hairdresser   teacher

1 A _____ serves food in a restaurant.
2 My cousin's a _____ with American Airlines.
3 A _____ cooks the food in a restaurant.
4 A _____ works in a garage and fixes cars.
5 A _____ cuts hair.
6 If you have problems with your teeth, see a _____ .
7 My _____ helps me with my English.
8 My sister's a _____ . She works at a hospital in New York.

4 Put the words in the correct columns.

accountant   gloves   Brazil   Turkish   glasses
sunglasses   Mexican   American   doctor   lawyer
UK   taxi driver   Japan   Irish   tissues   Colombia

Jobs	Countries	Nationalities	Objects

Personal Best

Lesson 1A
Name five nationalities.

Lesson 2A
Name five jobs.

Lesson 1A
Write two sentences about yourself using the verb *be*: one affirmative, one negative.

Lesson 2A
Write three sentences about your friends using the simple present.

Lesson 1B
Write three simple statements with *be*.

Lesson 2C
Write a *yes/no* question using *do* or *does*.

Lesson 1C
Name five things in your bag.

Lesson 2C
Write three questions you can ask the first time you meet someone.

Lesson 1C
Write three sentences using *his*, *her*, and *their*.

Lesson 2D
Give two expressions for closing an informal email.

Lesson 1D
Give two expressions to ask for clarification.

Lesson 2D
Write one sentence with *but* and one with *or*.

21

UNIT 3
People in my life

LANGUAGE frequency adverbs and expressions ■ family

3A Time together

1 When and where do you spend time with your family? Tell your partner.

I see my family on the weekend. We have lunch together on Sundays.

2 Look at the pictures of different family activities. How many generations can you see? What are they doing together?

3 A Read the text. Complete it with the verbs in the box.

go   cook   make   see   play   watch

Family get-togethers

Once a year, my whole family meets at my parents' house for a weekend of fun, music, and great food. We're a big family, and there are four generations of us!

In the morning, we often ¹_____ games with the children in the park. My brother Ben has a boy and a girl. My niece and nephew are crazy about soccer, so we usually play that.

In the afternoon, we ²_____ for a walk or stay at home. We sit in the backyard, and we sometimes ³_____ things with the children. My sister-in-law Lois teaches five-year-olds, and she always brings lots of paper and pens.

In the evening, we ⁴_____ dinner. Food's always an important part of the weekend! Our food's very international – my grandmother's Brazilian, my dad's Colombian, my sister-in-law's British, and my husband's Polish. We often have Mexican food because we all love it.

We never ⁵_____ television – we prefer to talk. My Uncle Paul and my cousins Joe and Megan play music. Uncle Paul and Joe play the guitar, and Megan sings and plays the piano. They're really good.

I don't ⁶_____ my family often because we all live in different parts of the country, but I love these weekends. They're really special.

B ▶ 3.1 Listen and check your answers.

4 A Read the text again and choose the correct options.
1 The writer is Ben's *sister / aunt*.
2 Lois is Ben's *sister / wife*.
3 Paul is Joe's *father / grandfather*.
4 Megan is Paul's *son / daughter*.

B Look at the main picture in the text. What relation to the writer do you think the people are?

Go to Vocabulary practice: family, page 140

22

frequency adverbs and expressions ■ family   **LANGUAGE**   **3A**

5 ▶ 3.4 Listen to Ben and match the activities with the people and the frequency expressions.

1 play tennis	son	every day
2 read stories	grandmother	once a week
3 go out for coffee	son and daughter	once a month
4 watch TV	cousin	three times a week
5 go out for dinner	wife	every evening
6 buy food	brother-in-law	twice a month

6 A Underline the frequency adverbs in the text on page 22. Complete the rule.

Frequency adverbs go *before* / *after* the verb *be* and *before* / *after* other verbs.

B Look at the frequency expressions in exercise 5. Which word means "one time"? Which word means "two times"? Then read the Grammar box.

📖 **Grammar** | frequency adverbs and expressions

Frequency adverbs:

Frequency expressions:

once/twice/three times | a | day/week/month/year
                       | every |

Go to Grammar practice: frequency adverbs and expressions, page 116

7 A ▶ 3.6 **Pronunciation:** sentence stress Listen to the sentences. Underline the stressed words or syllables. Are the frequency adverbs and expressions stressed?

1 I sometimes play the guitar.
2 He's often late.
3 We never watch television.
4 They eat out once a week.
5 She sees her grandparents three times a year.
6 I listen to the radio every day.

B ▶ 3.6 Listen again and repeat the sentences. Copy the rhythm.

8 A Write five sentences about you and your family. Use different frequency adverbs and expressions.

I often go out for coffee with my mother-in-law.   *I sometimes watch TV with my grandparents.*
I play soccer with my brother once a week.

B In pairs, say your sentences. Do you do the same activities with the same people?

Go to Communication practice: Student A page 159, Student B page 168

9 A Ask and answer questions with your classmates about how frequently you do the activities.

go to (the movies)   play (a sport)   cook   meet (your cousins)   drive a car   go running

A *How often do you go to the movies?*   **B** *Once a month. What about you?*   **A** *I never go to the movies.*

B Complete the sentences about your classmates.

1 _____ never goes _____.
2 _____ sometimes plays _____.
3 _____ cooks _____.
4 _____ meets his/her _____.
5 _____ drives a car _____.
6 _____ goes running _____.

Personal Best Draw your family tree. Choose five people in your family and write a sentence about each of them.

23

3B A new group

1 Look at the picture. In pairs, talk about how you usually meet new people in your town or city.

> **Skill** scanning a text
>
> Scanning means reading quickly to find specific information; for example, you scan a TV guide for a program, or a schedule for a train's arrival time. You don't read everything. You only look for the information you want.

2 A Read the Skill box. Imagine that you like art and photography. Scan the website to find groups that are suitable for you.

B You are free on Monday and Wednesday evenings. Which art or photography group can you join? Scan the website again.

3 Read the website again and read for detail. Are the sentences true (T) or false (F)?

1 The Walking Club meets on the weekend. ____
2 The Drawing Club always meets in a studio. ____
3 The Italian Club sometimes goes to Italy. ____
4 The Camera Club has an exhibit once a year. ____
5 In the International Friends Club, people cook at different homes every week. ____
6 Children and young people watch the Drama Club's shows. ____
7 The Cooking Club meets once a week. ____
8 The Movie Club always meets every Saturday evening. ____

> **Text builder** *also* and *too*
>
> *Also* and *too* are adverbs that we use to add extra information. *Also* often goes after the verb *be* and before other verbs. *Too* usually goes at the end of the sentence. We use a comma before *too*, but not before *also*.

4 A Read the Text builder. <u>Underline</u> examples of *also* and *too* on the website.

B Choose the correct words to complete the sentences.
1 She plays the guitar, and she *also / too* writes stories.
2 I want to join the Camera Club and the Cooking Club, *also / too*.
3 We go to the movies once a month, and we sometimes go to the theater, *also / too*.
4 They go to a restaurant twice a week, and they *also / too* get takeout once a week.

5 In pairs, discuss which club on the website you like most. Why?

6 A Plan a new club for the website. Think about the following:
What does it do? How often does it meet? Where does it meet?

B Tell the class about your new club and listen to your classmates' clubs. Decide which new club you like most.

scanning a text ■ *also* and *too* **READING** | **SKILLS** | **3B**

Clubs near you

WALKING CLUB

We're a walking club for people who love the country. We go on lots of walks of different lengths and levels of difficulty. We start at 9:30 a.m. on Sunday mornings, and we usually finish at about 5 p.m.

INTERNATIONAL FRIENDS CLUB

We're a friendly group that meets every week on Tuesdays. We usually meet at a restaurant, and we often go to the movies and theater. We want to learn about other countries and cultures, and have a good time, too!

DRAWING CLUB

This is a club for art lovers of all ages. Beginners are very welcome! We don't have a teacher, but we all learn from each other. We work in a studio on Thursday evenings, and we also go outside to draw once a month.

DRAMA CLUB

We're a big group, but we always welcome new members. We perform three shows a year at the local arts center and at local schools, too. We meet on Wednesday evenings at 7:30.

ITALIAN CLUB

Buongiorno! We're a group of people who speak Italian and who are interested in Italian culture. We meet at an Italian restaurant once a month, on a Friday evening. We also watch Italian movies together.

COOKING CLUB

We meet every Saturday to cook together at someone's home and then enjoy a great meal! We try lots of new and delicious foods, and we also meet other people who love cooking.

CAMERA CLUB

Do you like photography? If so, come and join our camera club! We meet every Monday at 7 p.m. We have talks and discussions about different kinds of photography, and we show each other our own photos.

MOVIE CLUB

We don't have a regular meeting! Members post a message on the website and invite others to join them for a movie. After watching the movie, we usually go out for coffee and talk. It's a great way to enjoy movies and make new friends, too.

Personal Best — Describe a club that you're in now or when you were a child.

3 LANGUAGE — love, like, hate, enjoy, don't mind + noun/-ing form ■ activities (2)

3C Opposites attract

1 Which activities are good for a couple to do together? In pairs, choose five activities and explain why.

> going on vacation   visiting relatives   playing sports   going bike riding
> playing computer games   visiting museums   relaxing at home   studying

Go to Vocabulary practice: activities (2), page 141

2 **A** Read the text about Cara and Chris. What do they do together?

B Discuss the questions in pairs.
1 Are Cara and Chris happy that they are very different? Why/Why not?
2 Do you think opposites attract?

Do opposites really attract? Or is it better to find someone similar to you? We ask one couple why they are together when they are so different from each other.

OPPOSITES attract

CARA
My boyfriend Chris and I are very different. He's always out, and he loves playing sports. He likes running, and he loves playing tennis. I don't mind tennis, but I hate running! I like different activities: I enjoy doing yoga in the park, and I love reading. But I think we're a great couple. Why? We both like living in the city. We enjoy good restaurants, and we love seeing our friends on the weekend, but I sometimes prefer to spend a quiet evening with him at home.

CHRIS
I think it's great that Cara and I have our own interests. I enjoy being active: I play tennis and go running every day. Cara enjoys relaxing at home, and she loves visiting museums and galleries. I don't mind visiting museums, but I hate art! We do some things together – we both love going bowling, for example, but I don't want a girlfriend who's just like me. They say "opposites attract," and I agree!

3 **A** Work in pairs. Read the text again. Student A: write about Cara. Student B: write about Chris. Complete the sentences.

Student A
1 Cara loves _____.
2 She enjoys _____.
3 She likes _____.
4 She doesn't mind _____.
5 She hates _____.

Student B
1 Chris loves _____.
2 He enjoys _____.
3 He likes _____.
4 He doesn't mind _____.
5 He hates _____.

B ▶ 3.8 Tell your partner your answers. Listen and check.

love, like, hate, enjoy, don't mind + noun/*-ing* form ■ activities (2) **LANGUAGE 3C**

4 Look at the sentences in exercise 3. Choose the correct option to complete the rule. Then read the Grammar box.

After *love, like, hate, enjoy,* and *don't mind,* we usually use
a a noun or *-ing* form.
b a *to* infinitive.

📖 **Grammar** *love, like, hate, enjoy, don't mind* + noun/*-ing* form

love, like, etc. + noun:
I *love* TV.
I *like* books.
I *enjoy* music.
I *don't mind* tennis.
I *hate* museums.

love, like, etc. + *-ing* form of verb:
I *love watching* TV.
I *like reading* books.
I *enjoy listening* to music.
I *don't mind playing* tennis.
I *hate visiting* museums.

Go to Grammar practice: *love, like, hate, enjoy, don't mind* + noun/*-ing* form, page 117

5 A ▶ 3.10 **Pronunciation:** *-ing* forms Listen and repeat the verbs.

watching   reading   visiting   doing   going   being   playing   running

B ▶ 3.11 Say the sentences. Listen, check, and repeat.
1 I don't mind visiting museums.
2 She doesn't like going bowling.
3 I love reading magazines.
4 He hates going to the gym.
5 We enjoy doing yoga.

6 A Complete Stephanie's profile with the correct form of the verbs in the box.

get   talk   watch   cook   be   play

About me:
Stephanie Ellis

In the evening, I usually make dinner because I don't mind ¹_____. After dinner, I walk my dog Bruno for an hour. It's very relaxing, and I enjoy ²_____ to other dog walkers. I love ³_____ exercise, and sometimes I go running with a friend. I also love ⁴_____ at home with Bruno, but I don't like ⁵_____ TV, and I hate ⁶_____ computer games.

B Look again at the text on page 26. Who do you think is Stephanie's friend: Cara or Chris?

Go to Communication practice: Student A page 159, Student B page 168

7 A Write two true sentences for you for each verb. Use nouns and *-ing* forms.
• I love …
• I like …
• I enjoy …
• I don't mind …
• I don't like …
• I hate …

B Compare your sentences with a partner. Are you similar or different?
A *I enjoy swimming in the sea.*   **B** *I don't like swimming. I enjoy …*

Personal Best Choose someone you know. Write about what he/she loves, likes, and hates doing.

3 SKILLS SPEAKING — making plans ■ accepting or declining an invitation

3D A night out

1 A Look at the clocks. Match them with the times.

1 It's ten thirty. ____
2 It's a quarter after ten. ____
3 It's ten o'clock. ____
4 It's twenty-five after ten. ____
5 It's seven minutes after ten. ____
6 It's a quarter to eleven. ____
7 It's five after ten. ____
8 It's twenty after ten. ____
9 It's twenty-five to eleven. ____
10 It's ten to eleven. ____

B ▶ 3.12 Listen and check. Listen again and repeat.

2 ▶ 3.13 Watch or listen to the first part of *Learning Curve*. What's Penny's main problem?

a She is late.
b Ethan is late.
c They don't know what time it is.

3 ▶ 3.13 Watch or listen again. Choose the correct times.

1 Penny's watch says it's five minutes *to/after* ten.
2 The clock on the wall says it's *seven/eleven* minutes after ten.
3 The clock on Penny's computer says it's *a quarter past/half after* ten.
4 Ethan wants to meet Penny at *ten to/ten after* eleven.
5 Ethan's phone says it's ten *thirty/forty*.

4 ▶ 3.14 Watch or listen to the second part of the show and answer the questions.

1 What two activities do they all want to do?
2 What time does Penny arrange to meet Taylor and Ethan?

making plans ■ accepting or declining an invitation **SPEAKING** | **SKILLS** | **3D**

Conversation builder **making plans**

Suggesting an activity:
Would you like to ...?   Do you want to ...?   How about having dinner/How about we have dinner ...?
Let's go together.   Do you have plans after ...?   Are you free for lunch on Thursday?

Agreeing on a time:
What time is good for you?   Let's say 8 p.m.   How about we meet tomorrow at six?
About seven?   Can we go at 8 p.m.?

5 A ▶ 3.14   Read the Conversation builder. Match the two parts to make complete sentences. Watch or listen again and check.

1	What time is	**a**	at five thirty in front of our building?
2	How about we meet	**b**	to come?
3	Do you want to	**c**	seven o'clock?
4	Would you like	**d**	good for you?
5	Are you both free	**e**	for dinner?
6	Can we go at	**f**	go bowling tonight?

B Who says questions 1–6? Write M (Marc), E (Ethan), T (Taylor), or P (Penny). Watch or listen again to check if necessary.

1 ____   3 ____   5 ____
2 ____   4 ____   6 ____

6 In pairs, make plans to see a movie and go shopping together. Take turns suggesting the activity.

Skill **accepting or declining an invitation**

When you accept or decline an invitation, it's important to be polite.
• When you accept, be enthusiastic:
  Sure. I like bowling!   *Yes, I'd love to.*   *Cool!*

• When you decline, explain why, and say that you're sorry:
  I'd really love to, but I'm busy tonight.
  Tonight? I'm sorry, I can't. How about another day?

• Use intonation to sound enthusiastic or sorry.

7 A ▶ 3.15   Read the Skill box. Listen to the conversations. Does speaker B accept (✔) or decline (✗) the invitations?

1 **A** Would you like to go out for dinner tonight?   **B** ____
2 **A** Do you want to have a barbecue this weekend?   **B** ____
3 **A** How about going swimming tomorrow?   **B** ____
4 **A** Do you want to have lunch on Saturday?   **B** ____

B ▶ 3.15   Listen again. Repeat speaker B's words. Copy his/her intonation.

Go to Communication practice: Student A page 159, Student B page 168

8 A PREPARE   Think of an activity you want to do with a friend. Use the places in the boxes or your own ideas.

movies   bowling alley   café   restaurant   shopping center   museum   gallery   gym

B PRACTICE   Invite your partner to do your activity, and accept or decline your partner's invitation politely. Agree on a time and place if you accept.

C PERSONAL BEST   In groups of four, repeat your conversations, and listen to the other pair. Do they use the phrases from the Conversation builder and Skill box correctly?

Personal **Best**   How often do you go out in the evening during the week? Describe what you normally do.

29

UNIT 4
Home and away

LANGUAGE prepositions of time ■ daily routine verbs

4A 24 hours in the dark

1 Do you usually do these things in the morning? Discuss in pairs.

check e-mails   go to the gym   take a bath   take a shower   have breakfast

Go to Vocabulary practice: daily routine verbs, page 142

2 **A** Look at the title of the lesson and the pictures in the text. Which countries sometimes have 24 hours of darkness?

B Read the text. Match the headings in the box with paragraphs A–E.

Light and dark   Summer activities   Our daily routine   My city   Winter activities

24 hours of night – or day!

by Tom Sanders

A _____
I'm from New York, but I now live in the north of Norway in a small city called Tromsø. I like living here. I have an interesting job, and I like the people.

B _____
I work from 8:00 in the morning to 4:00 in the afternoon. I usually wake up at 6:00 and get up at 6:15. I take a shower and get dressed. At 6:45, I have breakfast and check my e-mails. I leave home at 7:15. My wife and children leave home at 8:00. The children start school at 8:30 and finish at 2:30. I get home at about 5:00.

C _____
Our lives are different in the summer and the winter. In the summer, there are 60 days when the sun doesn't set. From May to July, it's light at midnight. And in the winter, we have 60 days of night. From November to January, it's dark at noon!

D _____
It's very dark, but it's not a bad time of year. On the weekend, we spend time together as a family, or we go skiing. We sometimes see the Northern Lights at night. They're really beautiful.

E _____
In the summer, we spend a lot of time outdoors. In the evening, we often have a barbecue on the beach and, on Friday nights, we sometimes go to outdoor concerts. In July, we go on vacation. We usually visit my family in New York and also spend some time with my wife's family in the mountains.

30

prepositions of time ■ daily routine verbs   LANGUAGE   4A

3 A Read paragraph B again. Cover the text. Ask and answer questions about Tom and his family's daily routine with the verb phrases in the box. What can you remember?

wake up   have breakfast   leave home   start work/school   finish work/school   get home

A *When does Tom wake up?*   B *I think he wakes up at 6:00.*

B In pairs, compare your daily routine with Tom's. What is the same? What is different?

I have breakfast at home, too.   I don't check my e-mails at home.   I get home at six o'clock, not five o'clock.

4 Choose the correct prepositions to complete the sentences. Use the text to help you. Then read the Grammar box.

1 I leave home *at / in* 7:15.
2 *In / From* May *on / to* July, it's light *at / in* midnight.
3 We sometimes see the Northern Lights *in / at* night.
4 *At / In* the summer, we spend a lot of time outdoors.
5 *On / At* Friday nights, we sometimes go to outdoor concerts.

Grammar — prepositions of time

in:	on:	at:	from ... to:
the morning(s)	Saturday(s)	5:30	... Monday ... Friday
the winter	Friday night(s)	midnight/noon	... November ... January
July	Monday morning(s)		... 9:00 a.m. ... 5:00 p.m.
	the weekend		

Go to Grammar practice: prepositions of time, page 118

5 A Read about Tom's daughter, Mia. Complete the sentences with the correct prepositions.

1 I usually wake up _____ 5:45 on weekdays.
2 I swim _____ 6:30 _____ 7:30. _____ the weekend, I get up _____ the afternoon!
3 _____ Fridays and Saturdays, I go to bed late.
4 _____ the summer, I often go to concerts _____ night. They don't finish until 2:00 _____ the morning, but it's still light.

B ▶ 4.3 Listen and check your answers. What does Mia love doing? Do you enjoy this activity?

6 ▶ 4.4 **Pronunciation:** sentence stress   Listen and repeat the sentences. Which words are stressed?

1 I get up at six in the morning.
2 I work from Monday to Friday.
3 I go swimming on Wednesday evenings.
4 I walk to work in the summer.
5 My wife gets home at midnight.
6 We have dinner at 8:30.

7 A Complete the sentences so that they are true for you. Write one false sentence.

1 I get up at _____.
2 I work from _____.
3 I _____ evenings.
4 I _____ the summer.
5 I don't _____ the weekend.

B In pairs, say your sentences. Guess the false sentences.

Go to Communication practice: Student A page 160, Student B page 169

8 A Read and answer the questions. Are you a morning person or an evening person?

1 What time do you usually get up on the weekend?
2 What time do you usually go to bed on the weekend?
3 When do you like working or studying?
4 When do you enjoy getting exercise?

B Find a classmate who is like you. Discuss what you like doing in the morning or in the evening. Tell the rest of your class.

David and I are morning people. We like getting up early and going to the gym before work.

Personal Best Think of someone that you know well. Describe his/her daily routine during the week and on the weekend.

31

4 SKILLS LISTENING listening for the main idea ■ sentence stress ■ the weather and the seasons

4B Weather around the world

1 Complete the sentences with the words in the box.

> snowing   hot   cold   raining   cloudy   foggy

1 It's _____.   2 It's _____.   3 It's _____.   4 It's _____.   5 It's _____.   6 It's _____.

Go to Vocabulary practice: the weather and the seasons, page 142

2 A Complete the chart. Then tell your partner about the activities that you do during different seasons.

Season	Months	Weather	My activities

B What is your favorite season? Why? Tell your partner.

> **Skill   listening for the main idea(s)**
>
> **It is important to understand the main idea when someone is speaking.**
> - Use any pictures to help you understand what the topic is.
> - Think about who is speaking and what the situation is.
> - Don't worry if you don't understand everything. Listen for the important words.

3 ▶ 4.6 Read the Skill box. Watch or listen to the first part of *Learning Curve*. Match places 1–4 with the types of weather a–d.

1 New York   a rainy and very cloudy
2 Mount Emei   b usually warm
3 Bay of Bengal   c very rainy
4 Rome   d sometimes snowy in winter

4 ▶ 4.6 Watch or listen again. For 1–3, check (✓) the correct sentence, a or b.

1
a ☐ It never snows in the fall in New York.
b ☐ Ethan wears his snow boots every day in the winter.
2
a ☐ It rains a lot in Mount Emei, but it rains more in the Bay of Bengal.
b ☐ It's very cloudy in the Bay of Bengal.
3
a ☐ It doesn't often snow in Rome.
b ☐ When it snows in New York, the schools always close.

listening for the main idea ■ sentence stress ■ the weather and the seasons   LISTENING   SKILLS   4B

5 ▶ 4.7 Watch or listen to the second part of the show. For each sentence, write M (Marina), S (Sam), or J (Jenny).

Marina

Sam

Jenny

1 Once in 100 years, there's snow! _____
2 I get about 100 days of sun a year. _____
3 It's like this 200 days a year. _____
4 I love it. Winter is here! _____
5 I sleep early and wake up early. _____
6 We don't usually talk about the weather. _____

6 ▶ 4.7 Watch or listen again. Choose the correct options to complete the sentences.

1 Marina says it's *17°C / −7°C / 18°C*.
2 She goes to her sister's house *after breakfast / in the afternoon / in the evening*.
3 Sam says it's *sometimes / usually / always* hot and sunny in Egypt.
4 His advice is to *wear a hat / wear boots / carry an umbrella* in hot weather.
5 Jenny says the weather forecast is good for *Saturday / Monday / Tuesday*.
6 She *likes / doesn't like / hates* living in Newfoundland.

7 In pairs, think of some advice for visitors to your country for different seasons.
In the winter, it's a good idea to wear warm clothes.

Listening builder | sentence stress

In English, we usually stress the most important words in a sentence. These stressed words are usually nouns, verbs, adjectives, and adverbs. You can usually understand the general idea if you only hear these words:
<u>Mount Emei</u> in <u>China</u> gets <u>twenty-seven feet</u> of <u>rain</u> in a <u>year</u>.
In the <u>evening</u>, we have <u>dinner</u> at my <u>sister's house</u>.

8 A Read the Listening builder. Read the text and <u>underline</u> the most important words.

Patagonia is a beautiful part of South America. It's always windy in Patagonia. The wind is sometimes very strong – about a hundred and twenty kilometers an hour. You can't walk when it's so windy.

B ▶ 4.8 Listen and check which words are stressed.

9 Discuss the questions in pairs.

1 Do people in your country talk about the weather a lot?
2 Do you talk about the weather a lot? Who do you talk about it with?
3 What kinds of weather do you like? (sunny weather, rainy weather, etc.)
4 What kinds of weather do you hate?
5 What do people do in your country when the weather is bad?
6 Do you sometimes have strange weather? Describe it.

Personal Best Write a guide to the weather in your country for tourists.

4 LANGUAGE — present continuous

4C A long weekend

1. What do you like doing when you visit a new city? Tell your partner.

2. **A** In pairs, look at the pictures of Charlotte and Pete's trip. Which city are they in?
   B Read Charlotte's posts. Which famous places does she mention?

3. Read the posts again. Answer the questions.
   1. Do they like their apartment?
   2. What's the weather like?
   3. How do they travel around?
   4. Do they like the food?

a. We're going away for a long weekend. I'm so excited! We're sitting on the train, and we're waiting to leave for Paris on the Eurostar. I'm having a good time already!

b. We're here. We're staying in a private apartment with a view of the city. It's so romantic!

c. Today, we're visiting the Rodin Museum. We're walking around the beautiful gardens in the warm spring sunshine.

d. Look, it's the Eiffel Tower! I feel like a real tourist. We're having a sandwich and waiting in line.

e. I'm having a good time, but Pete isn't happy. We're going shopping on the Champs-Élysées. He's carrying my bags. I'm feeling hungry – time for lunch.

f. We're at a lovely little restaurant. I'm having the steak! The weather's lovely and warm. What's Pete doing? He's trying to speak French to the waiter.

g. It's late. We're tired, and we're taking a taxi back to the apartment after a great night out. The city lights are amazing!

h. It's our last day. We're buying some food to take home. It's raining, but we don't mind.

4. Match Pete's posts 1–8 with pictures a–h.
   1. I'm looking for some French cheese as a present for my mom.
   2. The weather's great. We're having a fun time at the museum.
   3. We're going to Paris!
   4. What a cool apartment! Charlotte's taking a shower, and I'm relaxing after the trip.
   5. We're visiting a very famous monument. I want to take a selfie at the top.
   6. I'm not enjoying this! I hate shopping!
   7. We're going back to the apartment now. Fantastic night out!
   8. Finally, I'm sitting down! What's for lunch?

5. **A** Underline the verbs in exercise 4. Which ones describe an action that is happening now?
   B Choose *be* or *have* to complete the rule. Then read the Grammar box.

   We form the present continuous with the verb *be* / *have* + *-ing* form.

present continuous **LANGUAGE** **4C**

📖 Grammar   present continuous

Affirmative:
I'm having a good time.
He's carrying my bags.
We're taking a taxi home.

Negative:
I'm not enjoying this.
It isn't raining.

Questions and short answers:
What's Pete doing?
Are you eating steak?
Yes, I am.   No, I'm not.

Go to Grammar practice: present continuous, page 119

6 A ▶ 4.10 **Pronunciation:** linking consonants and vowels Listen and repeat the sentences.

I'm getting‿up.   It‿isn't raining.   He's‿eating‿a sandwich.

B ▶ 4.11 Listen and <u>underline</u> the words that are linked. Listen, check, and repeat.

1 What are you talking about?
2 He's enjoying this game.
3 We're sitting in a café.
4 They're going away for a weekend.

7 Complete the dialogues with the present continuous form of the verbs. Then act out the dialogues in pairs.

1 A What _____ you _____ (do) here?   B I _____ (wait) for my friends.
2 A _____ it _____ (snow)?   B No, it _____. It _____ (rain).
3 A Why _____ James _____ (wear) a suit? B He _____ (go) to a job interview.
4 A _____ your friends _____ (leave) now? B Yes, they _____. They _____ (look) for their umbrellas.
5 A Who _____ Ben _____ (call)?   B I don't know. He _____ (not / talk) to Alex because Alex is here!

Go to Communication practice: Student A page 160, Student B page 169

8 Work in groups. Take turns miming and guessing the actions.

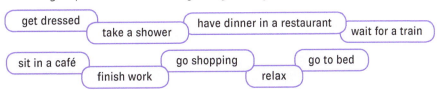

get dressed   take a shower   have dinner in a restaurant   wait for a train
sit in a café   finish work   go shopping   relax   go to bed

A *Are you getting dressed?*   B *No, I'm not.*   A *Are you taking a shower?*   B *Yes, I am!*

9 A Charlotte calls her friend, Olivia. Complete the conversation with the correct form of the verbs in the box. Who is Nacho?

visit   have   do   make   play   wait

Olivia   Hi, Charlotte! How are you?
Charlotte Hi, Olivia! I'm good, thanks. I'm in Paris with Pete! We ¹_____ a great time!
Olivia   Paris! That's fantastic. What ²_____ right now?
Charlotte We're at the Eiffel Tower. We ³_____ to go up. Where are you?
Olivia   Nacho and I ⁴_____ my in-laws with the girls. They ⁵_____ in the backyard with Nacho's mom. And Nacho's dad ⁶_____ lunch for us.
Charlotte That sounds nice.

B ▶ 4.12 Listen and check your answers.

10 Imagine you are on vacation. Decide where you are. Call your partner and tell each other where you are, who you are with, and what you are doing.

A *Hello, Ana. It's Daniel.*   B *Hi! Where are you?*   A *I'm in New York. I'm going for a walk in Central Park.*

Imagine your long weekend. Write eight sentences to describe what you're doing.

35

SKILLS   WRITING   describing a photo ■ using personal pronouns

4D A vacation with friends

1 Ask and answer the questions in pairs.
1 When do you go on vacation?
2 Where do you usually go?
3 Who do you go with?
4 What do you like doing there?

2 **A** Look at the pictures. Guess where the people are.
B Read the e-mail and check.

Hi Lucy,

¹ How are you? How's work? I hope everything's OK.

² I'm in Argentina! I'm visiting Leo and María in Buenos Aires, and I'm having a wonderful time. The weather's amazing! It's 25 degrees, and it's never cloudy. It's hot all day and warm at night. It's so nice after the cold fall weather at home.

³ Most days I get up early here, and I go running with Leo before breakfast. He loves getting exercise in the morning. Then we return home and have breakfast. Leo and María start work at 8:30, and I leave the apartment with them. I go into the city and visit different places like Casa Rosada and Teatro Colón. In the evening, we go for a walk and then have dinner. The restaurants are great here, and the steaks are fantastic!

⁴ I'm sending you a couple of photos that I took. The first photo's of some colorful houses in an area called La Boca. It's a really cool part of town with some amazing buildings. In the second photo, you can see Leo and María. We're having coffee in a local café near their apartment. They have great coffee and delicious pastries there.

My flight's on Friday. See you at work on Monday!

Love, Gemma

---

3 Read the e-mail again. In which paragraph does Gemma …
1 write about the weather? _____
2 describe the pictures? _____
3 ask Lucy questions? _____
4 write about her daily routine on vacation? _____

 Skill describing a photo

When you send a photo, describe who or what the photo shows. If it shows people, describe what they are doing:
The first photo's of some colorful houses. In the second photo, you can see …
In this photo, I'm in the park with my friends. We're playing soccer.
This photo's of my sister. She's playing the piano. Here's a photo of our new car.

4 Read the Skill box. Look at Gemma's e-mail again. How does she describe the pictures?

describing a photo ■ using personal pronouns   **WRITING**   **SKILLS**   **4D**

5 A Match the two parts to make complete sentences.

1 In this photo, I'm with
2 Here's a photo
3 In this photo, we're
4 Here's a photo of us in

a Red Square in Moscow!
b fixing our bikes.
c of Sydney at night.
d my niece, Eliza. We're reading a story.

B Match the completed sentences with pictures a–d.

Text builder | using personal pronouns

We often use personal pronouns (*he*, *she*, *it*, etc.) to avoid repeating words and names:
*I'm with Sergio and Ana. **We**'re eating fish. **It**'s delicious!*
*Eleni's helping me with my French homework. **She** speaks really good French.*

6 A Read the Text builder. Read paragraphs 3 and 4 in the e-mail again and underline the personal pronouns. What do they refer to?

B Complete the sentences with the correct personal pronouns.

1 I'm with Theo. _____'re waiting for the train.
2 This is the hotel pool. _____'s on top of the hotel.
3 Theo's shopping. _____'s spending all his money!
4 Katie's in bed. _____'s sleeping!
5 The kids are out. _____'re on their bikes.

7 A PREPARE Imagine you're on vacation. Decide where you are, what the weather's like, how you're feeling, who is with you, and what to do every day. Imagine two or three photos of your vacation.

B PRACTICE Write an e-mail to a friend. Use personal pronouns to avoid repeating words/names.
- Begin your e-mail.
- Paragraph 1: Ask your friend how he/she is.
- Paragraph 2: Describe where you are, what the weather is like, and who is with you.
- Paragraph 3: Describe your daily routine on vacation.
- Paragraph 4: Describe two or three photos of your vacation.
- Finish your e-mail.

C PERSONAL BEST Exchange e-mails with a partner. Does his/her e-mail contain personal pronouns to avoid repeating words/names? Can you add any more?

Personal Best Find a photo of people on vacation. Describe their vacation. Where are they? What are they doing?

3 and 4 · REVIEW and PRACTICE

Grammar

1 Choose the correct options to complete the sentences.

1 This week _____ in Washington, D.C.
- **a** I stay
- **b** I staying
- **c** I'm staying

2 What _____ right now?
- **a** do you do
- **b** are you doing
- **c** doing you

3 My grandfather always _____ on Sunday afternoons.
- **a** is visiting
- **b** visit
- **c** visits

4 _____ do you see your cousins?
- **a** How many
- **b** How often
- **c** How about

5 My sister's birthday is _____ Friday.
- **a** at
- **b** in
- **c** on

6 My brother's in his room with a friend. _____ computer games.
- **a** They playing
- **b** They're playing
- **c** They play

7 I _____ on the weekend.
- **a** play always soccer
- **b** always play soccer
- **c** play soccer always

8 When _____ go shopping?
- **a** do you usually
- **b** usually do you
- **c** are you

2 Complete the dialogue with the correct form of the verb in parentheses.

A How [1]_____ (be) the new job?

B It's good. Right now, I [2]_____ (work) on a new project.

A Where?

B Near Miami. We [3]_____ (build) a new hotel.

A Where [4]_____ (live) right now?

B I'm living with friends from Monday to Friday, and then I always [5]_____ (come) home on the weekend.

A Are you OK with that?

B I don't mind [6]_____ (travel), and I enjoy [7]_____ (work) on a small team.

A No problems at all?

B Well, I hate [8]_____ (get up) early on Monday mornings!

3 Complete the text with the words in the box.

> flies   at   often   arrives   stays
> checks   starts   spends

☰ / ✎ / 📅 / 🔖 FEATURED   🔖 SITE

I live in six cities

Barbara Fiala is the owner of Baobab, a communications company, based in New York. She [1]_____ travels for work and spends around two months a year in Europe. She [2]_____ to London and then visits Berlin, Budapest, and Warsaw. She usually [3]_____ three nights in each city and then starts again. She [4]_____ in the evening, so she's ready to work the next day. "I often go for a walk or go to the gym [5]_____ 6 a.m," she says. She [6]_____ work around 7 a.m. and [7]_____ her e-mails and makes some telephone calls before her meetings. In London, she [8]_____ with her sister, but in the other cities she stays at hotels. She does yoga and reads books to relax.

Vocabulary

1 Circle the word that is different. Explain your answer.

1 son	father	niece	brother
2 fall	rain	spring	winter
3 yoga	barbecue	picnic	dinner
4 golf	bowling	volleyball	dancing
5 cold	snowy	warm	icy
6 gallery	museum	gym	violin
7 aunt	grandmother	son	mother
8 karate	swimming	shopping	running

38

2 Make words to describe the weather.

What's the weather like? It's _____.

1. d y o c u l   _____
2. n d w y i   _____
3. t h o   _____
4. g y o g f   _____
5. m r w a   _____
6. y u n s n   _____
7. i a n r y   _____
8. w g o n n s i _____

3 Put the words in the correct columns.

summer   school   son   swimming   gym   spring
shopping   sister   home   winter   running
uncle   fall   cousin   yoga   museum

Seasons	Relatives	Activities	Places

4 Complete the sentences with the correct form of the verbs in the box.

do   finish   start   walk   get   play   go   have

1. My father _____ up in the morning at six o'clock.
2. He works in a factory and _____ work at 7:30 a.m.
3. I usually _____ to work at 10:00 a.m. on Fridays.
4. To stay in shape, I _____ karate at lunchtime.
5. I _____ work at five in the evening and ride my bike home.
6. In the evening, I _____ my dog for an hour.
7. My sister _____ the violin.
8. We often _____ dinner together.

39

UNIT 5

What are you wearing?

LANGUAGE simple present and present continuous ■ clothes ■ ordinal numbers

5A Party time

1 Look at the pictures in the text. What are the people wearing? Choose from the words in the box.

a dress   a shirt   pants   boots   a jacket   sandals   a hat   a suit

Go to Vocabulary practice: clothes, page 143

2 A Read the text. Match pictures a–c with names of celebrations 1–3.

B Match sentences 1–5 with the three celebrations.

1 This celebration takes place in Brazil.   _____
2 A lot of people wear red for this celebration.   _____
3 This celebration starts on a Friday.   _____
4 This celebration happens in the winter.   _____
5 Animals take part in this celebration.   _____

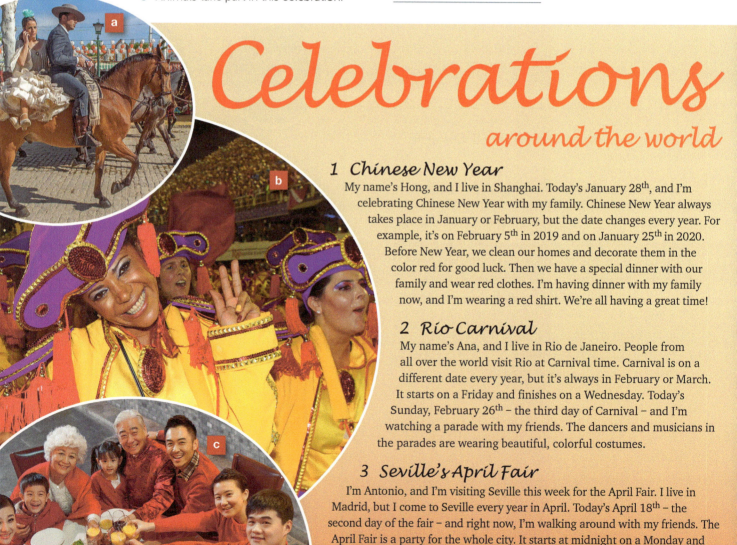

Celebrations
around the world

1 Chinese New Year

My name's Hong, and I live in Shanghai. Today's January 28th, and I'm celebrating Chinese New Year with my family. Chinese New Year always takes place in January or February, but the date changes every year. For example, it's on February 5th in 2019 and on January 25th in 2020. Before New Year, we clean our homes and decorate them in the color red for good luck. Then we have a special dinner with our family and wear red clothes. I'm having dinner with my family now, and I'm wearing a red shirt. We're all having a great time!

2 Rio Carnival

My name's Ana, and I live in Rio de Janeiro. People from all over the world visit Rio at Carnival time. Carnival is on a different date every year, but it's always in February or March. It starts on a Friday and finishes on a Wednesday. Today's Sunday, February 26th – the third day of Carnival – and I'm watching a parade with my friends. The dancers and musicians in the parades are wearing beautiful, colorful costumes.

3 Seville's April Fair

I'm Antonio, and I'm visiting Seville this week for the April Fair. I live in Madrid, but I come to Seville every year in April. Today's April 18th – the second day of the fair – and right now, I'm walking around with my friends. The April Fair is a party for the whole city. It starts at midnight on a Monday and finishes on a Sunday. The women wear flamenco dresses, jewelry, and flowers in their hair, and the men wear suits and hats. Some people ride horses. The atmosphere's fantastic!

simple present and present continuous ▪ clothes ▪ ordinal numbers | **LANGUAGE** | **5A**

3 **A** Underline the verbs in the simple present and circle the verbs in the present continuous in the text.

B Complete the rules with *simple present* or *present continuous*. Then read the Grammar box.

1 We use the _____ to talk about facts and things that happen regularly.

2 We use the _____ to talk about things that are happening now or temporary actions.

📖 **Grammar** | **simple present and present continuous**

For things that happen regularly or are always true, we use the simple present:
*It always **happens** in January or February.*   *I **live** in Shanghai.*

For things that are happening now or temporary actions, we use the present continuous:
*I'**m having** dinner with my family now.*   *I'**m visiting** Seville this week.*

Go to Grammar practice: simple present and present continuous, page 120

4 **A** Complete the interview with the correct form of the verbs in parentheses. Which person from the text is the interview with?

A Hello. I'm from 103 FM Radio. ¹_____ you _____ a good time? (have)

B Yes, it's amazing! We ²_____ every year. (come)

A What ³_____ you _____ right now? (do)

B We ⁴_____ the local people go by on their horses. (watch) The women look beautiful!

A What ⁵_____ they _____? (wear)

B Long flamenco dresses with special sandals, lots of jewelry, and flowers in their hair. People at the fair always ⁶_____ traditional clothes like that. (wear)

A ⁷_____ you _____ here? (live)

B No, I ⁸_____ just _____ the city this week. (visit) It's my favorite festival in the whole country.

A Great to talk to you! Enjoy the rest of the celebration.

B ▶5.3 Listen and check your answers.

Go to Communication practice: Student A page 161, Student B page 170

5 Match festivals 1–5 with dates a–e.

1 New Year's Day	**a** March 8th	
2 U.S. Independence Day	**b** October 31st	
3 Halloween	**c** January 1st	
4 Valentine's Day	**d** July 4th	
5 International Women's Day	**e** February 14th	

Go to Vocabulary practice: ordinal numbers, page 143

6 **A** ▶5.5 **Pronunciation:** dates Listen and repeat the dates. Which words are stressed?

It's July fourteenth.   *It's August twenty-fifth.*   *It's the second of May.*   *It's the third of June.*

B ▶5.6 In pairs, say each date in two different ways. Listen, check, and repeat.

It's April first.   *It's the first of April.*

1 April 1	5 October 31	9 February 26
2 July 4	6 November 20	10 March 5
3 August 8	7 December 30	
4 September 12	8 January 16	

7 **A** Ask different classmates about their birthdays. Who has a birthday in the same month as you?

A *When's your birthday?*   **B** *My birthday's on March 7th.*

A *What do you usually do on your birthday?*   **B** *I usually go out for lunch with my family. What about you?*

B Tell the class about your classmates' birthdays.

Elena's birthday's on June 4th. She always goes out with her friends.

Personal Best | Write sentences about some of your classmates. What do they usually wear to class? What are they wearing today? | 41

5 SKILLS READING identifying facts and opinions ■ adjectives

5B Don't tell me what to wear

1 Read the introduction of the text and discuss the questions in pairs.

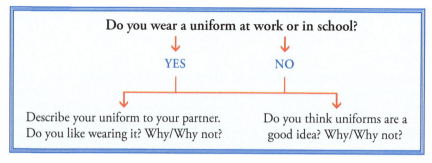

> **Skill** identifying facts and opinions
>
> Texts often include both facts and opinions.
> A fact is a piece of true information: *New Year's Day is on January 1st*.
> An opinion is what someone thinks about something. You can express an opinion with:
> a verb: *I think (that) …, I don't think (that) …, I agree, I don't agree*
> a positive or negative adjective: *good, fun, fantastic, bad, horrible*

2 A Read the Skill box and the text. Find one fact for each person.

1 Richard _____
2 Maria _____
3 Saif _____
4 Nikki _____
5 Hannah _____

B In pairs, say your facts. Do you remember which person says them?

A *I wear a uniform on my job – a hat, a shirt, and pants.* B *That's Hannah.*

3 Read the text again and answer the questions.

Which person/people think(s) that …
1 uniforms aren't for everyone? _____
2 his/her uniform's not nice? _____
3 his/her uniform is nice? _____, _____
4 his/her uniform's not interesting? _____
5 uniforms are a good idea in his/her situation? _____, _____, _____, _____

> **Text builder** adjectives
>
> Adjectives often show someone's opinion:
> *It's pretty **boring**.*   *We have a **nice** uniform at the bank.*   *The hat's **terrible**.*
>
> Adjectives come before a noun and after the verb *be*:
> *We wear a **great** uniform.*   *The uniform's **great**!*

4 Read the Text builder. Find more examples of adjectives in the text. Does each one come before a noun or after the verb *be*?

5 Look at the pictures. Imagine you wear one of the uniforms. Write a paragraph about your uniform. Give facts and opinions.

42

UNIFORMS

ARE YOU A FAN?

Uniforms are common for schoolchildren, police officers, firefighters, soldiers, and a lot of other jobs. But do people like wearing uniforms? Does a uniform make you feel part of a group, or do people dislike looking exactly the same? Here, five readers give us their opinions.

Richard, 16

I wear a uniform to school every day. The uniform for boys is black shoes or sneakers, black pants, a white shirt, and a blue sweater. It's pretty boring, but I don't mind wearing it. I think it's OK to have a school uniform. It means my parents don't need to buy lots of clothes.

Maria, 27

I work in fashion, and clothes are a big part of my life. I always wear fashionable suits to work. It's important to look good on my job – your clothes say a lot about you. Uniforms are fine for some people, but not for me. I don't want someone telling me what to wear.

Saif, 40

Everyone knows we wear a uniform in the fire department. We wear special boots, pants, jackets, gloves, and helmets because we need them. It also shows people that we're firefighters – we're there to help them. I think our uniform's great! It makes me feel part of the fire department.

Nikki, 35

We have a nice uniform at my bank – the women all wear an attractive jacket, a white shirt and scarf, and pants or a skirt. It makes life simple because you don't need to choose your clothes in the morning! I think the uniform's very fashionable, too – it's similar to my own clothes.

Hannah, 21

I wear a uniform on my job – a hat, a shirt, and pants. I don't like my uniform. I don't like the fabric, and the hat's terrible. But I agree that uniforms are necessary on my job because they often get dirty, and I don't want to wear my own clothes at work.

5 LANGUAGE *can* and *can't* ■ hobbies

5C Do the things you love

1 Work in pairs. Match the verbs in the box with pictures 1–5 in the text.

> sew   bake   take photos   paint   make jewelry

Go to Vocabulary practice: hobbies, page 144

2 A Read the web page. Which people don't have another job?

B Read the web page again and answer the questions.

1. How does Sandra make money?
2. What does Paul paint?
3. Do people buy Alexa's photos directly from her?
4. Where does Edith sell her clothes?
5. Where do people buy Alain's cakes?

MONEY MONTHLY
Do the things you love

Do you have a hobby? Perhaps you write a blog, collect stamps, or play chess. Or maybe you draw or paint. These are all great hobbies, and many people enjoy doing them for pleasure, but can you make money from your hobby? Read this week's article and find out.

Meet Sandra, Paul, Alexa, Edith, and Alain. They all make money from their hobbies.

SANDRA works full time in an office, but in her free time, she makes jewelry. She started making jewelry when she was a girl and now makes earrings, bracelets, and rings, and sells them online. She can earn about $150 a month from her hobby. She also wears some of the things she makes.

PAUL's a teacher and, in his free time, he paints. He paints beautiful paintings of animals. People often ask him to paint their pets. He usually goes to their homes to see the pets, draws a picture, and then finishes the painting in his studio at home. He sells about ten paintings every year.

ALEXA's a nurse and her hobby is photography. She has three different cameras. She usually visits interesting places on weekends. She takes great photos, and she often uploads her photos to photo libraries. People can't use them for free, but they can pay to download them.

EDITH AND ALAIN are retired. Edith can sew and make dresses, shirts, and pants. She sells her clothes at the local market. Alain loves cooking, and he bakes delicious cakes. He sells them to local cafés, and people love them. "It's great," he says. "I can make money simply by doing what I love!"

3 Complete the sentences from the text with the phrases in the box.

> can't use   can pay   can make   can earn

1. She _____ about $150 a month.
2. People _____ them for free.
3. They _____ to download them.
4. I _____ money simply by doing what I love.

can and *can't* ■ hobbies   LANGUAGE   **5C**

4 Look at the sentences in exercise 3. Choose the correct options to complete the rules. Then read the Grammar box.

1 We put the base form of a verb *with / without* "to" after *can*.
2 The *he* and *she* form of *can* is *the same as / different from* the other forms.
3 The negative form of *can* is *can't / don't can*.

> **Grammar** *can* and *can't*
>
> ***can*** to talk about ability:
> He **can** make money by doing what he loves.
> She **can** sew.
>
> ***can*** to talk about possibility:
> People **can** pay to download them.
> You **can** buy Alain's cake at this bakery.
>
> ***can*** to talk about permission:
> You **can** park here.   We **can** sit here.
>
> Negative:
> People **can't** use them for free.
>
> Questions and short answers:
> **Can** you make money from your hobby?
> Yes, I **can**.   No, I **can't**.

Go to Grammar practice: *can* and *can't*, page 121

5 A ▶ 5.9 **Pronunciation:** *can* and *can't* Listen and repeat.

1 My brother can speak Italian.
2 I can ride a bike.
3 My sister can't play the violin.
4 You can't sit there.
5 **A** Can you knit? **B** Yes, I can.
6 **A** Can John play chess? **B** No, he can't.

B ▶ 5.10 Say the sentences. Listen, check, and repeat.

1 I can't swim.
2 You can sell your cakes here.
3 **A** Can I ask you a question? **B** Yes, you can.
4 David can't sew.
5 Ellie can sing.
6 **A** Can you cook French food? **B** No, I can't.

Go to Communication practice: Student A page 161, Student B page 170

6 A Imagine you are the manager of a store. Decide the rules for your salesclerks. Complete the sentences with *can* or *can't*.

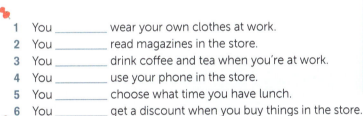

1 You _____ wear your own clothes at work.
2 You _____ read magazines in the store.
3 You _____ drink coffee and tea when you're at work.
4 You _____ use your phone in the store.
5 You _____ choose what time you have lunch.
6 You _____ get a discount when you buy things in the store.

B In pairs, ask and answer questions about your rules. Do you want to work in your partner's store? Why/Why not?

A Can I wear my own clothes at work?   **B** No, you can't. Everyone wears a uniform.

7 A Match sentences 1–5 with headings a–e.

1 You can't go swimming in the ocean here because we don't have a beach.
2 I can bake really good cookies.
3 You can drive a car if you're over eighteen.
4 You can visit the Science Museum.
5 I can't speak Japanese.

a Your abilities: things that you can do
b Your abilities: things that you can't do
c Things that people can do in your town or city
d Things that people can't do in your town or city
e Things that you can do in your country if you're over eighteen

B Think of more sentences that are true for you in pairs.

In our city, you can watch a soccer game at the national stadium.

Personal Best Write about your favorite hobby. When do you do it? Do you do it with other people? Can you earn money from it?

5 SKILLS SPEAKING shopping for clothes ■ offering help

5D Can I try it on?

1 A Do you enjoy shopping for these things? Why/Why not? Tell your partner.

books   food   clothes   shoes   jewelry   sports equipment   birthday presents

B Do you like shopping in these places?

department stores   supermarkets   markets   local stores   online   shopping malls

2 ▶ 5.11 Watch or listen to the first part of *Learning Curve*. Are the sentences true (T) or false (F)?

1 Simon, Kate, and Jack all want some new clothes. ____
2 They have a big event next week. ____
3 They want to order things online. ____

3 ▶ 5.11 Watch or listen again. Choose the correct options to complete the sentences.

1 Simon *likes / loves / doesn't mind* shopping for sports equipment.
2 He *likes / doesn't like / doesn't mind* shopping for birthday presents.
3 He *likes / doesn't like / doesn't mind* shopping at department stores.
4 The big event is a special *dinner / show / party*.
5 "First in Web TV" is a *prize / video channel / website*.

4 ▶ 5.12 Watch or listen to the second part of the show and check (✓) the clothes that Simon, Jack, and Kate try on.

1 coat ☐   6 scarf ☐
2 top ☐   7 shirt ☐
3 skirt ☐   8 dress ☐
4 tie ☐   9 pajamas ☐
5 suit ☐   10 shorts ☐

5 ▶ 5.12 Match the two parts to make complete sentences. Watch or listen again and check.

1 Do you have it   a sell pajamas?
2 What colors   b this credit card here?
3 Do you   c in a size 38?
4 Where are the   d are there?
5 How much   e these on, please?
6 Can I pay with   f is it?
7 Can I try   g women's changing rooms, please?

46

shopping for clothes ■ offering help **SPEAKING** **SKILLS** **5D**

Conversation builder — shopping for clothes

Asking for information:
Do you have this (suit)/these (jeans) in (blue/a size 38/a medium)?
What colors are there?
Do you sell (pajamas)?
Where are the women's changing/dressing rooms, please?
How much is it/are they?

Asking for permission:
Can I try this (suit) on, please?
Can I pay with cash/by credit card?

this/that/these/those:

I like this (shirt).

I like these (shirts).

I like that (shirt).

I like those (shirts).

6 Read the Conversation builder. Choose two items in the box. In pairs, take turns asking and answering questions about them. Ask about the prices, sizes (small, medium, or large), and colors.

dress   shirt   jacket   jeans   pajamas   shorts

A *Do you have this dress in a small?*   B *No, I'm sorry, we don't. We only have it in a large.*

Skill — offering help

If someone needs something, we can offer to help them:
- Ask if they need help: *Are you all right? Do you need any help?*
- Ask if you can help: *Can I help you?*
- Say what you will do: *Just a minute. I'll check.   I'll show you (where they are). Let me ask someone. I'll be right back.*

7 5.13   Read the Skill box. Complete the conversation. Listen and check.
A ¹_____?
B Yes, please. I'm looking for jackets.
A ²_____.
B Thank you. Do you have this jacket in a large?
A ³_____. I'll be right back. ... Yes. Here you are.
B Thank you very much.

Go to Communication practice: Student A page 161, Student B page 170

8 A PREPARE In pairs, read the situations. Choose your roles. Think about what you need to say.

	Situation 1	Situation 2
Student A	You are a customer. You want to buy a blue T-shirt in a medium. You can spend $20. Ask to try the T-shirt on. Ask about the dressing rooms.	You are a salesclerk in a shoe store. You have shoes in black, brown, and blue, in every size. They are all $40. Offer to help the customer.
Student B	You are a salesclerk in a department store. You have white, blue, and black T-shirts, in small and medium. They are $19.99. Offer to help the customer.	You are a customer. You want to buy some brown shoes in a size 9. Ask about the price. If it's OK, ask to try the shoes on.

B PRACTICE Act out your conversations.

C PERSONAL BEST Find a new partner and act out your conversations again. Is your conversation better this time?

Personal Best Write a conversation between a customer and a salesclerk in a clothing store or department store.

UNIT 6

Homes and cities

LANGUAGE *there is/there are, some/any* ■ prepositions of place ■ rooms and furniture

6A A small space

1 Look at these rooms and items of furniture. Which of them do you have in your home? Can you think of more?

> kitchen   bedroom   living room   stove   closet   armchair   sofa   mirror

Go to Vocabulary practice: rooms and furniture, page 145

2 **A** Look at the title of the text and the pictures. How is the apartment special?
B Read the text and check.

3 Read the text again and answer the questions.
1 What is Gary's job?
2 How does Gary make the different "rooms"?
3 Where is his bed?
4 Where can guests sleep?
5 According to the text, what free-time activities can Gary do in the apartment?

24-room micro-apartment

HONG KONG is a busy and exciting city with a population of more than seven million. Like most people in Hong Kong, architect Gary Chang lives in a small apartment. But Gary's apartment has a difference – he can move the walls. It's only 32 square meters, but he can create a lot of new "rooms" inside it.

When you come into the apartment, you see just one room. There's a wall with a TV on it. If you move this, you find a kitchen with a sink and stove. Next to the kitchen, there's a small wall with a washing machine behind it.

Back in the main room, are there any chairs? No, there aren't any armchairs, but there's a small sofa on a wall. You can lift the sofa, pull down the wall, and it becomes a double bed! There are some shelves for books next to the bed, and there's a desk under the shelves.

Another wall in the main room has shelves for Gary's 3,000 CDs. If you move this wall, you find a bathroom behind it. Is there space for visitors? Gary can cover the bathtub to make a bed for guests.

In total, Gary can make 24 different "rooms," including a dining room, a study, and a movie room. There's no balcony, but Gary doesn't mind. He has enough space to have dinner with friends, do yoga, and even have a party!

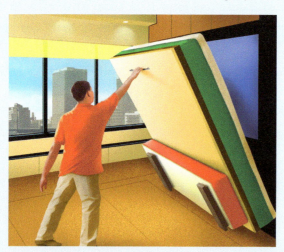

there is/there are, some/any ■ prepositions of place ■ rooms and furniture | **LANGUAGE** | **6A**

4 A Complete the sentences. Check your answers in the text.

1 There _____ a wall with a TV on it.
2 There _____ some shelves for books.

3 There _____ balcony.
4 There _____ any armchairs.

B Choose the correct options to complete the rules. Then read the Grammar box.

We can use *some* and *any* with plural nouns. They mean "more than one."

1 We use *some* / *any* in affirmative sentences.
2 We use *some* / *any* in negative sentences and plural questions.

📖 **Grammar** *there is/there are, some/any*

Singular

Affirmative:
There's a TV.
There's an armchair.

Negative:
There's no sofa.
There's no balcony.

Questions:
Is there a washing machine?
Yes, there is. No, *there's not.* (*No, there isn't.*)

Plural

Affirmative:
There are some cabinets.

Negative:
There are no/There aren't any stairs.

Questions:
Are there any shelves?
Yes, there are. No, *there aren't.*

Look! We usually use the contraction *there's* for *there is*. We don't contract *there are*.

Go to Grammar practice: *there is/there are, some/any*, page 122

---

5 A ▶ 6.4 **Pronunciation:** *there's/there are* Listen to the sentences and notice how *there's* and *there are* are pronounced. Listen again and repeat.

1 There's a balcony.
2 There are two armchairs.

3 There's no sofa.
4 There aren't any shelves.

B ▶ 6.5 Say the sentences. Listen, check, and repeat.

1 There are five rooms in the apartment.
2 There's a big table in the kitchen.

3 There are no chairs in the living room.
4 There's no garage.

6 A ▶ 6.6 Listen to the description of an apartment. Complete it with the prepositions in the box. Which room is the speaker describing?

behind   in front of   across from   under   next to

This is my favorite room. There's a window ¹_____ the door. There are some chairs and a table ²_____ the window. We have two comfortable armchairs – they're ³_____ the TV, and there's a small table between them. There are some shelves ⁴_____ the armchairs. We have some books and a clock on the shelves. There's a cabinet ⁵_____ the TV.

B Underline two other prepositions of place in the text in exercise 6A. Then read the Grammar box.

📖 **Grammar** prepositions of place

We use prepositions of place to say where something or someone is:
*Beth's **in** the backyard.*   *The bathroom's **across from** the bedroom.*   *Our photos are **on** the shelves.*

Go to Grammar practice: prepositions of place, page 122

Go to Communication practice: Student A page 162, Student B page 171

7 Think of a room in your house. What furniture is there? What other objects and possessions are there? Describe it to your partner and ask him/her to draw a plan of it.

Personal Best Write a paragraph about your classroom. Describe what there is.

6 SKILLS LISTENING identifying key points ■ contractions ■ common adjectives

6B Amazing homes

1 Match pictures a–h with the adjectives in the box.

> clean narrow light traditional heavy wide modern dirty

Go to Vocabulary practice: common adjectives, page 145

2 Think of the homes of your friends and family. Describe them to your partner with the adjectives.

My parents' apartment has a modern kitchen and bathroom. There's an old armchair in the living room.

3 A In pairs, look at the pictures from the show. What adjectives can you use to describe each house?

a house in the Czech Republic   b house in the Philippines

B ▶ 6.9 Watch or listen to the first part of *Learning Curve* and check your answers.

4 ▶ 6.9 Watch or listen again. Which house in exercise 3 do sentences 1–5 describe? Write a or b.

1 This house can move up and down. ____
2 This house is on an island. ____
3 This house changes with the weather. ____
4 This house can get bigger. ____
5 This house is above the ground because it's dry there. ____

🔧 Skill identifying key points

When people speak, listen for the important things they say.
- Don't worry if you don't understand every word.
- People often give an example of the key points using *for example*, *such as*, or *e.g.*
- Listen to which words are stressed. People often emphasize the most important ideas.

identifying key points ■ contractions ■ common adjectives   LISTENING   SKILLS   6B

5 ▶ 6.10   Read the Skill box. Then watch or listen to the second part of the show. Complete the key points with the names.

Josh

Charlotte

Danielle

Manu

1 _____'s home is very big and very old.
2 _____'s home is small, and it's not expensive.
3 _____'s only living in this home for a short time.
4 _____'s home has both modern and traditional things.

6 ▶ 6.10   Watch or listen again. Are the sentences true (T) or false (F)?
1 There aren't any windows in Josh's apartment.   ____
2 It's quiet in his apartment at night.   ____
3 Charlotte has some new things in her kitchen.   ____
4 Her wardrobe's very expensive.   ____
5 Danielle's house is in Canada.   ____
6 She's cleaning the shelves right now.   ____
7 Manu lives in his beach house for nine months every year.   ____
8 He's a teacher in California.   ____

7 Discuss the questions in pairs.
1 Do you live in a house or an apartment? How old is it?
2 Are there old or new things in it?
3 Describe your favorite room.
4 Do you live in your house or apartment all year?

Listening builder   contractions

When people speak, they usually contract verbs:
He is calling from California! → He**'s** calling from California!
My home is not big. → My home **isn't** big.
I do not understand. → I **don't** understand.

---

8 A Read the Listening builder. In pairs, complete the sentences from the show with the contractions in the box.

don't   there's   it's   I'm   bed's   they're

1 When _____ cold, the house turns and moves up, and gets a lot of sun.
2 I _____ mean a garage at a house.
3 There are about 300 small apartments. And _____ very cheap.
4 My _____ opposite the kitchen.
5 There are four bedrooms, and _____ a bathroom next to each bedroom.
6 _____ a teacher!

B ▶ 6.11   Listen and check.

9 Discuss the questions in pairs.
1 What do you remember about the homes in the video?
2 Which homes in the video do you like? Why?
3 Which homes don't you like? Why?
4 Do you prefer modern or traditional homes? Why?
5 Do you know someone who lives in an unusual home? Can you describe it?

Personal Best   Write a paragraph about your home or another person's home.

6 LANGUAGE — modifiers ■ places in a city

6C The Big Apple

1 A Think of a city from these continents and regions. Write a fact about each city.

Europe   Asia   Africa   Latin America   Australasia

B In pairs, tell each other about your cities. Are any of your facts the same?

2 A Look at the pictures. What do you already know about New York City? Make a list in pairs.

B Read the text. What information about New York City is new to you?

So you want to visit …
New York City?

New York — "the Big Apple" — is my favorite city in the world. I love the streets, the modern skyscrapers, and old apartment buildings. It's full of really famous sights, and even on a short visit, you can see a lot of amazing things.

For many people, number one on the list of places to see is the Empire State Building. It's a very famous skyscraper, and there are great views of the city from its 86th and 102nd floors. Another interesting skyscraper is 4 Times Square (formerly the Condé Nast building). It's not beautiful at all, in my opinion, but it's an important "green" building. New York has very cold winters and pretty hot summers, but 4 Times Square produces its own comfortable temperature for most of the year.

For a fantastic view of Manhattan and the Statue of Liberty, visit the Brooklyn Bridge. It's great for taking photos, but it's really busy, with hundreds of cars, bikes, and people. If you get stressed out by the noise, go back to Manhattan and relax in City Hall Park for a while. It's a pretty small park, but it's very special. You can have your lunch there and decide what to do next: see a show on Broadway, go shopping on Fifth Avenue, or go for a walk in Central Park. It's impossible to be bored in this incredible city!

by Harry Fuller

3 Read the text again. What adjectives does the writer use to describe the places?
1 the Empire State Building
2 4 Times Square
3 the Brooklyn Bridge
4 City Hall Park

4 Match sentences 1–5 with pictures a–d. Two sentences match one picture. Then read the Grammar box.
1 This restaurant is very busy.
2 This restaurant's not very busy.
3 This restaurant is pretty busy.
4 This restaurant is really busy.
5 This restaurant's not busy at all.

modifiers ■ places in a city **LANGUAGE** **6C**

 Grammar modifiers

We use modifiers with adjectives:
There are **really** beautiful views of the city.
It's **really** hot in the summer.
It's a **pretty** famous building.

It's not a **very** big park.
It's **not** a beautiful building **at all**.

Go to Grammar practice: modifiers, page 123

5 Look at the sentences in exercise 4. Rewrite them beginning with *This is*.

This restaurant is very busy. → This is a very busy restaurant.

6 John is staying in a hotel in New York City. Look at his feedback form about the hotel and complete the sentences with *is/isn't* and *very/really* (✓✓), *pretty* (✓), *not very* (X), or *not ... at all* (X X).

In your opinion, this hotel is ...								
comfortable	✓	modern	X	nice	✓	clean	✓✓	expensive	✓✓	quiet	X X

John says that the hotel ...
1 _____ comfortable.
2 _____ clean.
3 _____ modern.
4 _____ expensive.
5 _____ nice.
6 _____ quiet _____.

7 A ▶ 6.13 **Pronunciation:** sentence stress. Listen and underline the stressed words in the sentences. Listen, check, and repeat.

1 This is a really interesting city.
2 The bridge is pretty wide.
3 Our office isn't very nice.
4 The café isn't cheap at all.
5 Their new house is very traditional.
6 It's a really famous monument.

B ▶ 6.14 Say the sentences. Listen, check, and repeat.

1 This apartment is really modern.
2 Pizza Palace isn't a very expensive restaurant.
3 Boston is a pretty nice city.
4 This square is very popular.
5 We live in a really old house.
6 This building's not beautiful at all.

Go to Communication practice: Student A page 162, Student B page 171

8 Complete definitions 1–3 with the words in the box.

square   cathedrals   apartment buildings   skyscrapers   mosques   market

1 Religious buildings like _____ and _____ are often very beautiful.
2 _____ are very tall buildings. They can be hotels, office buildings, and _____.
3 A _____ is an open area in a town or city. There's often a _____ there where you can go shopping.

Go to Vocabulary practice: places in a city, page 146

9 A ▶ 6.16 Listen and match the places with the cities.

mosque
square
stadium
market
theater
cathedral
skyscraper

Cairo

Brasília

B ▶ 6.16 Listen again and make notes about the places in Cairo and Brasília. Talk about what you can remember in pairs.

You can buy clothes and jewelry at the market in Cairo.

Personal Best Choose three or four interesting buildings in your city. Write a description of them for a travel website.

53

6 SKILLS WRITING topic sentences ▪ describing places

6D Beautiful places

1 A In pairs, match capital cities 1–8 with countries a–h.

1 Kathmandu	a Kenya
2 Wellington	b Poland
3 Lima	c Nepal
4 Warsaw	d Bulgaria
5 San José	e Costa Rica
6 Nairobi	f New Zealand
7 Kingston	g Peru
8 Sofia	h Jamaica

B Think of ten more capital cities.

2 Read the description of Lisbon. Match pictures a–e with paragraphs 1–5.

a _____

b _____

c _____

d _____

e _____

Lisbon a city by the sea

1 Lisbon's the capital city of Portugal. It's on the River Tejo, and it's next to the sea. Lisbon's a pretty small capital city – about 550,000 people live there.

2 Lisbon has some very old areas. Alfama and Graça are beautiful old districts with narrow streets, small squares, and interesting shops. Above them is the castle of São Jorge. There are wonderful views of the city from the castle. You can walk to Alfama and Graça, or you can take the streetcar. It's a great way to see this part of the city.

3 If you want to go on a day trip, take the streetcar to Belém. It's the last district before the beach. There are some interesting museums, a cultural center, and some really beautiful parks. You can try Belém's famous *pastel de nata*, too. These are delicious custard pastries – perfect with coffee.

4 There are lots of places to eat and go out in Lisbon. Bairro Alto's a good place, and there are lots of restaurants and stores. It's pretty noisy at night sometimes. If you want a traditional Portuguese restaurant, go to Alfama or Graça.

5 You can visit Lisbon during any season. It's not very cold in the winter. Spring and fall are lovely times to visit because it's usually warm and sunny. Summer in Lisbon's very hot, but you can go swimming in the sea to cool down!

3 Write the paragraph number for each topic.

1 old parts of Lisbon ____
2 when to visit ____
3 geographical information ____
4 an interesting day trip ____
5 where to eat and go out ____

54

topic sentences ■ describing places **WRITING** **SKILLS** **6D**

Skill: topic sentences

When you write a text, give each paragraph one main topic. The first sentence of the paragraph introduces the topic – we call it a "topic sentence."
For example, in paragraph 1, the "topic sentence" is: *Lisbon's the capital city of Portugal*.

4 A Read the Skill box. <u>Underline</u> the topic sentences in paragraphs 2–5 of the description of Lisbon.

B In pairs, write a topic sentence for each paragraph about Madrid.

1 _____. It's in the middle of the country, and it's on the River Manzanares. Madrid is the capital of Spain and an important political, economic, and cultural center.

2 _____. A really old park is El Capricho. This park has a river, a lake, and some interesting statues and fountains. Another famous park is El Retiro. This is very popular with families.

3 _____. You can go to Plaza de Santa Ana, where there are a lot of fantastic bars and restaurants. Other great areas for going out are La Latina, Malasaña, and Chueca.

Text builder: describing places

Describing a place's location and geography:
... is the capital city of ...
... is in the middle of the country/on the River ... /next to the ocean.
... people live there.

Recommending places:
There are wonderful views of ... from ...
If you want to go on a day trip, go to ...
... is a good place for ...
... is a great way to ...
There are lots of places to ...

5 Read the Text builder. Complete the sentences about the city of Santiago.

1 Santiago _____ Chile. _____ River Mapocho.
2 _____, go to Pomaire.
3 _____ the city and the mountains from San Cristóbal Hill.
4 Bike riding _____ get to the top of the hill.
5 _____ go out in the evening. Barrio Bellavista _____ restaurants.

6 A PREPARE Choose a town or city that you know well. Make notes about the following:

- the location and population
- interesting areas to visit
- places with good views
- places nearby to go on a day trip
- good areas to go out (restaurants, stores, etc.)
- the weather in different seasons

B PRACTICE Write a description of your town or city. Begin each paragraph with a topic sentence.

- Paragraph 1: Give geographical information about the location and population.
- Paragraph 2: Describe an interesting area in the city to visit.
- Paragraph 3: Describe a place near the city where people can go on a day trip.
- Paragraph 4: Talk about some good areas to go out.
- Paragraph 5: Talk about the best time to visit.

C PERSONAL BEST Read your partner's description. Choose a paragraph that you like. What do you like about it? Is there a topic sentence? Can you improve the paragraph?

Personal Best Write about your favorite area in your town or city. Why do you like it? What can you do there?

5 and 6 — REVIEW and PRACTICE

Grammar

1 Choose the correct options to complete the sentences.

1 I usually work in Budapest, but this month _____ in Prague.
   a I work
   b I working
   c I'm working

2 What _____ on the weekend?
   a do you do
   b you do
   c doing you

3 My father _____ speak three languages.
   a can to
   b can
   c is

4 _____ three people in the picture.
   a They're
   b There are
   c There's

5 The letter M is _____ L and N in the alphabet.
   a between
   b behind
   c under

6 I'm sorry, but I _____ come this evening.
   a am not
   b can't
   c don't

7 _____ a good restaurant near here?
   a Is it
   b There's
   c Is there

8 The books are _____ a shelf in the kitchen.
   a at
   b in
   c on

2 Rewrite the sentences with the tense in parentheses.

1 She plays tennis. (present continuous)
_____

2 They're living in Dubai. (simple present)
_____

3 What are you doing? (simple present)
_____

4 We don't work. (present continuous)
_____

5 Where do you live? (present continuous)
_____

6 He wears shorts. (present continuous)
_____

7 She's not listening. (simple present)
_____

8 Are you playing tennis? (simple present)
_____

3 Complete the text using the words in the box.

| eat   between   can't   are   on   in   very   can |

Inside a luxury plane

This is the Embraer Lineage 1000E. It ¹_____ carry 90 passengers, but this one carries nineteen. There's a living area with leather seats and a wool carpet ²_____ the floor. There ³_____ five TVs and four blu-ray players. The seats turn so four people can ⁴_____ around a dining table. The kitchen has two ovens, an espresso machine, and a $75,000 dishwasher! There's a ⁵_____ large bed ⁶_____ the bedroom and a shower. There are two bathrooms and, ⁷_____ the cockpit and the living area, there's another cabin for the crew. For nineteen passengers, there are two flight attendants and two pilots. For luxury, you ⁸_____ do better than the Embraer Lineage.

Vocabulary

1 Circle the word that is different. Explain your answer.

1	attic	desk	bathroom	kitchen
2	living room	bedroom	kitchen	apartment
3	sew	stove	knit	bake
4	boots	shorts	pants	belt
5	three	second	fourth	first
6	theater	stadium	concert hall	bridge
7	armchair	desk	sofa	chair
8	narrow	heavy	modern	wide

2 Match definitions 1–8 with nouns a–h.

1 kitchen furniture with a door where you keep things
2 you put books on these
3 shoes for hot weather or the beach
4 bedroom furniture where you keep clothes
5 a building where you can read and borrow books
6 a room under the house
7 earrings, necklace, etc.
8 where you keep the car

a basement
b library
c closet
d cabinet
e garage
f jewelry
g sandals
h shelves

3 Put the words in the correct columns.

armchair   jeans   bake   hall   play chess   study
sofa   socks   kitchen   take photos   closet
scarf   bathroom   skirt   knit   bed

Furniture	Hobbies	Clothes	Rooms

4 Complete the sentences with the words in the box.

department stores   bake   jeans   tie
backyard   paint   shorts   monument

1 In my office, all the men wear a _____ .
2 I don't like shopping for _____ . I can never find my size.
3 In the park in our town, there's a _____ made of stone.
4 On the weekend, I love sitting in our _____ .
5 My wife likes to _____ in a modern style.
6 I like local stores, but I hate _____ .
7 In the winter, I _____ bread and cakes.
8 I often wear _____ in the summer.

REVIEW and PRACTICE **5** and **6**

Personal Best

Lesson 5A Describe what you're wearing today.

Lesson 5A Name five other items of clothing.

Lesson 5C Name three hobbies with the word *play*.

Lesson 5C List three things you can do well.

Lesson 5C Write three sentences about things you can't do in college or at work.

Lesson 5D List three phrases for shopping for clothes.

Lesson 6A Name five rooms in a house.

Lesson 6A Write four sentences about your home, with *there's*, *there's no*, *there are*, *there are no*.

Lesson 6B List four pairs of opposite adjectives.

Lesson 6C Name four adjectives to describe cities.

Lesson 6C Write a sentence with *pretty* or *really*.

Lesson 6D Write three sentences to describe your city.

57

UNIT 7
Food and drink

LANGUAGE countable and uncountable nouns + *some/any* ■ food and drink

7A Food to your door

1 A Discuss the questions in pairs.
1 Where do you usually go food shopping?
2 How often do you buy food?
3 Do you enjoy food shopping? Why/Why not?

B Look at the pictures on the page. Which items of food can you name?

Go to Vocabulary practice: food and drink, page 147

2 Read the text. What types of food are very popular in food boxes?

What should we have for dinner?

Do you hate supermarkets? Do you like eating healthy meals? A lot of companies in different countries now deliver food boxes to your house. You can find boxes with all different types of food: fresh fruit and vegetables, meat and fish, vegetarian and vegan food, and even desserts, cookies, and cakes. Fruit and vegetables are very popular, especially if it's the season when they're fresh. You usually can't choose the food in the box – it's a surprise!

3 A ▶ 7.2 Listen to James and Fran. What do they cook for their dinner?

B ▶ 7.2 Listen again. Which two types of food aren't in the food box?

| fruit | potatoes | eggs | peas | rice |
| beef | onions | peppers |

4 A ▶ 7.3 Listen and complete the sentences.
1 We need _____ pepper.
2 There's _____ beef.
3 There isn't _____ rice.
4 You have _____ tomatoes, strawberries, and potatoes.
5 Are there _____ onions?
6 There aren't _____ peppers.

B Read the sentences again and complete the rules with *singular* or *plural*. Then read the Grammar box.
1 Uncountable nouns like *rice* and *beef* only have a _____ form.
2 Countable nouns like *tomato* and *onion* can be singular or _____.
3 We use *some* and *any* with uncountable and _____ countable nouns.

58

countable and uncountable nouns + *some/any* ■ food and drink   **LANGUAGE**   **7A**

📖 **Grammar** countable and uncountable nouns + *some/any*

Countable nouns:

two apples
three eggs
two strawberries

Uncountable nouns:

rice
meat
pasta

There are **some** onions.
Are there **any** tomatoes?
We don't need **any** potatoes.

There's **some** fruit.
Do we have **any** pasta?
There isn't **any** juice.

Go to Grammar practice: countable and uncountable nouns + *some/any*, page 124

5 A ▶ 7.5 **Pronunciation:** *some/any* Listen to the sentences. How do we say *some* and *any*? Are they stressed?

1 I have some fruit in my bag.
2 We need some carrots.
3 There are some crackers on the plate.
4 We don't have any bread.
5 I don't want any peas.
6 Is there any milk?

B ▶ 7.5 Say the sentences. Listen again, check, and repeat.

6 A Look at the pictures and name the items. Are they countable (C) or uncountable (U)?

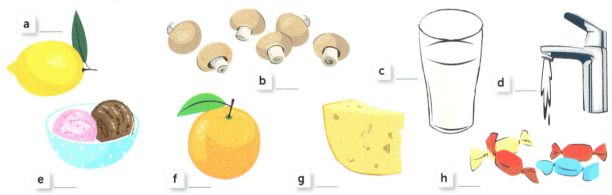

a ___   b ___   c ___   d ___
e ___   f ___   g ___   h ___

B In pairs, make sentences about the food and drink in 6A. Use *a*, *an*, or *some*.

There are some mushrooms.

7 A Imagine you are preparing a fresh-food box for a family. Choose the following food and drink to go in it:

(three types of fruit) (three types of vegetables) (some protein (meat, fish, etc.)) (something sweet)

B Guess what's in your partner's box. Ask questions with *Is there/Are there …?* Who can guess the most items?

A *Is there any cheese?*   B *No, there's not. My turn. Are there any strawberries?*
A *Yes, there are!*

Go to Communication practice: Student A page 162, Student B page 171

8 Ask and answer the questions in pairs.

1 What do you usually have for breakfast, lunch, and dinner?
2 What food do you need for your favorite meal?
3 What food is in your fridge at home right now?

Personal Best Think of someone you know and make the perfect food box for him/her. Describe it.

| **7** | SKILLS | **READING** | skimming a text ■ pronouns and possessive adjectives |

7B Stopping for lunch

1 A How important is it for you to stop for a lunch break every day? Mark the line.

| 1 | 2 | 3 | 4 | 5 | 6 | 7 | 8 | 9 | 10 |

Very important   Not important at all

B In pairs, discuss the questions. How long is your lunch break? Where do you usually have lunch?

> ### Skill   skimming a text
>
> **When we skim a text, we read it quickly to understand the main ideas.**
> - Read the first sentence of each paragraph to get an idea of the topic.
> - Read the rest of each paragraph quickly. Don't worry if you don't understand every word.
> - Try to understand the general idea or ideas in the text.

2 Read the Skill box. Skim the text and match the countries with the sentences.

> the U.S.   Italy   Kenya

1 People often have lunch with their colleagues.   _____
2 People often have a quick lunch.   _____
3 Lunch breaks in cities are different from in the country.   _____

3 Read the text again and answer the questions.

1 What do people like in their sandwiches in the U.S.?
2 What does Carla do when she has lunch?
3 Why is lunch very important in Kenya?
4 Where does Joseph like sitting for lunch?
5 What happens to a lot of stores in small towns in Italy at lunchtime?
6 What does Andrea sometimes do after lunch?

4 Match the places from the text with the sentences.

1 A lot of working people in the U.S. eat their lunch here._____, _____
2 People in the U.S. often buy sandwiches here.   _____, _____, _____
3 A lot of popular food in Kenya comes from here.   _____
4 Italians in the country often eat their lunch here.   _____

5 In pairs, discuss the people in the text. Whose lunch break is similar to yours? Which do you think is the best and why?

> ### Text builder   pronouns and possessive adjectives
>
> **We use pronouns and possessive adjectives to avoid repeating nouns and names:**
> *I usually buy a **sandwich**. I eat **it** at my desk.*
> ***Working people** usually have a long, sociable lunch. **They** often go to **their** favorite restaurant.*

6 Read the Text builder. Look at the sentences from the text. What do the <u>underlined</u> pronouns and possessive adjectives refer to?

1 My lunch break is an hour, but <u>it</u>'s longer on Fridays.
2 The quality of the food is very important to Italians, even if <u>their</u> lunch break is short.
3 My wife is an excellent cook. <u>She</u> usually makes some pasta with beef and tomato sauce.

7 In pairs, think about different people and their jobs in your country. How long is their lunch break? Where do they go for lunch? What do you think they have?

60

skimming a text ■ pronouns and possessive adjectives   READING   SKILLS   7B

Lunches around the world

THE U.S.
In the U.S., a lot of working people take a short lunch break. They eat lunch in their office or even at their desk. Sandwiches are the most popular lunch, and they're often filled with cheese or meat, such as chicken. People bring their own sandwiches or buy them from a supermarket, delicatessen, or café. A lot of places also sell salads and soup to take out.

CARLA, 34, ACCOUNTANT
"I rarely take more than ten to fifteen minutes to eat my lunch. I usually buy a sandwich from a coffee shop near the office. I then eat it at my desk and read the news on the Internet. After that, I continue working."

KENYA
In Kenya, lunch is a very important meal because people leave home very early, and they don't have time for breakfast. Working people usually have a long, sociable lunch. They often go to their favorite restaurant with their colleagues. People eat a lot of fish, and the most popular dishes come from the west of Kenya.

JOSEPH, 39, IT WORKER
"My lunch break is an hour, but it's longer on Fridays. I usually go for lunch with some friends from work, and we like sitting outside in the sun to eat. It's nice to have lunch together. I usually order the same dish: fish with vegetables in a creamy sauce."

ITALY
In small towns and villages in Italy, people usually take a long lunch break. Stores and businesses close for two or three hours, and families have a big lunch together at home. It's different in big cities – people take a shorter lunch break and usually don't go home. The quality of the food is very important to Italians, even if their lunch break is short.

ANDREA, 43, STORE OWNER
"I always close my store for lunch and eat with my family. My wife is an excellent cook. She usually makes some pasta with beef and tomato sauce, and then we have chicken or fish with fresh vegetables. I sometimes have a nap (a short sleep) after lunch. I open the store again at 4 p.m."

Personal Best — Write a paragraph about a typical lunch on a work day for you.

61

7 LANGUAGE
quantifiers: (how) much, (how) many, a lot of, a few, a little ■ containers and portions

7C Are you hungry?

1 Look at the picture and discuss the questions in pairs.
1 What can and can't you eat or drink when you're on a diet?
2 Do you know any unusual diets?

2 A Read the text. Why is the diet called the "5:2 diet"? Do you think it is a good idea?

B Complete the chart with the food and drink that Gary eats every week.

	Vegetables	Fruit	Meat	Dairy products	Drinks	Other food
Five days a week						
Two days a week						

The 5:2 diet

Do you know about the 5:2 diet?

For some people, this amazing diet really works. On the 5:2 diet, you can eat normally for five days a week. You are only on the diet for two days a week, but, on those two days, you can only eat 500 calories a day if you're a woman and 600 if you're a man.

How much is 600 calories? Here are some examples:

1 large burger   2 small bars of chocolate

3 bags of potato chips   2 bowls of rice

6 tins of tomatoes   6 bananas

Gary is on the 5:2 diet.
FIVE DAYS a week, he has:
- Breakfast – two eggs, three slices of toast with butter, a cup of coffee with milk and sugar
- Snack – a few cookies
- Lunch – a bag of nuts, two sandwiches
- Snack – a small bag of potato chips, a carton of juice
- Dinner – pasta with beef and tomato sauce, peas
- Drinks – five cups of coffee with sugar and milk, three bottles of cola

TWO DAYS a week, he has:
- Breakfast – a slice of toast with no butter, a cup of coffee with no milk
- Snack – water, an apple
- Lunch – salad
- Snack – an orange
- Dinner – chicken and cabbage
- Snack – a few grapes

3 A Label the items from Gary's list.

a _a slice of toast_   b _____   c _____   d _____   e _____   f _____

quantifiers: *(how) much, (how) many, a lot of, a few, a little* ■ containers and portions   **LANGUAGE 7C**

B Cover page 62 and answer the questions in pairs.
1 What do you remember about Gary's diet?
2 What can he eat two days a week?
3 What can he eat five days a week?

Go to Vocabulary practice: containers and portions, page 148

4 A ▶ 7.7 Listen to Gary talking to his friend Amy about his diet. Is it a "5" or a "2" day today?

B ▶ 7.7 Listen again and complete the sentences and questions.
1 I normally have a lot of _____ for breakfast.
2 How much _____ can you have?
3 I only have a little _____ – not a lot.
4 How many _____ of coffee do you have on a "5" day?
5 I don't eat much _____, and I don't eat many _____.
6 I have a few _____ in the morning for my snack.

5 A Look again at 4B and complete the sentences with *much, many,* and *a lot of*. Then read the Grammar box.
1 We use How _____ to ask about countable nouns.
2 We use How _____ to ask about uncountable nouns.
3 We use _____ in affirmative sentences and questions.
4 We use _____ and _____ in negative sentences.

B Which phrase in 4B means "a large amount"? Which phrase means "a small amount"? Which phrase means "a small number"?

📖 **Grammar**   quantifiers: *(how) much, (how) many, a lot of, a few, a little*

Countable nouns:
I eat **a lot of** vegetables.
I have **a few** cookies with my coffee.
I don't eat **many** potato chips.
Do you eat **many** vegetables?
How **many** eggs do you eat? Not **many**./A **few**./A **lot**.

Uncountable nouns:
I eat **a lot of** fruit.
I put **a little** milk in my coffee.
I don't eat **much** meat.
Do you drink **a lot of** coffee?
How **much** fruit do you eat? Not **much**./A **little**./A **lot**.

Go to Grammar practice: quantifiers: *(how) much, (how) many, a lot of, a few, a little,* page 125

6 A ▶ 7.9 **Pronunciation:** weak form *of* Listen and repeat the phrases.
1 a lot of pasta
2 a cup of coffee
3 a bottle of water
4 a lot of salad
5 a glass of orange juice
6 a piece of cake

B ▶ 7.10 Say the sentences. Listen, check, and repeat.
1 I don't eat a lot of cookies.
2 Can I have a bag of potato chips, please?
3 There's a can of peas in the kitchen cabinet.
4 I drink a lot of coffee.

7 A Complete the questions with *How much* or *How many*.
1 _____ rice do you eat a week?
2 _____ pasta do you eat a week?
3 _____ glasses of water do you have a day?
4 _____ cups of coffee do you have a day?
5 _____ sugar do you have a week?
6 _____ cartons of juice do you buy a week?

B Ask and answer the questions in pairs.
A *How much rice do you eat a week?*   B *I have rice about once a week. How about you?*

Go to Communication practice: Student A page 163, Student B page 172

8 A Do you have a healthy diet? Score your typical daily diet 1–10 on the scale below.

junk food lover 1 2 3 4 5 6 7 8 9 10 healthy eater

B Compare your scale with a partner. Discuss your typical daily diet.
A *I have a pretty healthy diet. I don't eat many cookies or a lot of cake. I don't eat junk food.*
B *Me, too. I eat a lot of fresh fruit and vegetables, but I sometimes have soft drinks, such as cola.*

Personal Best Plan a new diet to help people be healthier. What can you eat and drink each day or week?

63

7 SKILLS SPEAKING in a restaurant ■ asking politely for something

7D Out for dinner

1 Look at pictures a–d. In which pictures are the people:

1 asking for the check?   _d_
2 ordering food?   ____
3 arriving at a restaurant?   ____
4 reserving a table?   ____

2 A ▶ 7.11 Watch or listen to the first part of *Learning Curve*. Which activity in exercise 1 do you see or hear?

B ▶ 7.11 Watch or listen again and answer the questions below.

1 What is the name of Jack and Lance's restaurant?
2 Why is the restaurant called this?
3 What day and time does Simon want to reserve a table for?
4 How many people does he want the table for?

3 ▶ 7.12 Now watch or listen to the second part of the show. Who orders the following food and drink? Write K (Kate) or S (Simon).

1 small salad   ____
2 chicken soup   ____
3 goulash with rice   ____
4 chicken   ____
5 chips, peas, and carrots   ____
6 chocolate ice cream   ____
7 a cup of tea   ____

Conversation builder — in a restaurant

Reserving a table:
Do you have a table for ... please?
It's for ... people.

Arriving at a restaurant:
We have a table reserved in the name of ...

Ordering food:
I'd like the (chicken), please.
I'll have ...
Could/Can I have ...?
The same for me, please./Me too.

Paying the check:
Could/Can we have the check, please?

4 A Read the Conversation builder and complete the mini-conversations.

Waiter Hello, Harry's Restaurant. How can I help?
Dimitri ¹ _____ Saturday for lunch, please?

Dimitri Hello. ² _____ Aristov.
Waiter No problem. Follow me, please.

Waiter Would you like a starter?
Dimitri Yes. ³ _____ the vegetable soup, please.

Waiter And for you?
Svetlana ⁴ _____ the five-bean salad, please?

Svetlana ⁵ _____, please?
Waiter Would you like to pay by cash or credit card?
Svetlana By card.

B In groups of three, practice saying the conversations. Take turns being the waiter, Dimitri, and Svetlana.

in a restaurant ■ asking politely for something **SPEAKING** **SKILLS** 🎥 **7D**

5 ▶ **7.12** Watch or listen again and complete the sentences.

1 Kate doesn't want _____ or _____ in her starter.
2 Jack's goulash has _____, _____, vegetables, and spices in it.
3 Simon wants to have _____ scoops of _____.
4 Kate wants to pay by _____, but Simon wants to pay by _____.
5 Jack says that the meals are "on the _____" – it means Simon and Kate don't need to pay.

🔧 **Skill** **asking politely for something**

It's important to use polite forms when you ask for something.
Instead of *I want*, use *I'd like*, *Can I have ...?* or *Could I have ...?*
I'd like a cup of coffee.
Could I have a large orange juice, please?
Can we have three slices of cake?

Use polite intonation, too.

6 **A** ▶ **7.13** Read the Skill box. Listen to three situations. Which customer is more polite, a or b?

1 ____   2 ____   3 ____

B Take turns asking and answering the waiter's questions politely. Use the food items and drinks below or your own ideas.

Would you like a starter?   Can I get you any drinks?   Anything else?   Are you ready to order your main course now?

bread

fish and chips   French onion soup   avocado salad   olives   bottle of mineral water   glass of orange juice

Go to Communication practice: Student A page 163, Student B page 172

7 **A** **PREPARE** Look at the menu. Decide when you want to go there for a meal, with how many people, and what you would like to eat.

> ## The Bell
>
> **STARTERS**
> Tomato soup, Garlic mushrooms, Bean and pasta salad
>
> **MAIN COURSES**
> Roast beef, Fish of the day, Fried chicken
> All served with seasonal vegetables and a choice of French fries,
> boiled potatoes, or rice.
>
> **DESSERTS**
> Chocolate cake, Local cheeses, Fresh fruit, Ice cream (choice of flavors)

B **PRACTICE** Decide who the waiter is and who the customer is.

CUSTOMER: Call the restaurant to reserve a table. Arrive at the restaurant, order your food, and ask for the check.

WAITER: Take the telephone reservation. Welcome the customers to the restaurant, take their order, and give them the check.

C **PERSONAL BEST** Exchange roles and repeat the conversation. Is it easier to be the waiter or the customer? Why?

Personal Best Plan a menu for your ideal restaurant. Describe it.

UNIT 8 In the past

LANGUAGE past of *be* ■ simple past: irregular verbs ■ inventions

8A Technology through the ages

1 Match the inventions with the words in the box. Do you have any of these things in your home?

video player   digital camera   microwave   TV   smartphone   CD player

a _____   b _____   c _____   d _____   e _____   f _____

Go to Vocabulary practice: inventions, page 149

2 Which inventions are important to you? Choose your top three and tell a partner.

I can't live without my smartphone, GPS, and TV.

3 A When do you think most people in the U.S. first had these things in their homes? Write *1930s*, *1960s*, or *1990s*.

washing machine _____   black-and-white TV _____   telephone _____   CD player _____
radio _____   vacuum cleaner _____   the Internet _____   freezer _____

B Read the text. When did Ethel, George, and Jessica have these things in their homes?

The 1930s

In the 1930s, life at home wasn't easy. There was a lot of housework to do, and we didn't have a lot of things to help us like we do now. There wasn't a vacuum cleaner, an electric iron, or a washing machine in our home. We didn't have a private telephone, but there was a phone that we shared with other families. We didn't make many telephone calls! We had a radio, but we didn't have a TV. In my free time (we were always busy, so there wasn't much free time!), I read a lot of books.

Ethel

The 1960s

My first house was very different from my parents' house. The furniture was very colorful, and there was a lot of technology. We had a telephone and a TV. The TV was black and white, and there were a lot of different programs, but there weren't many channels. We had some modern appliances in our kitchen – a fridge, a freezer, an electric stove, a toaster, and a washing machine, and we always had a vacuum cleaner.

George

The 1990s

In the 1990s, a lot of my friends had TVs in their bedrooms. TVs and other electrical items weren't expensive, and I had a TV and a video player in my room. I had both a cassette player and a CD player to listen to music. In 1997, I bought my first cell phone. There was a computer in our house. I didn't use it much, but in 1998, we got the Internet at home. We were so excited! I can't imagine life without the Internet now. Can you?

Jessica

past of *be* ■ simple past: irregular verbs ■ inventions   **LANGUAGE**   **8A**

4 **A** Complete the sentences from the text with the correct form of *be*.

1 My first house _____ very different from my parents' house.
2 In the 1930s, life at home _____ easy.
3 We _____ so excited!
4 TVs and other electrical items _____ expensive.
5 There _____ a lot of technology.
6 There _____ many channels.

B Answer the questions. Then read the Grammar box.

1 Which are the two affirmative past forms of *be*? _____ and _____
2 What are the negative forms? _____ and _____
3 What are the past forms of *there is* and *there are*? _____ and _____

📖 **Grammar**   **past of *be*, *there was/there were***

Affirmative:
*I **was** two years old in 1934.*
*You **were** a child in the 1960s.*
*Life **was** difficult in the past.*
*We **were** happy.*

Negative:
*I **wasn't** alive in 1930.*
*You **weren't** an adult.*
*It **wasn't** easy.*
*My parents **weren't** rich.*

Past of *there is* and *there are*:
*There **was** a TV in our living room.*
*There **was no** private telephone in our house.*
*There **were** a lot of TV programs.*
*There **weren't** many TV channels.*

Go to Grammar practice: past of *be*, *there was/there were*, page 126

5 ▶ 8.4 **Pronunciation:** *was* and *were* Listen and repeat the sentences. Which verb forms are stressed: affirmative or negative?

1 The TV was in the living room.
2 There wasn't much free time.
3 There were two bedrooms and a bathroom.
4 Things were very different.
5 Dishwashers weren't in every home.
6 There weren't many cars.

6 **A** Look again at the text. Find the affirmative simple past form of these verbs.

1 have _____   2 read _____   3 buy _____   4 get _____

B Find the negative simple past form of these verbs from the text. Which verb form do we use after *didn't*? Then read the Grammar box.

1 have _____   2 make _____   3 use _____

📖 **Grammar**   **simple past: irregular verbs**

A lot of verbs have an irregular simple past affirmative form. You need to learn them.
Affirmative:
*In the 1930s, I **read** a lot of books.*
*We **had** a computer.*

Negative:
*We **didn't make** many phone calls.*
*I **didn't go** there much.*

Go to Grammar practice: simple past: irregular verbs, page 126

7 **A** ▶ 8.6 Complete the text with the simple past form of the verbs in the box. Listen and check.

buy (×2)   have   not use   not have

In the 1990s, I ¹_____ a cell phone, but I ²_____ a digital camera. I ³_____ a digital camera in 2001, but then, in 2005, I ⁴_____ a smartphone, so I ⁵_____ my digital camera after that.

B Tell your partner about yourself. Use the prompts.

(In the 1990s/2000s, I had a …) (I didn't have a …) (I bought a …) (I used …)

Go to Communication practice: Student A page 163, Student B page 172

8 Talk about your parents/grandparents when they were young. What did/didn't they have in their homes?

Personal Best   Think about your house when you were a child. Write about the gadgets and inventions you had.

67

8 SKILLS LISTENING listening for numbers, dates, and prices ■ phrases ■ life stages

8B Life stories

1 Match the phrases in the box with pictures a–f.

> get married   retire   go to college   be born   start school   get a job

2 Look at the chart. When do these life stages happen in your country? Discuss in pairs.

Life stage	Average age in the U.S.	Average age in the UK
start school	5 or 6	4 or 5
go to college	18 or 19	18 or 19
get married	28	31
have your first baby	26	30

In our country, people start school when they're four.

Go to Vocabulary practice: life stages, page 150

3 ▶ 8.8 Watch or listen to the first part of *Learning Curve*. Choose the correct options to complete the sentences.
1 Simon talks about the invention of the *satellite / GPS*.
2 Kate talks about the invention of *instant coffee / coffee filters*.

> **Skill** listening for numbers, dates, and prices
>
> We sometimes have to listen for numbers, dates, and prices:
> • Practice listening to numbers regularly on the radio or on television.
> • Be prepared to hear years and dates if someone is talking about the past.
> • Listen for the verbs *cost* and *spend*. We often use them to talk about prices.

4 A ▶ 8.8 Read the Skill box. Watch or listen again and complete the sentences with the correct numbers, dates, and prices.
1 Simon's taxi trip took _____ minutes. It cost about £_____.
2 In 19_____, Roger Easton worked at a research center in Washington, D.C.
3 In the 19_____s, he thought of putting clocks on satellites.
4 It cost about $_____ million to build the first GPS.
5 On February _____ 1978, the first GPS satellite went into space.
6 Melitta Bentz was born on January 31, _____.
7 In the early _____th century, people used little bags to make coffee.
8 Kate usually spends £_____ when she buys a cup of coffee.

B Discuss the questions in pairs.
1 Do you use the inventions in the program? How often do you use them?
2 Which invention do you think is more important? Why?

68

listening for numbers, dates, and prices ■ phrases ■ life stages **LISTENING** **SKILLS** **8B**

5 **A** Look at the irregular simple past forms in the chart. Write the base form of each verb. Then check in the Irregular verbs list on page 176.

	Base form	Simple past	Kate or Simon?		Base form	Simple past	Kate or Simon?
1		took		5		thought	
2		had		6		went	
3		told		7		made	
4		cost		8		gave	

B ▶ 8.8 Watch or listen again. Who says the irregular simple past forms in 5A? Write K (Kate) or S (Simon).

Go to Vocabulary practice: irregular verbs, page 150

6 ▶ 8.10 Watch or listen to the second part of the show. Match the people with the services that they mention. There is one service that you don't need.

cooking app   online language courses   sightseeing app   online fashion store

1 Vanessa: _____   **2** Marcello: _____   **3** Xander: _____

7 ▶ 8.10 Watch or listen again. Choose the correct options to complete the sentences.
  1 Vanessa's birthday is on May *10th / 12th / 28th*.
  2 It usually costs about *£11,000 / £23,000 / £33,000* to start a company.
  3 She got her degree in *2002 / 2010 / 2012*.
  4 Marcello got married *two / three / four* years ago.
  5 Xander finished his invention on April *1st / 3rd / 5th*.
  6 His invention costs about *$1.13 / $1.30 / $1.19*.

Listening builder phrases

People often use set phrases when they talk, especially in informal situations. Learn them as phrases, not just individual words:
I'm just in time.   Bye for now!

8 ▶ 8.11 Read the Listening builder. Complete the sentences with the phrases in the box. Listen and check.

First of all   a cup of coffee   Of course you can!   Bye for now!   What do you do?

  1 A _____   B I sell computers.
  2 A Can I ask you a question?   B _____
  3 A _____ See you tomorrow.   B See you!
  4 A Would you like _____ and a cookie?   B Yes, please.
  5 A How did you start writing books?
     B _____, I wrote a blog, and then I wrote a book.

9 In pairs, think of someone interesting that you know and talk about his/her life story.
My grandma was born in Lima in 1929. She got married to my grandfather when she was 18.

Personal Best Think of a famous person that you know about. Write a paragraph about his/her life story.

8 LANGUAGE   simple past: regular verbs and past time expressions

8C Life in the 1980s

1 A In pairs, look at the pictures. What do you know about life in the 1980s?

B Do you like the fashion and music from the 1980s? Why/Why not? Discuss in pairs.

2 Read the text. What is it about? Choose the best summary.
1 It's about a family who lived in the 1980s without any technology.
2 It's about a family who stopped living with modern technology.
3 It's about a family who didn't like 1980s technology.

BACK TO THE 1980s

In 2013, Canadian couple Blair and Morgan McMillan started to worry about their two young sons, Trey and Denton. The boys used a smartphone and a tablet, and they were always inside – they didn't want to play outside. Blair and Morgan wanted to change the situation, so they decided to live like a family in the 1980s for a year. They stopped using cell phones, tablets, the Internet, and cable TV!

Life changed a lot. Blair and Morgan stopped banking online; instead, they went to the bank in person. They used an old-fashioned camera, not a digital camera. At home, the family listened to cassettes and watched videos. There was an old games console from the 1980s, and the children played Super Mario Bros. on that. And they loved it! For their vacation, the family traveled across Canada using a map, not a GPS.

Some things were hard. Blair lost a business partner because he didn't use a computer or cell phone for his job. It was difficult for the family to communicate with their friends and relatives. They had a phone, but all their friends and family used the Internet or social media.

But a lot of things were better. The family saved a lot of money. Also, they enjoyed spending more time together in the evenings and on the weekend. The boys didn't play with their phones and computers all the time – they played with their toys in the living room, and Blair and Morgan talked on the sofa or watched 1980s TV programs.

3 Read the text again. Are the sentences true (T) or false (F)?
1 The boys liked playing outside before 2013. ____
2 Blair and Morgan stopped going to the bank in "the 1980s." ____
3 The family had a TV before 2013. ____
4 Blair didn't use modern technology in his work in "the 1980s." ____
5 The family didn't have much money in "the 1980s." ____
6 The family were together more often in "the 1980s." ____

4 Find the affirmative form of the sentences in the text.
1 Blair and Morgan didn't want to change the situation.
2 They didn't stop using cell phones.
3 They didn't use an old-fashioned camera.
4 The family didn't travel across Canada.
5 The family didn't save a lot of money.
6 They didn't enjoy spending more time together.

70

simple past: regular verbs and past time expressions LANGUAGE **8C**

5 **A** Look at the sentences in exercise 4. What ending do regular simple past affirmative forms have?

B <u>Underline</u> more regular simple past forms in the text. Then read the Grammar box.

> **Grammar** simple past: regular verbs and past time expressions
>
> **Affirmative:**
> They **listened** to cassettes.
> I **loved** playing video games.
>
> **Negative:**
> They **didn't watch** DVDs.
> Blair **didn't use** a computer for work.
>
> **Past time expressions:**
> **last** week, **last** month, **last** year, **last** summer
> a few years **ago**, a week **ago**, two days **ago**, three hours **ago**
> **yesterday** morning, **yesterday** afternoon, **yesterday** evening
>
> **Look!** We say **last night**, NOT **yesterday night**. We can also say **last evening**.

Go to Grammar practice: simple past: regular verbs and past time expressions, page 127

6 **A** ▶ 8.13 **Pronunciation:** -ed endings Listen and repeat the three verbs in the chart. Notice how we say the -ed endings.

/t/	/d/	/ɪd/
looked	changed	wanted

B ▶ 8.14 Add the verbs in the box to the chart. Listen, check, and repeat.

tried   decided   stopped   traveled   played   watched   waited   liked   ended

7 ▶ 8.15 Say the sentences. Listen, check, and repeat.
1 We traveled all night.
2 I watched a movie last night.
3 The family saved a lot of money.
4 You needed a new cell phone.
5 My father worked on the weekend.
6 I wanted a new computer.

8 **A** Write true sentences with affirmative or negative simple past verbs.
1 I _____ dinner last night. (cook)
2 I _____ a photo online yesterday. (post)
3 I _____ to the radio this morning. (listen)
4 I _____ two years ago. (move)
5 I _____ German at school. (study)
6 I _____ in a different city when I was younger. (live)

B In pairs, compare your sentences. Add more information.
A *I cooked dinner last night. I cooked lasagna.*   **B** *I cooked chicken last night.*

Go to Communication practice: Student A page 163, Student B page 172

9 **A** Write one thing for each point below.
• A TV program or movie you watched last week: _____
• A place you traveled to last year: _____
• A game or sport that you played last month: _____
• The job that you wanted to do when you were a child: _____

B Work with your classmates. Find someone with the same answer as you.
A *When I was a child, I wanted to be a vet. How about you?*
B *I didn't want to be a vet. I wanted to be a farmer.*

10 Tell your classmates about different people in your class.
Erica wanted to be a farmer when she was a child.

Personal Best Choose ten years of your life. Write one important thing that happened in each year.

71

8D What happened to you?

1 Think of something interesting that happened to you last week, last month, or last year. Tell your partner.

2 Read Tony's story. Did he get the job?

My nightmare job interview

Last week, I had a job interview. The interview was on Friday at 9:30 a.m. in New York City. On Thursday evening, I prepared a presentation on my laptop and checked the train times and the address of the company. Before the interview, I felt confident. I went to bed early because I wanted to sleep well.

On Friday morning, the problems started. First, I didn't hear my alarm, and I woke up late. I didn't have time to take a shower or have breakfast. I ran out of the house.

It started to rain, so I stopped to buy an umbrella. Then I ran to the station, but I missed my train!

I felt quite stressed, but there was another train in twenty minutes. I called the company, and they changed the interview to 10:30 a.m. I felt a bit more relaxed. Later, I arrived in New York, and I checked my phone to see where the company was. But my phone had no battery! I was very late when I arrived at their office.

After I got to the interview room, I opened my bag to take out my laptop, but it wasn't there! I felt really stressed, and I had a terrible interview. I wasn't surprised when I didn't get the job!
by Tony Smart

3 Read the story again. Order events a–h from 1–8.

a ☐ The interview started.
b ☐ Tony checked the address.
c ☐ They changed the interview time.
d ☐ He checked the train times.
e ☐ His phone didn't have any battery.
f ☐ It started to rain.
g ☐ He went to the station.
h ☐ He saw that he didn't have his computer.

> **Skill** planning and making notes
>
> Before you write a story about yourself, ask yourself the following questions and make notes:
> 1 When did it happen?
> 2 Where were you at the start?
> 3 What were the main events?
> 4 How did you feel at different times?
> 5 What happened in the end?

4 Read the Skill box. Imagine you are Tony and answer the questions in the Skill box.

planning and making notes ■ sequencers **WRITING** **SKILLS** **8D**

5 Match the notes with the different questions in the Skill box.

> a fell asleep on the bus to the airport, didn't get off the bus at the airport, missed the plane, slept at the airport
> b last month
> c London, on vacation
> d got a flight the next day
> e tired (on the bus), stressed and angry (at the airport), very tired, but happy (the next day)

Text builder | sequencers

We can connect events with words such as *first*, *then*, *later*, *before*, and *after*. We use these to show the time order of the events:
First, I got up late. *Then* I took a shower. *Later*, I went out for coffee.

We use *before* and *after* + a noun or verb phrase:
Before the interview, …
After I got to the interview room, …

6 Read the Text builder. <u>Underline</u> the sequencers in the story on page 72.

7 Choose the correct sequencers to complete the sentences.
1 I always walk my dog in the evening *before / after* I go to bed.
2 *First / Before*, I had a cup of coffee. Then I went shopping.
3 I felt very tired on the trip home. *Later / Before*, I fell asleep on the sofa.
4 We bought some food. *First / Then* we made a nice meal.
5 Are you coming before or *after / later* dinner?

8 Complete the text with the words in the box.

then   first   later   before   after (×2)

> I had a terrible day yesterday. ¹_____, the coffee machine broke – I always have a cup of coffee ²_____ I leave the house. ³_____ I couldn't find my car keys. ⁴_____ 30 minutes, I found them in my jacket pocket. ⁵_____, I had an argument with a colleague at work. It was awful, so I went to speak to my boss. ⁶_____ I spoke to her about the situation, I felt a lot better.

9 Write sentences about yesterday. Use the sequencers in exercise 8.
After I arrived at work, I made a large cup of coffee.

10 A PREPARE Think about a good/bad/strange experience you had. Make notes about these things:
• the introduction to the story: When did it happen? Where were you? Who were you with?
• the events of the story: What happened? What problems did you have? What did you do? How did you feel? What happened in the end?

B PRACTICE Write a story about your experience.

C PERSONAL BEST Read another student's story. Check that:
• the introduction is clear.
• the events of the story are clear.
• the verbs are in the correct simple past form.
• the sequencers show the order of events clearly.

Personal Best Choose a well-known movie and describe the events. Ask your partner to guess the movie.

73

7 and 8 REVIEW and PRACTICE

Grammar

1 Choose the correct options to complete the sentences.

1 How _____ fruit do you eat in a week?
   a many
   b often
   c much
2 I have _____ eggs every day for breakfast.
   a an
   b any
   c two
3 There isn't _____ milk in the fridge.
   a any
   b some
   c a
4 For this recipe, I need some peas and _____ .
   a any onions
   b some onions
   c a onion
5 How _____ are there for dinner?
   a much people
   b many people
   c many persons
6 There isn't _____ cheese.
   a lot of
   b a lot of
   c a lot
7 Last night, there _____ any bread in the store.
   a weren't
   b isn't
   c wasn't
8 My nephew doesn't like _____ green vegetables.
   a a
   b much
   c any

2 Rewrite the sentences with the simple past tense.

1 I sometimes work from home.
   Last Tuesday, I _____ .
2 He often goes to Paris.
   Three weeks ago, he _____ .
3 She often eats out.
   Last night, she _____ .
4 They sometimes play tennis.
   Last weekend, they _____ .
5 I get up early.
   Yesterday morning, I _____ .
6 We visit friends most weekends.
   Last weekend, we _____ .
7 I call my sister most days.
   This morning, I _____ .
8 They see their parents every month.
   Last month, they _____ .

3 Complete the text with the correct form of the verbs in parentheses.

The Brazilian Girl from Silicon Valley

Bel Pesce is a famous Brazilian entrepreneur. When she ¹_____ (be) seventeen she ²_____ (read) about the American university MIT and decided that she ³_____ (want) to study there. She ⁴_____ (find) the name of the only Brazilian graduate from the school and arranged to meet him. She ⁵_____ (take) a box of awards with her and ⁶_____ (spend) hours discussing her ideas with him. After that, she ⁷_____ (decide) to apply to MIT and, three months later, they ⁸_____ (accept) her. She completed her studies and then ⁹_____ (work) for Microsoft, Google, and other IT companies. She ¹⁰_____ (write) a book in 2013 called *The Brazilian Girl from Silicon Valley*.

Vocabulary

1 Circle the word that is different. Explain your answer.

1	apple	juice	pear	banana
2	slice	bottle	jar	box
3	fridge	microwave	GPS	dishwasher
4	cheese	beef	ice cream	milk
5	crackers	beans	carrots	peas
6	coffee	tea	cake	water
7	salad	cereal	pasta	rice
8	tablet	smartphone	freezer	laptop

REVIEW and PRACTICE 7 and 8

2 Match definitions 1–8 with objects a–h.
This is something for:

1 cooking something quickly a digital camera
2 talking to your friends b freezer
3 keeping food frozen c dishwasher
4 taking photos d GPS
5 helping you find your way e microwave
6 doing the dishes f smartphone
7 watching TV shows you missed g fridge
8 keeping things cold h video recorder

3 Complete the sentences with the correct form of the verbs in the box.

> meet finish get have go be born start retire

1 All of our children _____ in July.
2 My daughter _____ school when she was four years old.
3 You normally can't _____ school before you are sixteen.
4 In the UK, students usually don't live at home when they _____ to college.
5 To get a good job, you need to _____ a good degree.
6 People often _____ their partners at work.
7 My sister _____ her second baby last year.
8 My parents _____ in 2010 at the age of 60.

4 Put the words in the correct columns.

> cereal onions freezer carton fridge rice
> carrots pepper dishwasher bread bag
> glass cabbage microwave packet pasta

Vegetables	Containers	Kitchen equipment	Grains

Personal Best

Lesson 7A
Name five vegetables.

Lesson 8A
Name five kitchen objects.

Lesson 7A
Think of three kinds of food that are uncountable.

Lesson 8A
Write a sentence with *there weren't*.

Lesson 7B
Name two pronouns and two possessive adjectives.

Lesson 8B
Name six important life stages.

Lesson 7C
Write two questions, one with *How much …?* and one with *How many …?*

Lesson 8C
Write two sentences beginning *a few years ago*.

Lesson 7C
Write a sentence with *a few*.

Lesson 8C
List six regular verbs and put them in the simple past.

Lesson 7D
Give three phrases for ordering food in a restaurant.

Lesson 8D
Write three things you did yesterday with *first*, *then*, and *later*.

UNIT 9

Education, education!

LANGUAGE past of *be* and simple past: questions ■ school subjects and education

9A School days

1 Do you have these types of schools in your country? In pairs, discuss the ages when you start and finish each type of school.

We start nursery school when we're two and finish when we're four.

- nursery school
- kindergarten
- preschool
- elementary school (primary school)
- middle school
- high school (secondary school)

2 **A** Read the text. Do South Korean students study more or less than students in your country?

B Read the text again and answer the questions.
1 What is a *Hagwon*?
2 What do South Korean high school students say you can do if you sleep for three hours?
3 What do they say you can do if you sleep for six hours?
4 What lessons do elementary school students have?
5 What is *Hanja*?

3 Find five school subjects in the text.

School system in South Korea

Education is very important in South Korea. School days are long – students are often in school for eight hours. A lot of parents also send their students to a *Hagwon*, a private school where they have extra lessons before or after their normal school. Teachers give a lot of homework, too. All these hours, weeks, and years of study decide if students do well on their exams and can go to a good college, which is very important in South Korean society. High school students in their last year have a saying: sleep three hours and go to a top college. Sleep six hours and forget about college.

 Nursery school and kindergarten (ages 0–6)
Students can start going to school from a very young age. Playing games is an important part of lessons.

 Elementary school (ages 6–12)
As well as subjects like geography and math, students have lessons about how to be practical, how to enjoy life, and how to have good morals.

 Middle school (ages 12–15)
At this age, students start learning to write *Hanja*, the Chinese characters that are used in the Korean language.

 High school (ages 15–18)
There are different types of high schools, for example, science high schools, foreign language high schools, and art high schools.

Go to Vocabulary practice: school subjects and education, page 151

4 A ▶ 9.3 Listen to Ji-hoon. Are the sentences true (T) or false (F)?
1 He started nursery school when he was two years old. ____
2 He went to a *Hagwon* in middle school. ____
3 He was good at English. ____
4 He went to an arts high school. ____
5 He went to the library after school. ____
6 He didn't go to college. ____

76

past of *be* and simple past: questions ■ school subjects and education   **LANGUAGE**   **9A**

B ▶9.3 Listen again and complete the questions.

1 When _____ you _____ school?
2 _____ you _____ school?
3 What _____ your best subject?

4 _____ you good at English?
5 _____ you _____ a lot of homework?
6 _____ you _____ into college?

5 Look at the questions in 4B and complete the rules. Then read the Grammar box.

1 For the verb *be*, we make past questions with (question word) + _____ / _____ + subject.
2 For other verbs, we make past questions with (question word) + _____ + subject + infinitive.

> **Grammar**   past: questions
>
> **Past of *be*:**
> *Were you a good student?*
> *Was English your favorite subject?*
> *Who was your teacher?*
> *What were your worst subjects?*
>
> **Simple past:**
> *Did you enjoy school?*
> *Did your school have a swimming pool?*
> *What subjects did you study in high school?*
> *Where did you go to college?*

Go to Grammar practice: past: questions, page 128

6 A ▶9.5 **Pronunciation:** intonation in questions Listen to the questions. Do they have rising ↗ or falling ↘ intonation at the end?

1 Did you enjoy school?
2 Were you a good student?
3 Did you study music in school?

4 Where did you go to college?
5 What was your favorite subject?
6 Why did you study Russian?

B Match the beginnings of rules a–b with the endings.

a ↗ We use rising intonation for ...   questions with a question word.

b ↘ We use falling intonation for ...   questions with a *yes/no* answer.

7 ▶9.5 Say the questions from 6A. Listen, check, and repeat.

8 Complete the questions with *did*, *was*, or *were*. Then ask and answer the questions in pairs.

1 What subjects _____ you study in high school?
2 What _____ your favorite subject?
3 _____ there a lot of homework?
4 What subjects _____ you good and bad at?
5 When _____ you start and finish high school?
6 _____ you do well on your exams in school?

Go to Communication practice: Student A page 164, Student B page 173

9 A Look at the sentences. Decide what questions you need to ask.

1 Did you do homework before school?

Find a classmate who ...   **Name:**

1 did homework before school.   _____
2 studied until ten in the evening.   _____
3 was the best student in his/her class in school.   _____
4 had classes on Saturdays.   _____
5 was very good at math.   _____
6 played sports for his/her school.   _____
7 learned a musical instrument in school.   _____
8 didn't enjoy school.   _____

B Ask different classmates the questions. Try to find someone different for each sentence. Give more information when you answer the questions.

A *Did you play sports for your school?*   **B** *Yes, I did. I was on the school basketball team!*

Personal Best Find someone who went to school in another town or city. Ask him/her five questions about his/her school.

77

9 SKILLS READING understanding words that you don't know ■ *because* and *so*

9B Lifelong learning

1 A Look at the skills. Check (✓) the ones that you can do now. Cross out (**X**) the ones that you can't do.
- drive a car
- ride a bike
- speak German
- play a musical instrument
- sail a boat
- create a website

B Discuss how you learned to do each skill in pairs.

I took driving lessons when I was eighteen.

2 Read the introduction to each section in the text. Match the headings with the sections.

Adult learning   Homeschooling   Self-study

3 Work in groups of three. Each person reads one of the interviews. Close your books and tell your group about the person in the interview.

I read about Ana. Her parents homeschooled her because …

> **Skill**   understanding words that you don't know
>
> When you read a text, don't worry if there are words you don't understand. First, read the whole text to understand the main idea. Then look at the new words. Ask yourself these questions:
> - Are they verbs, nouns, or adjectives?
> - Do they look similar to words in your language?
> - Does the topic or sentence help you understand the meaning?

4 A Read the Skill box and look at the sentences from the text. Are the **bold** words verbs, nouns, or adjectives?
1. Some of the world's most **successful** people had parents who chose homeschooling. _____
2. I didn't enjoy it at first because I **missed** my friends. _____
3. He **cofounded** WhatsApp, the world's most popular messaging app, with Brian Acton. _____
4. Do you have any **advice** for people who want to teach themselves something? _____

B In pairs, discuss what you think the words mean. Use the text to help you. Check in a dictionary to see if you are right.

> **Text builder**   *because* and *so*
>
> **We use *because* to give a reason:**
> *I didn't enjoy it at first **because** I missed my friends.*
>
> **We use *so* to give a result:**
> *The lessons were really easy for me, **so** my parents decided to teach me at home.*

5 A Read the Text builder. Underline more reasons and results with *because* and *so* in the text.

B Match the two parts of the sentences and include *because* or *so* to complete them.
1. I found math difficult
2. My grandfather is getting a part-time degree
3. There are lots of self-study videos online
4. I wanted to be a lawyer when I was younger
5. I wanted to homeschool my children

a. I wanted to earn a lot of money!
b. he didn't go to college when he was younger.
c. I went to night school to take extra classes.
d. I left my job to teach them.
e. it's really easy to learn a new skill.

6 Discuss the questions about homeschooling, self-study, and adult learning in pairs.
1. What are the good and bad things about homeschooling?
2. Are you learning something by yourself right now, or would you like to? What activity or subject is it?
3. Would you like to go back to school when you're older? Why/Why not?

understanding words that you don't know ■ *because* and *so*   READING   SKILLS   9B

DIFFERENT PATHS →

Ana, 25, researcher

1 _____

In the U.S., about 2.5 million young people have their classes at home. Some of the world's most successful people had parents who homeschooled them: the scientist Michael Faraday, the rock group the Jonas Brothers, and Soichiro Honda, who started Honda cars.

Ana, why did you have classes at home?
In elementary school, classes were really easy for me – I helped the teacher! So my parents decided to teach me at home.

Did your mother or father teach you?
My mother taught me math and science, and my father taught me geography, history, and politics.

Did you like learning at home?
I didn't enjoy it at first because I missed my friends. But I really enjoyed studying with my two brothers.

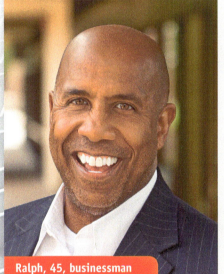

Ralph, 45, businessman

2 _____

A lot of successful people learn their skills themselves. David Karp, who started the photo blog website Tumblr, taught himself to program. Jan Koum is another programmer who learned through self-study. He cofounded WhatsApp, the world's most popular messaging app, with Brian Acton.

Ralph, why did you become interested in programming?
I loved making things and solving puzzles when I was a child. With programming, you can do both.

Did you learn programming in school?
No! I went to school in the 1980s. They only had one computer in the whole school, so I taught myself to program from books.

Do you have any advice for people who want to teach themselves something?
It can be hard without a teacher, so you need to love the subject that you're learning.

Eva, 73, retired secretary

3 _____

A lot of people go back to school later in life. In 2007, singer Shakira took a college course on the history of western civilization. Basketball star Shaquille O'Neal left college to play in the NBA. He went back to school in 2000, and by 2012, he was Dr. O'Neal. Next on his list? Law school.

Eva, when did you leave school?
I left school at 16. I got married and had four children. I worked part time.

Why did you start to study again?
I started going to night school because I wanted to learn a foreign language. I chose French.

When did you go to college?
When I retired, I went to college to study French. I graduated when I was 73!

Personal Best Describe what type of student you are. Do you find learning new things easy?

9C Change your life

1 A Read the introduction to the text. Did you make a New Year's resolution this year? Did you keep it? Discuss in pairs.

B Complete the text with the phrases in the box.

> get in shape   save money   improve your diet   get a new job   be more organized

Apps TO CHANGE YOUR LIFE

On January 1st every year, millions of us make New Year's resolutions – things that we want to change in our lives.

But only 8% of us are successful! Here are some top apps that can help you keep your resolutions.

MYWELLNESS
This app encourages you to [1]_____. If you join a gym and scan the code on the machines, it records all the exercise that you get. It also helps you plan your exercise goals.

ALLRECIPES
You can get bored eating the same food every day. You tell Allrecipes what's in your cabinets and fridge, and it gives you some new and healthy recipes. It's a great way to [2]_____.

TOSHL FINANCE
This app teaches people to [3]_____. It shows you how you spend your money and gives you ideas about how to save.

EVERNOTE
This is a great planning app for students who want to [4]_____. It organizes your study plans and gives you to-do lists. It can help you get good grades and pass exams.

SWITCH
This app can encourage you to [5]_____. If you see a job you like, you can contact the company. They see your profile but not your name, so you can keep it a secret from your manager!

2 In pairs, look at the apps again. Tell your partner which apps you think are good for you and why.

I think Allrecipes is a good app for me. I usually eat the same food every day.

Go to Vocabulary practice: resolutions, page 152

3 A ▶ 9.7 Listen to people talking about the changes they want to make. Match the people with the apps from the text.

1 Megan _____
2 Zafar _____
3 Tatyana _____
4 María _____
5 Raymond _____

B ▶ 9.7 Listen again. Complete the sentences with the verbs in the box.

> need (×2)   'm planning   want   'd like   hope

1 I _____ to learn how to cook some new things.
2 I _____ to save money for my vacation.
3 I _____ to get a new job this year.
4 I _____ to lose six kilos before the summer.
5 I _____ to go to college next year, so I _____ to get good grades and pass my exams.

verb patterns: verb + infinitive ■ resolutions   LANGUAGE   9C

4 Complete the rule. Then read the Grammar box.

After verbs like *want*, *need*, *hope*, and *plan*, we can use an _____.

> **Grammar** verb patterns: verb + infinitive
>
> I **want to improve** my diet.   I'm **planning to save** more money this year.
> I **need to get** more exercise every week.   I'**d like to get** a new job.
>
> **Look!** *'d like* is the contracted form of *would like*. It means *want*, not *like*.
> I'**d like to** join a gym this year. BUT I **like** going to the gym.

Go to Grammar practice: verb patterns: verb + infinitive, page 129

5 A ▶9.9 **Pronunciation:** *'d like* and *like* Listen and repeat.

I'd like	I would like	I like
you'd like	you would like	you like
we'd like	we would like	we like

B ▶9.10 Say the sentences. Listen, check, and repeat.

1 I'd like to speak French.
2 I like speaking French.
3 We'd like to play more sports.
4 We like playing sports.
5 They'd like to go on vacation.
6 They like going on vacation.

6 A Match the two parts to make complete sentences. Some items have more than one possible answer.

1 I didn't get any exercise last week. I need
2 I want to get a job in another country, so I need
3 I'm living in a new city. I hope
4 I have a test next week. I'm planning
5 I have a lot of free time. I'd like
6 I want to get a better job, but I need

a to make some new friends.
b to start a new hobby.
c to improve my English.
d to go to the gym this week.
e to improve my skills.
f to study every evening.

B Which of the sentences are true for you? Tell your partner.

I need to improve my English because I want to work in Canada one day.

Go to Communication practice: Student A page 164, Student B page 173

7 A Think of one idea for each option. Write your answers in the shapes.

- a person that you're planning to visit next week
- a place where you hope to go on vacation one day
- a language that you'd like to learn
- a person that you want to speak to today
- a place where you'd like to live one day
- something that you're planning to buy this year

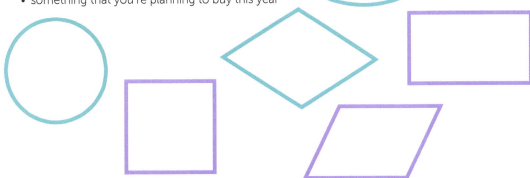

B Show your partner your answers. Ask each other questions about them and explain why you wrote them.

A *Why did you write "Barcelona"?*
B *Because I'd like to live in Barcelona one day. I think it's a really cool city.*

Personal Best Plan a new app to help people change their lives. What does your app do? Think of a name for it.

81

SKILLS **SPEAKING** making suggestions ■ sounding sympathetic

9D What's the problem?

1 A Match problems 1–5 with pictures a–e.
1 I'm stressed at work. ____
2 I'm always tired. ____
3 I'm homesick, and I miss my family. ____
4 My exams aren't going well. ____
5 I'm having problems with my boyfriend/girlfriend. ____

B Do you sometimes have these problems? Discuss in pairs.
I don't sleep well, and I'm always tired.

2 ▶ 9.11 Watch or listen to the first part of *Learning Curve*. What's Marc's problem? Choose the correct option.
a He didn't finish his final exam.
b He arrived late for his exam.
c He thinks he failed his exam.

3 ▶ 9.11 Watch or listen again. Are the sentences true (T) or false (F)?
1 Marc studied hard for this exam. ____
2 He has two jobs. ____
3 He's stressed, and he's always tired. ____
4 His sister sent him some candy for good luck. ____

4 A Look at Penny's text message to Marc. What two suggestions does she make? How does Marc respond?

> Hi Marc! I know you're stressed at the moment. Why don't you take a break from studying? How about meeting me and Ethan for coffee? We're waiting for you at the café. Penny

> That's a really good idea. Thanks, Penny! I'm on my way.

B Complete the sentences to make two more suggestions for Marc.
1 Why don't you …
2 How about …

Conversation builder | making suggestions

Making suggestions:
Why don't you talk with your family now?
What/How about visit**ing** your parents later this month?
Can you take some time off work?
Let's do something quiet tonight.

Responding to suggestions:
I'm not sure I should.
That's a (really) good idea.

making suggestions ■ sounding sympathetic **SPEAKING** **SKILLS** **9D**

5 Read the Conversation builder. In pairs, make suggestions for the problems in Exercise 1, and respond.

6 ▶9.12 Watch or listen to the second part of the show. Which problem from exercise 1 does Penny have? What two suggestions does Ethan make?

7 ▶9.12 Watch or listen again and complete the extracts with the words in the box.

awful   sorry   shame   no

Penny	My parents can't come to New York on holiday until next spring.
Ethan	Oh, I'm [1]_____ to hear that.
...	
Penny	I'm homesick!
Ethan	Oh! [2]_____ you!
...	
Marc	I couldn't remember the answer to one of the math problems. I was too tired.
Penny	That's a [3]_____.
...	
Marc	I was so tired I fell asleep on the train. I almost missed my exam!
Penny	How [4]_____!

🔧 **Skill**   sounding sympathetic

If someone has bad news or feels unhappy, we can show that we are sympathetic.

- Use falling intonation: *That's a shame!*   *How terrible!*   *Poor you!*
- Say you're sorry to hear his/her news: *Oh no! I'm sorry to hear that*.
- Show you understand that the situation is bad/difficult: *I'm sure it's difficult to (be so far away from your family)*.

8 **A** ▶9.13 Read the Skill box. Listen and repeat the expressions of sympathy when you hear the beeps.

B In pairs, take turns saying sentences 1–6 and respond with sympathy. Use intonation to sound sympathetic.

1 I don't sleep well because my neighbors are very noisy.
2 I can never find the time to study because I have two jobs.
3 My girlfriend/boyfriend isn't speaking to me.
4 I missed my nine o'clock class again, and the teacher wants to speak to me.
5 I have a $2,000 credit card bill!
6 I didn't get into college last year.

Go to Communication practice: Student A page 164, Student B page 173

9 **A** PREPARE Think of three problems you sometimes have or had in the past. Use the following ideas and your own ideas.

- problems at work/with education
- problems with your family or partner
- problems with your friends
- problems with money

B PRACTICE In pairs, take turns describing your problems. Show sympathy, make suggestions, and respond to the suggestions. Use a variety of phrases.

C PERSONAL BEST Repeat the activity with a different partner. Did they use different phrases from the Conversation builder? Did they sound sympathetic? Who made the best suggestions?

Personal Best   Write a short conversation between two friends about a problem one of them has.

83

UNIT 10 People

LANGUAGE comparative adjectives ■ adjectives to describe places

10A First dates

1 A Make pairs of opposite adjectives. Use them to describe the places in the pictures.

empty   unfriendly   safe   light   crowded   friendly   dark   dangerous

a   b   c   d   e

B Use the adjectives to talk about places in your town or city.

The subway is always really crowded.

The downtown area is safe during the day, but it can be dangerous at night.

Go to Vocabulary practice: adjectives to describe places, page 152

2 Read the definition of a first date. Choose three good places for a first date from the ideas below. Discuss in pairs.

first date: a meeting, usually at a restaurant, movie theater, etc., with a new person when you're looking for a boyfriend or girlfriend

a restaurant   a movie theater   a café   your house   a shopping mall   a club   a bowling alley

3 Read the text. Which three places are a bad idea for a first date? Which three places are a good idea?

Where NOT to go on a first date

You have a date with someone special, and you don't know where to go. Don't make the mistake of choosing the wrong place. Here are three places not to go!

1 A movie theater
Do you want to sit in a dark room in silence during your first date? No? Then don't go to the movies! How about going to the park instead? Nothing is more important than conversation on a first date, and a walk in the park gives you lots of time to talk and have fun together. It's more romantic than a movie theater, and it's also cheaper. In fact, it's free!

2 A club
Music, dancing, beautiful people … a date at a club sounds great! Or maybe not. It's impossible to talk, and a lot of people don't feel comfortable on a crowded dance floor. Why not go bowling? A bowling alley is quieter and more relaxed than a club, and it's cheaper!

3 An expensive restaurant
It's a popular first date, but a meal in an expensive restaurant is often a bad idea. It can be hard to relax and be yourself in a restaurant, especially if it's pretty quiet. It's better to meet in a café for a cup of coffee or lunch. It's more comfortable than a restaurant, and if things aren't going well, it's also easier to escape!

Our final piece of advice: don't be late. There's nothing worse than a late date!

comparative adjectives ■ adjectives to describe places **LANGUAGE** **10A**

4 Complete the sentences with words from the text.
1 It's _____ than a movie theater.
2 A bowling alley is _____ and _____ than a club.
3 It's _____ to meet in a café.
4 It's also _____ to escape!
5 There's nothing _____ than a late date!

5 Look at the sentences in exercise 4 and complete the grammar rules. Then read the Grammar box.
1 To make the comparative form of a short adjective, for example, *cheap*, we add _____.
2 To make the comparative form of a long adjective, for example, *comfortable*, we put _____ before it.
3 The comparative forms of *good* and *bad* are _____ and _____.

> **Grammar** comparative adjectives
>
> **Short adjectives (one syllable or two syllables ending -y):**
> It's **cheaper** than a movie theater.
> It's **harder** to relax in a restaurant.
> It's **easier** to escape.
>
> **Long adjectives:**
> Nothing is **more important** than conversation.
> A bowling alley is **more relaxed** than a club.
>
> **Irregular adjectives:**
> A café is **better** than a restaurant.
> A date in a movie theater is **worse** than in a park.

Go to Grammar practice: comparative adjectives, page 130

6 A ▶10.3 **Pronunciation:** *-er* endings Listen and repeat the adjectives and comparatives.
big – bigger   noisy – noisier   cheap – cheaper   empty – emptier

B ▶10.4 Say the sentences. Listen, check, and repeat.
1 Bangkok is cheaper than Singapore.
2 Tokyo is safer than Los Angeles.
3 Winters are darker in Iceland than in Sweden.
4 Zurich is quieter than Rome.
5 The market is friendlier than the shopping center.
6 The bus is busier than the train.

7 A ▶10.5 George and Lola are discussing restaurants for a first date. Match the adjectives with each restaurant. Listen and check.

cheap   crowded   expensive   good (food)
quiet   romantic   relaxed

B Compare Mimi's and Luigi's in pairs.
Mimi's is more romantic than Luigi's.

Mimi's

Luigi's

Communication practice: Student A page 165, Student B page 174

8 In pairs, think of places in your town or city. Discuss where to go and what to do for the special occasions below.
A *I think Pizza Palace is a good place for a second date.*
B *I'm not sure. I think a café like Coffee House is better because you can relax there.*

a second date   a friend's 30th birthday   your grandmother's birthday

your niece's second birthday   a big family get-together

a school reunion   other ideas

Personal Best Write ten comparative sentences about cities in your country.

85

10 SKILLS LISTENING — listening for detailed information (1) ■ weak forms ■ describing appearance

10B You look so different!

1 Match the words in the box with pictures a–c.

straight hair   beard   red hair   glasses   curly hair   elderly   middle-aged   blond hair   bald   young

Go to Vocabulary practice: describing appearance, page 153

2 In pairs, think of people you know and describe their appearance.

A *My father has a beard.*   B *My friend Amanda has blond hair. She's tall and slim.*

3 ▶ 10.7   Watch or listen to the first part of *Learning Curve*. Choose the correct definition of "disguise."

a A disguise is something that helps you look younger.
b A disguise is something that changes the color of your hair.
c A disguise is something that makes you look like a different person.

Skill   listening for detailed information (1)

It is often necessary to understand what someone says in detail.
- Read the questions before you listen and think about the possible answers.
- Listen for words that introduce the information that you need. For example, if you need the name of a movie, listen for the word "film" or "movie."
- Wait until the speaker has finished speaking before you answer the question.

4 **A** ▶ 10.7   Read the Skill box and questions 1–6 below. Watch or listen again. Complete the sentences.

1 Ethan mentions a movie called *The Master of* _____.
2 In the movie, the actor Dana Carvey becomes an overweight, _____ character.
3 In another scene, Dana is a middle-aged woman with _____ hair.
4 Dark lines on an actor's face can make him or her look _____.
5 Lucia Pittalis can make her eyes look smaller or her lips look _____.
6 A wig can make your hair look _____ or _____.

B Do you know any movies where someone has a disguise? Tell your partner about the movie.

listening for detailed information (1) ■ weak forms ■ describing appearance   LISTENING   SKILLS   10B

5 ▶10.8   Watch or listen to the second part of the show. Match the things that the people change in their makeovers with the names below. You can use one word more than once.

beard   eyes   hair   mustache

1 Ginny _____   2 Ron _____   3 Malika _____

6 ▶10.8   Watch or listen again. Are the sentences true (T) or false (F)?

1 Ginny wants straight hair. ____
2 She wants her lips to look bigger. ____
3 Ron wants a makeover because he has a new job. ____
4 After his makeover, he feels lighter. ____
5 Malika usually has long, curly hair. ____
6 Malika thinks she looks taller after her makeover. ____
7 Her boyfriend talked a lot when he saw her. ____
8 Ginny thinks she looks younger after her makeover. ____

7 Discuss the questions in pairs.

1 How important is your appearance to you? (1 = not important, 10 = very important)
2 How much time and money do you spend on your appearance each week?
3 Do you want to look different? If so, what do you want to change?

Listening builder   weak forms

In English, we don't usually stress words like articles and prepositions. These words sound shorter and weaker than important words like nouns, verbs, and adjectives:
One of the best makeup artists in the world is Kevin Yagher.
I have an interview for a new job later, in an art gallery.

8 A Read the Listening builder. Read the sentences and underline the words which you think have weak forms.

1 The people in the movie were very young.
2 His character was an elderly man with a long white beard.
3 She puts a lot of makeup on their faces.
4 I like your hair. I think the color looks great.
5 The name of her character was Emma.
6 My brother has a long beard and a mustache.

B ▶10.9   Listen and check.

9 A Look at the photos of two makeovers. In pairs, describe the photos from "before" and "after" the makeovers.

B In pairs, answer the questions.

1 How does the man/woman look different now?
2 Do they look better or worse after their makeovers in your opinion? Why?

Personal Best   Imagine you had a makeover. Describe your new appearance.

10 LANGUAGE — superlative adjectives ■ personality adjectives

10C The yearbook

1 Look at the adjectives in the box. Think of someone you know for each one. Tell your partner.

> smart   lazy   shy   polite   popular   kind   funny

My nephew is very smart. He's studying math in college.

Go to Vocabulary practice: personality adjectives, page 154

2 A Look at the pictures. Which famous person can you see? Read the text quickly. Which other famous people does it mention and why?

B Read the text again. Which of these things can you find in a yearbook? What else does a yearbook include?

- personal stories about people in the school
- exam results
- photos of students
- students' e-mail addresses
- students' plans for the future

3 Match the awards with the celebrities. There are three extra awards.

1 Renée Zellweger
2 Michael Jackson
3 Jack Nicholson

a the worst dancer
b the most beautiful girl
c the nicest personality
d the laziest student
e the shyest classmate
f the best actor

THE YEARBOOK

"The best athlete" … "The nicest personality"… "The worst dancer." Welcome to the yearbook, an important tradition in the U.S. and other countries. A yearbook is like a photo album, with photos of all the students in one year in a high school or college. Students write about sports teams and clubs, they remember funny stories about their classmates and teachers, and they write about their future plans.

A yearbook also includes awards. These can be for the friendliest teacher, the laziest student, the funniest laugh, and so on. In high school, Renée Zellweger was "The most beautiful girl," Jack Nicholson was "The best actor," and Michael Jackson was "The shyest classmate." Here's a surprising one – in his school, "The least likely to be successful" was … Tom Cruise!

Some people say that high school and college are the happiest days of our lives. And, for millions of students, the yearbook is an important way of remembering that time.

4 Look at the adjectives in exercise 3 and answer the questions. Then read the Grammar box.

1 What letters do we add to a short adjective to make the superlative form? _____
2 What word do we use before long adjectives? _____
3 What is the superlative form of *good* and *bad*? _____ and _____
4 What word comes before all superlative forms? _____

superlative adjectives ■ personality adjectives   LANGUAGE **10C**

📖 Grammar   superlative adjectives

Short adjectives (one syllable or two syllables ending -y):
She's **the nicest** person in our class.
High school and college are **the happiest** days of our lives.

Long adjectives:
She's **the most popular** girl in the school.
Our teacher is **the most interesting** person that I know.

Irregular adjectives:
He's **the best** dancer in the school.
This is **the worst** photo of me.

Go to Grammar practice: superlative adjectives, page 131

5 **A** ▶ 10.12 **Pronunciation:** superlative adjectives Listen and repeat the superlatives.

the nicest   the funniest   the most popular   the most relaxed

B ▶ 10.13 Say the sentences. Listen, check, and repeat.

1 You're the kindest person that I know.
2 He's the laziest person in the office.
3 She has the most beautiful voice.
4 It's the most exciting movie of the year.

Go to Communication practice: Student A page 165, Student B page 174

6 Complete the text about Ashrita Furman with the superlative forms of the adjectives in the box.

popular   high   strange   heavy   tall   fast

The **most world records** on the planet

The *Guinness Book of World Records* is one of the ¹_____ books on Earth. If you have a copy, you will probably notice the name Ashrita Furman. This is because Ashrita has ²_____ number of world records on the planet – more than 200! And his records are also some of the ³_____ records in the book. Here are a few:

The ⁴_____ shoes in the world
In November 2010, Ashrita walked around London in shoes that weighed 146.5 kg.

The ⁵_____ object balanced on the nose
In August 2015, Ashrita balanced a 15.95 m. pole on his nose in New York.

The ⁶_____ mile with a milk bottle on the head
In February 2004, in Indonesia, Ashrita ran a mile in 7 minutes, 47 seconds, balancing a milk bottle on his head.

7 **A** Write sentences that are true for you.

The kindest person that I know is my friend María.

The (kind) person that I know is …
The (old) person in my family is …
The (lazy) person that I know is …
The (funny) person on TV is …
The (good) movie of the year so far is …

The (interesting) show on TV at the moment is …
The (beautiful) place in my country is …
The (expensive) place in my town is …

B Ask and answer questions about your answers to exercise 7A in pairs.

Who's the kindest person that you know?

8 **A** In groups, create your own class awards. Discuss and choose an award for each student. Use the ideas in the boxes and your own ideas.

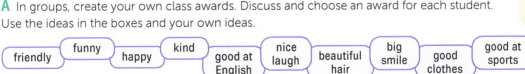

friendly   funny   happy   kind   good at English   nice laugh   beautiful hair   big smile   good clothes   good at sports

I think Eduardo always wears really cool clothes. Let's give him an award for the best clothes.

B Share your awards with the class.

We'd like to give Elena the award for "the friendliest student".

Personal Best   Write ten superlative sentences about people and places that you know.

10 SKILLS WRITING — writing a description of a person ■ clauses with *when*

10D Someone that I admire

1 Is there someone that you admire? It could be a friend, a family member, or someone famous. Why do you admire him or her? Discuss in pairs.

I admire my aunt. She's a surgeon, and she saves people's lives. It's a really difficult and important job.

2 A Read Hannah's description. Who does she admire and why?

B Read the description again and answer the questions.
1. What does Michaela look like?
2. What happened when she was three years old?
3. When did she move to the Dutch National Ballet?
4. Who does Michaela help?
5. What difficult situation did Hannah have?

A PERSON I ADMIRE
Michaela DePrince

Michaela DePrince is a ballet dancer from Sierra Leone. She's unusual in the world of ballet because there aren't many ballerinas from her country. She is slim and confident and has a beautiful smile. ¹_____

From a young age, Michaela's life was extremely difficult. When she was three years old, she lost both her parents in the civil war in Sierra Leone. But she survived her difficult past, and today she's one of the most talented young ballet stars in the world. She became the youngest dancer at the Dance Theatre of Harlem in New York when she was just seventeen and, in 2013, she moved to the Dutch National Ballet. ²_____

I admire Michaela because she's a very strong and brave person. As well as ballet dancing, she spends a lot of time helping young people who have problems in their lives. ³_____ When I didn't get the grades that I needed to study medicine in college, Michaela's story inspired me, and I didn't give up.

By Hannah Lee

> **Skill** writing a description of a person
>
> When you write a description of a person, organize your ideas into paragraphs, for example:
> **Paragraph 1:** where the person is from, his/her job, appearance, and personality
> *Ed Sheeran is a singer and musician from England. He has red hair and blue eyes, and is very popular.*
>
> **Paragraph 2:** information about his/her life and achievements
> *He was born in 1991 in Yorkshire. When he was a child, he learned to play the guitar. He made his first record when he was thirteen. Today, he is popular all over the world.*
>
> **Paragraph 3:** why you admire him/her
> *I admire him because he writes beautiful and honest songs, and he's very talented.*

3 Read the Skill box. Complete 1–3 in the description of Michaela DePrince with sentences a–c.
a. She shows that there is always hope for a better future.
b. In 2016, she danced in Beyoncé's visual album, *Lemonade*.
c. For a ballerina, she's not very tall.

writing a description of a person ■ clauses with *when* **WRITING** **SKILLS** **10D**

4 Organize the sentences about Lionel Messi into three paragraphs.

a He played his first game for Barcelona when he was seventeen and quickly became one of their most important players.
b When Lionel was a young boy, he began playing soccer. FC Barcelona soon noticed him and, when he was thirteen, he moved to Spain.
c He's 1.7 m. tall and has dark brown hair.
d Lionel Messi is not only a fantastic soccer player, but he's also a great person.
e He's generous and kind, and he does a lot to help children's charities.
f Lionel Messi is a soccer player from Argentina. He plays for FC Barcelona in Spain and for his national team, Argentina.

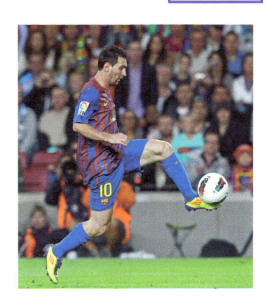

Text builder clauses with *when*

We use a clause with *when* to talk about two things that happened in the past:
When she was three years old, she lost both her parents.
She became the youngest dancer at the Dance Theatre of Harlem *when* she was just seventeen.

We use the clause with *when* for the action that happened or started first:
When she arrived in the U.S., she joined the Dance Theatre of Harlem.

5 A Read the Text builder. Choose the correct option to complete the rules.

1 When a clause with *when* comes before the main clause, we *use / don't use* a comma.
2 When a clause with *when* comes after the main clause, we *use / don't use* a comma.

B Join the two sentences with a clause with *when*. Write two versions for each sentence.

He was eighteen. At that time, he moved to Australia.

When he was eighteen, he moved to Australia.

He moved to Australia when he was eighteen.

1 She finished college. After that, she became a photographer.
2 His mother died. After that, he went to live with his aunt.
3 I was a student. At that time, I met my wife.
4 I had a problem at work. That's when my best friend gave me some good advice.
5 She was thirty. At that time, she had her first baby.
6 He retired. He learned to play the guitar.

6 A PREPARE Make notes about a person that you admire. Think about these questions:
• What does he/she do? What does he/she look like? What is he/she like?
• What do you know about his/her life and achievements?
• Why do you admire him/her?

B PRACTICE Write a description. Use the heading *A person that I admire*.

Paragraph 1: Describe the person.
Paragraph 2: Describe the most important events of his/her life.
Paragraph 3: Describe why you admire the person.

C PERSONAL BEST Read your partner's description. Correct any mistakes and give suggestions for improvement.

Personal Best Think of a famous person who is unusual in his/her profession. Write some facts about him/her.

9 and 10 REVIEW and PRACTICE

Grammar

1 Cross out (**X**) the sentence that is NOT correct.

1 a Where did you go last weekend? ____
  b Where went you last weekend? ____
  c Where were you last weekend? ____

2 a Were you study English in elementary school? ____
  b Did you study English in elementary school? ____
  c Were you happy in elementary school? ____

3 a He wanted finish the job. ____
  b He agreed to finish the job. ____
  c He decided to finish the job. ____

4 a We're planning to go away this weekend. ____
  b We would like to go away this weekend. ____
  c We need going away this weekend. ____

5 a My sister's older than me. ____
  b I'm younger than her. ____
  c She's more old than me. ____

6 a This question's more easy than the others. ____
  b This question's easier than the others. ____
  c This question's the easiest. ____

7 a This hotel's the most expensive in the town. ____
  b This hotel's the more expensive in the town. ____
  c It's also the most comfortable. ____

8 a Who's the better player in the world? ____
  b Who's the best player in the world? ____
  c Who's the most popular player in the world? ____

2 Make comparative sentences with the adjectives in parentheses.

1 John's 20 and Sophie's 21. (young)
   _____

2 Flight A's $400 and Flight B's $300. (expensive)
   _____

3 The cheetah has a top speed of 95 km. an hour, and the lion about 80 km. an hour. (fast)
   _____

4 A mile's about 1,500 m., and a kilometer is 1,000 m. (long)
   _____

5 A bike's lighter than a car. (heavy)
   _____

6 The Nile's 6,800 km., and the Yangtze's 6,500 km. (short)
   _____

7 My mother's 70. My father's 68. (old)
   _____

8 Player A's number 1 in the world. Player B's number 25. (good)
   _____

3 Complete the questions in the dialogue.

The man who beat Pokémon Go

1 Q Congratulations! H_____ l_____ d_____ i_____ t_____ y_____?
  A It took me just over two weeks.

2 Q H_____ m_____ d_____ y_____ c_____?
  A I caught 142.

3 Q W_____ d_____ y_____ f_____ t_____?
  A I found them in New York City.

4 Q H_____ m_____ d_____ y_____ s_____?
  A I spent about $200.

5 Q H_____ f_____ d_____ y_____ w_____?
  A I walked about 200 km.

6 Q So it was a healthy activity. D_____ y_____ l_____ any weight?
  A Yes, I did. I lost about five kilos.

7 Q W_____ d_____ y_____ p_____ i_____?
  A I played it for my work. I work for a tech company in Manhattan.

8 Q W_____ y_____ a Pokémon fan as a child?
  A Yes, I was. I played it in 1996 on my Game Boy.

Vocabulary

1 Circle the word that is different.

1	chemistry	physics	history	biology
2	take	get into	pass	fail
3	get in shape	get a job	lose weight	get exercise
4	short	slim	empty	tall
5	crowded	dark	dangerous	kind
6	curly	young	gray	straight
7	lazy	nice	polite	brave
8	school	college	gym	kindergarten

92

REVIEW and PRACTICE 9 and 10

2 Match definitions 1–8 with adjectives a–h.

1	between 45 and 60	a	funny
2	too heavy	b	elderly
3	not dangerous	c	safe
4	over 80	d	in shape
5	spends money on others	e	overweight
6	has little or no hair	f	middle-aged
7	makes people laugh	g	bald
8	healthy and gets regular exercise	h	generous

3 Put the words in the correct columns.

overweight preschool curly college
straight kindergarten lazy unfriendly
school long ugly brown

Places of learning	Types of hair	Other adjectives

4 Complete the conversation with the words in the box.

lazy funny blond tall cheerful
long young short

Jack   How's your new colleague?
Victoria She's really [1]_____ . Always telling jokes!
Jack   Do I know her? What does she look like?
Victoria She's [2]_____ and slim. Only about 1 m. 55.
Jack   With [3]_____ hair?
Victoria Not at all. She has short hair.
Jack   Brown?
Victoria No. [4]_____ , actually. What about your new boss?
Jack   She's OK. She's [5]_____ – only about thirty. She's pretty [6]_____ – about 1 m. 70. She's [7]_____ – you know, she smiles a lot. She works long hours. Not like the [8]_____ manager we had before.

Personal Best

Lesson 9A List five school subjects.

Lesson 10A List five adjectives to describe places.

Lesson 9A Write two simple past questions about someone's school days.

Lesson 10A Write two sentences comparing two towns or cities.

Lesson 9B Write a sentence with *because*.

Lesson 10B List five adjectives to describe people's appearance.

Lesson 9C Write a question using *need to*.

Lesson 10C Write two sentences about you and your family with superlative adjectives.

Lesson 9D Think of five expressions for making suggestions.

Lesson 10C List five adjectives to describe personality.

Lesson 9D Think of three expressions for sounding sympathetic.

Lesson 10D Write a sentence with *when* to link two events in the past.

93

UNIT 11 On the move

LANGUAGE *have to/don't have to* ■ travel and transportation

11A Getting to work

1 A What forms of transportation can you see in pictures a–d? What other forms of transportation can you think of?

B How do you usually travel to these places? Tell a partner.
- your work or place of study
- your English class
- the supermarket

A *I always go to my English class by bus.*   B *Really? I drive.*

Go to Vocabulary practice: travel and transportation, page 155

2 A Read the introduction to the text. Complete the three definitions with the correct words.

1 _____ (verb): to travel to work
2 _____ (noun): the trip to work
3 _____ (noun): people who are traveling to work

B Read the rest of the text. Which forms of transportation does it mention?

THE WORLD'S coolest commutes

Do you have a long trip to work? Do you have to sit in traffic for hours or fight with thousands of other commuters for a place on the subway? It doesn't have to be stressful to commute. Here are three of the world's coolest commutes.

Chris Roberts is a doctor with Australia's Royal Flying Doctor Service. He spends about 90 minutes every day on a plane, and he often has to fly to some of the most remote places in Australia – places where there are no airports. "I love flying to work," he says, "but we have to look out for kangaroos when we land, especially at night."

Inger Bojesen is a journalist in Copenhagen, Denmark. Her trip to work is a 30-minute bike ride. In Copenhagen, 45% of people go to work by bike. There are bike lanes and special traffic lights for bicyclists, so they don't have to wait with all the cars and buses. And it's very safe. "I love my commute," says Inger. "It's really fast, and it's free!"

John Douglas is an engineer at a power plant on beautiful Lake Manapouri in New Zealand. There are no roads to the power plant, so John has to drive to the ferry, and then he and his coworkers have to travel across the lake by boat. It's called the "Z" boat because "zzzz" is the sound of workers sleeping during the trip! "It's a great way to start the day," says John.

3 Read the text again. Who do you think says the following about his/her commute: Chris, Inger, or John?

1 It's a really quiet commute, and the scenery is beautiful. _____
2 Sometimes I see some interesting animals during my trip. _____
3 I love getting some exercise on my way to work. _____
4 I take two different forms of transportation to get to work. _____
5 I can also go to work by car or bus if I want. _____
6 I travel at different times of the day. _____

have to/don't have to ■ travel and transportation   **LANGUAGE 11A**

4 A Complete the sentences and question with words from the text.
1 We _____ look out for kangaroos when we land.
2 Bicyclists _____ wait with all the cars.
3 John _____ drive to the ferry.
4 _____ you _____ sit in traffic for hours?

B Choose the correct option. Then look at the examples in the Grammar box and check.
After *have to* or *has to*, we use the *base / -ing* form of the verb.

> **Grammar** *have to/don't have to*
>
> We use *have to/has to* to say that something is necessary:
> We **have to go** there by plane.
> She **has to drive** to work.
> **Do** you **have to take** the train to work?
>
> We use *don't have to/doesn't have to* to say that something isn't necessary:
> You **don't have to go** to work by car.
> It **doesn't have to be** stressful to commute.

Go to Grammar practice: *have to/don't have to*, page 132

5 A ▶11.3 **Pronunciation:** *have to/has to* Listen and repeat.
1 I don't have to go by boat.
2 Do you have to work today?
3 He has to go by bike.
4 She has to get up early.

B ▶11.4 Say the sentences. Listen, check, and repeat.
1 You have to go to work by subway.
2 We don't have to work today.
3 She has to wear a uniform.
4 He doesn't have to go to school on Sundays.
5 Do you have to go home by bus?
6 Does she have to drive to work?

6 A Look at the signs and complete the sentences. Use the verbs in the box with *have to/don't have to*.

pay   turn off   leave

1 You _____ your phone.
2 You _____ to go in.
3 You _____ your dog outside.

B In pairs, explain what the signs mean. Use *have to* and *don't have to*.

a

b

c

Go to Communication practice: Student A page 165, Student B page 174

7 A Ask and answer questions about your partner's commute to work or place of study.
How do you get to work? I have to drive because there are no buses.

B Work with a different partner. Tell him/her about your first partner's trip.
Ana works at the airport. She goes there by subway. It's usually very busy, and she has to stand.

Personal Best Write a paragraph about your favorite form of transportation and why you like it.

11	**SKILLS**	**READING** reading for detail ■ adverbs of probability

11B Looking for Elizabeth Gallagher

1 A Imagine you can go on a trip to anywhere in the world for three weeks. Write down the countries you'd like to visit.

B In pairs, compare your lists. Say one thing you'd like to do in each country.

2 Read the text about Jordan Axani and Elizabeth Gallagher. What was unusual about their trip?

> 🔧 **Skill**   reading for detail
>
> When you read a text, first look at the pictures and title, and then skim the text to understand the main ideas. After that, read the questions carefully. <u>Underline</u> any key words. Find the part of the text with the information you need, and read it slowly and carefully. The questions may repeat key words from the text, or they may express the ideas in a slightly different way.

3 Read the Skill box. Answer the questions.
  1 When did Jordan and his girlfriend's relationship end?
  2 What did Jordan do about their vacation when their relationship ended?
  3 What happened when Jordan placed an ad on Reddit?
  4 How was Jordan and Elizabeth's relationship at the end of the trip?
  5 What did Jordan do after the trip?

4 Match the questions to the paragraphs. Then write the answers.
  1 How old is Jordan?   *2*
  2 How long was the around-the-world trip? _____
  3 How many people responded to Jordan's ad? _____
  4 Where did Jordan and Elizabeth spend New Year's Day? _____
  5 Which city was Jordan and Elizabeth's favorite? _____

5 Read the Text builder. Complete the chart with the adverbs in the box.

> 🧩 **Text builder**   adverbs of probability
>
> We use adverbs of probability to say how certain we feel about something.
> *Maybe* and *perhaps* usually come at the beginning of a sentence:
> *Maybe one day there will be a movie about their adventures.*
>
> Other adverbs of probability usually come before the main verb, but after the verb *be*:
> *Things **definitely** felt a little strange at first.*   *Prague was **possibly** their favorite place.*

definitely   maybe   perhaps   possibly   probably   certainly

It's certain	It's almost certain	It's not certain

6 A Look at the list of activities below. Check (✔) the ones you'd definitely like to do, put a question mark (**?**) next to the ones you'd possibly like to do, and a cross (**X**) next to the ones you definitely wouldn't like to do.

ride an elephant ☐	fly in a helicopter ☐	learn an instrument ☐
climb a volcano ☐	appear on TV ☐	run a marathon ☐
write a book ☐	learn a new skill ☐	do a parachute jump ☐

B Compare your ideas in pairs.

A *I'd definitely like to ride an elephant.*   **B** *Really? I definitely wouldn't want to do that! I'd like to climb a volcano.*

96

reading for detail ● adverbs of probability **READING** SKILLS 11B

LOOKING FOR
Elizabeth Gallagher

1 It's like a story in a movie: a couple plans a romantic trip around the world, but then they break up. The boyfriend doesn't want to go on the trip by himself, but he can't change the names on the tickets. He has to go alone … or he has to find another woman with the same name as his ex-girlfriend. So he starts looking for one …

2 That's exactly what happened to 28-year-old Jordan Axani from Canada. He reserved a three-week-long vacation with his girlfriend, but their relationship ended a month before the vacation started. Jordan didn't want to cancel his vacation but he didn't want to go alone. The airline told Jordan that it was impossible to change the names on the tickets, so he decided to find a woman with a Canadian passport and with the same name as his ex-girlfriend: Elizabeth Gallagher.

3 Jordan placed an ad on the website Reddit, and about 1,200 women contacted him. Of those 1,200 women, eighteen had the name Elizabeth Gallagher and a Canadian passport. Jordan chose a 23-year-old student from Nova Scotia to come with him on the trip.

4 Jordan and Elizabeth had an amazing trip; they saw some beautiful places and met some great people. They went to New York, Paris, Venice, and Bangkok. They spent the New Year in Hong Kong. Prague was possibly their favorite place. Did they become friends? Yes, they did. Elizabeth thought that things definitely felt a little strange at first, but, after a while, they were like brother and sister. Elizabeth had a boyfriend back in Canada, so she and Jordan probably got along better because of this.

5 So, what's next for Jordan and Elizabeth? Elizabeth went back to her life in Nova Scotia. But Jordan is writing a book and – who knows – maybe one day, there really will be a Hollywood movie about their adventures together.

Imagine you are Jordan or Elizabeth. Write an e-mail to a friend at home telling him/her about your trip.

97

11 LANGUAGE — *be going to* and future time expressions ■ vacation activities

11C Road trip

1 A Complete the questions about vacations with the verbs in the box.

visit   go (×3)   relax   stay

1 Do you prefer to _____ to the beach or to the mountains?
2 Do you prefer to _____ at a hotel or at a campsite?
3 Do you prefer to _____ sightseeing or _____ by the pool?
4 Do you prefer to _____ a castle or _____ shopping for gifts?

B Ask and answer the questions in pairs.

Go to **Vocabulary practice:** vacation activities, page 156

2 Read the text. What is the connection between the two pictures?

RADIO 7
The best road trip

In the early 1940s, Sullivan Richardson, a journalist from Detroit, got into his white Chrysler with two friends and drove 14,000 miles from North America to the very tip of South America.

It's one of the greatest car adventures of all time. There were no roads for a lot of their trip. The three men drove over mountains and through deserts and jungles. At night, they camped next to the car. People said the trip was impossible, but after nine months and one day, they finally reached their destination in Chile. It was the trip of a lifetime! Now, more than 75 years later, friends Jack Reid and Ben Davis are going to take a similar trip along the longest road in the world – the Pan-American Highway, but in a comfortable camper!

3 ▶ 11.6 Listen to an interview with Jack and Ben. Complete the chart with information about the trip.

	Sullivan Richardson's trip	Jack and Ben's trip
Starting point	Detroit	1
Length of trip	nine months	2
Where / stay?	camped next to the car	3
Sightseeing?	no	4

4 A ▶ 11.6 Listen again and complete the sentences.

1 We're going to _____ from Arizona.
2 We're not going to _____ all the way to Chile.
3 Where are you going to _____?
4 Are you going to _____ the same places as Sullivan?
5 We're going to _____ a volcano in Guatemala.
6 We're going to _____ hiking in Costa Rica.

B Choose the correct options to complete the rules. Then read the Grammar box and check.

1 We use *be going to* to talk about the *present / future*.
2 After *be going to*, we use the *-ing / base* form of the verb.

98

be going to and future time expressions ■ vacation activities **LANGUAGE 11C**

Grammar: *be going to* and future time expressions

We use *be going to* + the base form of the verb to talk about future plans:
I'm going to visit the beaches in Brazil.
We're going to drive 14,000 miles.
She's not / She isn't going to go by bus.

We're not / We aren't going to travel all the way to Chile.
Where are you going to stay?
Is your friend going to come with you?

Look! We use future time expressions with *be going to*.
She's going to get a new job **next year**.

Go to Grammar practice: *be going to* and future time expressions, page 133

5 A ▶11.8 **Pronunciation:** sentence stress Listen to the sentences. Listen again and repeat.
1 She's going to travel by train.
2 We're not going to go to the beach.
3 Are you going to stay with friends?

B ▶11.9 Say the sentences. Listen, check, and repeat.
1 I'm going to visit the castle.
2 You're not going to come with me.
3 We're going to travel by boat.
4 He's not going to relax by the pool.
5 Are you going to visit South America?
6 Is she going to stay at a hotel?

6 A Complete the conversation with the verbs in the box and the words in parentheses. Use *be going to*.

stay   visit   do   go (×2)   take   come   watch

Nuria Where ¹_____ (you and Tim) on vacation this year?
Mona Cape Town in South Africa.
Nuria Really? I went last year – it's amazing! What ²_____ (you) there?
Mona ³_____ (we) Robben Island, and ⁴_____ (we) hiking up Table Mountain. ⁵_____ (I) a rugby game, but ⁶_____ (Tim) with me – he's not interested in sports. I think ⁷_____ (he) some photos of the city.
Nuria It sounds great. Where ⁸_____ (you)?
Mona We're not sure yet. Do you know any good hotels?

B Act out the conversation in pairs.

Communication practice: Student A page 166, Student B page 175

7 A In pairs, plan your own "vacation of a lifetime." Make notes about your plans.

Which country? One place or different places? (forest, city, coast, etc.)	
Travel to your destination? (plane, ferry, car, etc.)	
Length of stay? (one week, two weeks, one month, etc.)	
Accommodations? (hotel, apartment, campsite, etc.)	
Places to visit? (museums, castles, stores, etc.)	
Activities? (sports, hiking, surfing, etc.)	

B Work with a different partner. Talk about your vacation plans. Ask him/her for more information.
  A We're going to go to China on vacation. We're going to stay there for two weeks, and we're going to visit a lot of different places.
  B That sounds interesting. Which places are you going to visit?

Personal Best You are going to go on a road trip. Write an e-mail to a friend about your plans for the trip.

99

SKILLS **SPEAKING** arriving at a hotel ■ checking information

11D At a hotel

1 A Look at the reasons why people stay at hotels. Can you think of more?
- You're on vacation.
- You have a very early flight at an airport.
- You're on a business trip.

B In pairs, discuss the questions.
1. What do you enjoy about staying at hotels?
2. Is there anything that you don't like about hotels? What?
3. When did you last stay at a hotel? Describe your experience.

2 ▶ 11.10 Watch or listen to the first part of *Learning Curve*. Check (✔) the type of room that Ethan and Penny have.

	Standard room	Deluxe room
Ethan		
Penny		

3 ▶ 11.10 Watch or listen again. Are the sentences true (T) or false (F)?

1. Ethan's going to reserve a hotel room in New York. ____
2. He has a meeting there. ____
3. He reserves a room for three nights. ____
4. Breakfast is included in the price. ____
5. There's a discount for all the rooms. ____
6. Penny spells her first name for the receptionist. ____
7. Her room's on the seventh floor. ____

Conversation builder — arriving at a hotel

Hotel receptionist:
Welcome to the … Hotel.
(Are you) Checking in?
Could you spell your last name, please?
Could/Can I have your identification/ID/credit card, please?
Can you sign this form, please?
Here's your room key/passport/credit card.

Hotel guest:
I reserved a room under/in the name of …
I have a reservation under/in the name of …
Which floor did you say?
What's the WiFi password?

4 A Read the Conversation builder. Order the sentences from 1–9 to make a conversation.
a ☐ Here you are. Here's my passport.
b ☐ Sure.
c ☐ OK. Here's your room key. Room number 1203, on the twelfth floor.
d ☐ Thank you. Could I have your ID, please?
e ☐ Thanks. Which floor did you say? The tenth?
f ☐ Great. Can I have your credit card, please?
g ☐ Yes. I reserved a room under the name of Lucía Espinosa.
h ☐ No, the twelfth floor.
i ☐ Welcome to Park Road Hotel. Checking in?

B In pairs, act out the conversation. If you want, use your own names and change the other details.

arriving at a hotel ■ checking information **SPEAKING** **SKILLS** **11D**

5 ▶ 11.11 Watch or listen to the second part of the show. Who enjoyed their stay at the hotel? Who didn't enjoy it?

6 ▶ 11.11 Watch or listen again. Choose the correct options to complete the sentences.

1 Penny says she'd like to *check in / check out / change rooms*.
2 Penny's stay was *horrible / comfortable / lovely*.
3 Ethan paid *more than / less than / the same as* Penny.
4 The WiFi in Ethan's room was *awful / pretty good / very good*.

7 A Read the Skill box. Complete mini-conversations 1–4 with a phrase to check the information.

> **Skill** checking information
>
> If you aren't sure if information is correct, you can check it with the person who said it.
> **Formal:**
> *You're going on May 11. Is that correct?   He's over eighteen. Is that correct?*
> **Neutral:**
> *Did you say one room for one night?   Did you say the fourth floor?*
> **Informal:**
> *That's with the discount, right?   Breakfast is at seven, right?*

1 **A** I'd like to reserve a double room for two nights.
  B You want a double room. _____?
2 **A** I'd like a standard room for three nights. Arriving on April 19th.
  B _____ two nights from April 19th?
3 **A** The price for a deluxe room is $100 a night.
  B The price includes breakfast, _____?
4 **A** There's a 20 percent discount for advance reservations.
  B _____ a 20 percent discount?

B ▶ 11.12 Listen and check. Pay attention to the intonation. Then act out the conversations in pairs.

Go to Communication practice: Student A page 166, Student B page 175

8 A PREPARE In pairs, look at the diagram and discuss what you could say at each stage. You can make notes.

```
            Receptionist                              Guest

  Greet the guest. Ask if he/she is checking in.  →  Give details of your reservation.

  Ask the guest for his/her documents.            →  Give the documents.

  Give the guest his/her room                     →  Take the key. Ask about breakfast, WiFi,
  key and say what floor.                            and anything else that you want to know.

  Give the information.                           →  Thank the receptionist.
```

B PRACTICE Repeat the conversation until you can say it without looking at the diagram or your notes. Check any information that you're not sure about.

C PERSONAL BEST Work with another pair. Listen to their conversation. Did they check any information? What was good about their conversation?

Personal Best Ethan is checking into a hotel in your town/city. Write the conversation.

101

UNIT 12 Enjoy yourself!

LANGUAGE present perfect with *ever* and *never* ■ entertainment

12A Going out

1 A Complete the chart with the words about entertainment.

fan   game   play   opera house   actor   club

People	Places	Events

B In pairs, add more words about entertainment that you know to the chart.

Go to Vocabulary practice: entertainment, page 157

2 A Read the interview. Who is the person in the picture? What is he going to try for the first time?

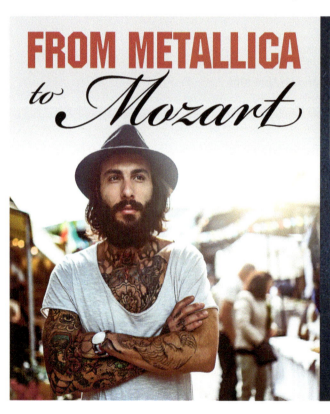

FROM METALLICA to Mozart

What happens when a heavy metal fan goes to an opera for the first time?

Have you ever been to a baseball game? Have you ever acted in a play? Is there a new experience that you'd like to try? Each week, we ask a guest to try something new for the first time. Our guest this week is Steve Bryant, a journalist with the heavy metal magazine, *Metal World*. Steve has never been to an opera.

So you've never been to an opera, Steve – is that right?
That's right. I've been to music festivals and rock concerts, but not to an opera. I've walked past the opera house, but I've never been inside.

We know you love heavy metal. What other music do you listen to?
I like a lot of different styles of music, from rock to blues and soul, and singer-songwriters like Neil Young and Bruce Springsteen.

What are your thoughts about opera music?
I've never really listened to it, and I don't know much about it. So this is going to be an interesting experience. I don't know if I'm going to like it!

B Read the interview again. Are the sentences true (T) or false (F)?
1 Steve has never been to a music festival. ____
2 Steve has never been inside an opera house. ____
3 He's only interested in heavy metal music. ____
4 He knows a lot about opera. ____

3 A Complete the sentences from the interview.
1 _____ you _____ to a baseball game?
2 Steve _____ never _____ to an opera.
3 I _____ past the opera house.
4 I _____ never _____ inside.

B Complete the rules. Then read the Grammar box.
1 We form the present perfect tense with the verb _____ + past participle.
2 We often use the adverb _____ in questions to ask about someone's experiences.
3 We often use the adverb _____ in negative sentences about experiences.

present perfect with *ever* and *never* ■ entertainment   **LANGUAGE**   **12A**

Grammar: present perfect with *ever* and *never*

We use the present perfect to talk about experiences in our lives.
Affirmative: I'**ve been** to music festivals and rock concerts.
Negative: He **hasn't listened** to an opera — He'**s never listened** to an opera.
Questions: **Have** they (**ever**) **acted** in a play?   Yes, they **have**. / No, they **haven't**.

Look! Regular past participles are the same as simple past forms. They end in -*ed*: act**ed**, walk**ed**, listen**ed**.
The past participle of *go* is *gone*, but we often use *been* for experiences:
*I went to London again last year. I've already **been** three times.*

Go to Grammar practice: present perfect with *ever* and *never*, page 134

4 A ▶12.3 **Pronunciation:** sentence stress Listen and repeat.
1 I've been to an opera.
2 I haven't been to a tennis game.
3 I've never sung in a band.
4 Have you ever bought a lottery ticket?

B ▶12.4 Say the sentences. Listen, check, and repeat.
1 Have you ever been to New York?
2 I've acted in a play.
3 I've never had a pet.
4 I haven't flown business class.

5 ▶12.5 Listen to part 2 of the interview with Steve. Complete the sentences.
1 I _____ about going to an opera.
2 I _____ a lot of bands.
3 Now I can say that _____ to an opera!
4 Most of my colleagues _____ an opera.

6 A Complete the sentences with the past participles of the verbs in the box.

see   cook   work   fly   fail   go   cry   arrive

1 I've _____ during a movie.
2 I've never _____ a Shakespeare play.
3 I've _____ to a ballet.
4 I've never _____ an exam.
5 I've _____ Chinese food.
6 I've never _____ late for my English class.
7 I've _____ as a waiter in a café.
8 I've never _____ in a helicopter.

B In pairs, say which sentences are true for you.
A *I've cooked Chinese food.*   **B** *That's not true for me! I've never cooked it.*

Go to Communication practice: Student A page 166, Student B page 175

7 A In pairs, ask and answer the questions in the questionnaire.
A *Have you ever been to a soccer game?*   **B** *Yes, I have. How about you?*

Are you adventurous?

Do you like to try new things? How adventurous are you?
Try our questionnaire to find out.

HAVE YOU EVER ...
1 (go) to a soccer game?
2 (see) your favorite band in concert?
3 (be) in a carnival?
4 (play) in a band or orchestra?
5 (visit) an art gallery?
6 (go) to an opera?
7 (dance) salsa?
8 (climb) a mountain?

YOUR SCORE
7–8 You're very adventurous. Is there anything you haven't done?!
4–6 You're pretty adventurous, but there's a lot more that you can try in life.
1–3 You haven't done many things, but don't worry! Why not try something new this weekend?

B Find your partner's score and tell the class about him/her.
Sofia is pretty adventurous. She's been in a carnival, but she's never climbed a mountain.

Personal Best Write about five things that you have done this year.

12B The book was better!

1 Complete the sentences with the words in the box.

> terrible   sad   amazing   fun   scary   strange

1 This is _____!   2 This movie is really _____!   3 What a _____ picture!

4 Our team is _____ today.   5 This view is _____!   6 This book is so _____.

2 Think of an example for each of the adjectives in exercise 1. Tell your partner.

Walking in the forest at night is scary.

Go to Vocabulary practice: opinion adjectives, page 157

3 12.7 Watch or listen to the first part of *Learning Curve*. Which sentence isn't true?

1 Kate knows more about *Frankenstein* than Simon.
2 There are lots of different *Frankenstein* movies.
3 *The Lord of the Rings* movies were created before the books.

Skill   listening for detailed information (2)

It is often necessary to understand what someone says in detail.
- Listen carefully to all the speakers. Sometimes one person corrects another person's information.
- Listen for people's names. Often you hear important information about the person immediately after you hear the name.
- Listen for key nouns and adjectives.

4 A 12.7 Read the Skill box. Then read the sentences below and watch or listen again. Are the sentences true (T) or false (F)?

1 Kate says Dr. Frankenstein is a monster.   ____
2 The most famous Frankenstein's monster is from the 1931 movie.   ____
3 In the book, Frankenstein's monster never speaks.   ____
4 Boris Karloff's special boots made the monster very tall.   ____
5 There are three *The Lord of the Rings* books.   ____
6 They made the first movie in 274 days.   ____
7 Some characters are funnier in the movie than in the books.   ____
8 The location of the films was Australia.   ____

B In pairs, discuss *Frankenstein* and *The Lord of the Rings*. Have you seen or read them? If not, would you like to see or read them? What do you think of them?

listening for detailed information (2) ■ linking ■ opinion adjectives   **LISTENING**   **SKILLS**   **12B**

5 ▶ 12.8   Watch or listen to the second part of the show. Choose the correct options to complete the sentences.

 Andy
 Millie
 Holly
 Yiannis

1 Andy thinks _____ is amazing.
  a *The Lord of the Rings*   b the original *Mad Max* movie   c the third *Mad Max* movie
2 Millie has seen all the *Harry Potter* movies _____ .
  a 10 times   b 15 times   c 20 times
3 Holly explains that Jane Austen didn't write _____ , but it has the same story as one of her books.
  a *Emma*   b *Clueless*   c *Pride & Prejudice*
4 Yiannis thinks that _____ were the best ones.
  a the first *James Bond* movies   b the first *James Bond* books   c the later *James Bond* movies

6 ▶ 12.8   Watch or listen again. Correct the mistakes in the sentences.
1 The original *Mad Max* movie is American. _____
2 Andy says that *Mad Max: Fury Road* is a happy movie. _____
3 In *Harry Potter*, they play Quidditch in the dining hall. _____
4 Charlie, Percy, and Bill are Ron Weasley's younger brothers. _____
5 The book *Emma* is about people in a high school. _____
6 *Bridget Jones's Diary* was a movie before it was a book. _____
7 The first *James Bond* movies were very different from the books. _____
8 Ian Fleming was a spy in the *James Bond* books. _____

7 A Make notes in the chart about some books you know that are also movies.

Book	Opinion of book	Movie	Opinion of movie

B In pairs, discuss the books and movies.
I love the book The Great Gatsby. It's beautiful and sad. But I think the 2013 movie is terrible.

Listening builder | **linking consonants and vowels**

When a word ends in a consonant sound and the next word starts with a vowel sound, we usually link them together:
The Lord‿of the Rings was‿a very popular series‿of books.
I can talk‿about James Bond‿all day!

8 ▶ 12.9   Read the Listening builder. Look at the sentences from the program and mark the links between words. Then listen and check.
1 Let's talk about the movie of another book.
2 I thought it was exciting!
3 She's a big fan of Jane Austen's books.
4 I'm sure a lot of people agree with us!
5 I've read all the books and seen all the movies.

9 A Prepare a one-minute talk about a movie. Use these questions to help you.
• What is the movie about?   • Was the location important?   • Did the idea for the movie come from a book?
• Who were the actors?   • What's your opinion of it?

B In pairs, give your talks. Ask your partner questions about his/her movie.

Personal Best   Choose two films and write a paragraph comparing them. Which movie is better/sadder/more exciting/funnier?   105

12 LANGUAGE present perfect and simple past

12C A famous voice

1 A Look at the picture and answer the questions.
1 Who is the character on the right?
2 What cartoon series is he from? Have you ever seen it?
3 Who do you think the woman on the left is?

B Read the text and check your answers.

NANCY CARTWRIGHT

As one of the most famous voices in the world, Nancy is the voice of Bart Simpson, from the American TV cartoon, *The Simpsons*. Naughty schoolboy Bart and his family are some of the world's most popular TV characters. Listen to today's program to find out more.

2 A ▶ 12.10 Listen to the radio program. When did Nancy start playing Bart?

B ▶ 12.10 Listen again and answer the questions.
1 Who did Nancy want to play at first?
2 What awards has Nancy won?
3 Has she ever acted in a movie?
4 What did Nancy say about her job on *The Simpsons*?

3 A Look at the extracts from the program. Underline the present perfect sentences, and circle the simple past sentences.

> **Rob** When did Nancy start playing Bart?
> **Chrissie** She started playing Bart in 1987.
>
> **Rob** Has Nancy ever won an award?
> **Chrissie** Yes, she's won a lot of awards. In 1992, she won an Emmy.

B Answer the questions. Then read the Grammar box.
1 Which two time words does Rob use in the box above?
2 Which tense does he use with these time words?

Grammar present perfect and simple past

Present perfect (talking about experiences in our lives, when we don't say when something happened):
She's **acted** in movies.   I've **been** to New York.   **Have** you ever **won** an award?

Simple past (asking for and giving more detail about past events):
She **was** in Godzilla **in 1998**.   I **went** to New York **last year**. I **went** with my dad.
When **did** she **win** an award?   **Did** you **have** a good time there?

Go to Grammar practice: present perfect and simple past, page 135

present perfect and simple past **LANGUAGE 12C**

4 Match the base forms, simple past forms, and past participles. Which past participles are the same as the simple past forms?

buy – bought – bought

Base form	Simple past	Past participle
buy drink drive eat	ate met saw drank	won eaten met read
fly meet read see	wrote flew spoke wore	worn written flown spoken
speak wear win write	drove won read bought	driven bought drunk seen

5 A ▶12.12 **Pronunciation:** vowels Listen and repeat the past participles in exercise 4.

B ▶12.13 Make pairs of past participles with the same vowel sound. Listen, check, and repeat.

w<u>o</u>n, dr<u>u</u>nk

6 A Write the conversations in full. Use the present perfect and simple past.

1
A you / ever / meet / a famous actor?
B yes
A who / you / meet?
B I / meet / Salma Hayek / last year.
A oh, really? where / you / meet / her?
B I / meet / her on a flight from Paris to London.

2
A you / ever / try / dangerous sport?
B yes
A what / you / try?
B I / try / rock climbing.
A you / enjoy / it?
B yes, it / be / great!

B In pairs, act out the conversations. Ask more questions to get more information.

Go to Communication practice: Student A page 166, Student B page 175

7 A Check (✓) the sentences that are true for you.

1 I've had a big party at my house. ☐
2 I've walked out of a movie theater before the end of a movie. ☐
3 I've bought clothes online. ☐
4 I've stayed awake all night. ☐
5 I've tried a dangerous sport. ☐
6 I've traveled first class. ☐
7 I've sung on stage. ☐
8 I've been on TV or in a newspaper. ☐

B Now work in groups. Ask *Have you ever* questions about the activities. Then ask simple past questions to find out more.

(What …?) (When …?) (Where …?) (Who …?) (How …?) (How much/many …?) (Did you …?)

A *Have you ever had a big party at your house?*
B *Yes, I have.*
A *How many people did you invite?*

Personal Best Think of an interesting experience you've had. Write a conversation like in exercise 6 to explain what happened.

107

12 SKILLS WRITING — writing and replying to an invitation ■ articles

12D Would you like to come?

1 Match pictures a–d with the events in the box. What other types of parties can you think of?

| a housewarming party a dinner party a wedding reception an office party |

2 Look at the party invitation below. Why are Amy and Will having a party?

Amy and Will
are having a
going-away party

We'd love you to join us as we say "Goodbye U.S." and "Hello Australia!"

When: Saturday, July 2nd, from 12:30 to 4:30 p.m.
Where: 17 Park Avenue
Children are welcome. No presents please.
RSVP: amyj81@net.com or 917-555-2392.

3 Now read three replies. Who is going to go to the party? Who can't go?

Dear Amy and Will,
Thanks so much for the invitation. I'm really sorry, but we can't make it because we're on vacation then. Hope you have a great time, and good luck in Australia! Keep in touch. We'd love to come and visit you!
Best wishes,
Kate and Ian xx

Hi Amy, hi Will,
Thank you for the invitation. We'd love to come to the party, and both of the kids would love to come, too! We can't wait to see you.
Lots of love,
Ed and Fiona

Dear Amy and Will,
Thanks very much for the invitation. I can definitely make it. I'm probably going to be a bit late as I'm going to drive back from Boston that day. Can I bring anything? Food? Something to drink?
All the best,
Jim

108

writing and replying to an invitation ■ articles   **WRITING**   SKILLS   **12D**

🔧 Skill   writing and replying to an invitation

When you write an invitation, say what sort of party it is, where it is, what time it starts, and the date. Give people your contact details:
We're having a (going-away) party.
Hope you can come. / Hope you can make it.
Please reply. / RSVP (from the French expression: *répondez s'il vous plaît*)

When you reply, thank the person who has invited you, and accept or decline the invitation.
If you decline, explain why you can't come:
I'd love to come.
I'd love to come, but … / I'm really sorry, but we can't come.

4 A Read the Skill box. Then read the invitation and replies again, and answer the questions.
  1 Which of the phrases do Amy and Will use?
  2 Find another phrase to invite someone to a party.
  3 Find another phrase for accepting an invitation.
  4 Find another phrase for declining an invitation.

  B Rewrite the replies. Use phrases from the Skill box.

a ● ● ●

Hi Amy and Will,

I can't come. ☹ Exam that day.

George

b ● ● ●

Amy, Will,

Thanks. See you on the 2nd.

Jess and Matt

🧩 Text builder   articles: *a/an*, *the*, or no article

We use *a/an* before singular nouns when we talk about a person or thing for the first time:
*Amy and Will are having **a** going-away party.*

We use *the* if we have already mentioned the person or thing:
*We'd love to come to **the** party.*

We use no article when we talk about things in general:
I love parties!

5 Read the Text builder and complete the sentences with *a/an*, *the*, or – (no article).

Lucy	I moved into ¹_____ new apartment last week, and I'm having ² _____ housewarming party next Friday. Would you like to come?
Joe	I'd love to! What time's ³_____ party?
Lucy	It's at eight o'clock. ⁴_____ apartment is 12A, Lancaster Street.
Joe	Great. Do you like ⁵_____ cake?
Lucy	Yes! Especially chocolate cake.
Joe	Great. I can make ⁶_____ orange and chocolate cake for the party.

6 A PREPARE Choose a type of party from exercise 1 or use your own ideas. Plan the details of your party.

  B PRACTICE Write an invitation to your event. Then exchange it with a partner and write two replies: one accepting and one declining the invitation. Use information and phrases from the Skill box and exercise 3 on page 108.

  C PERSONAL BEST Read your partner's replies to your invitation. Do they use phrases from the Skill box? Do they use articles correctly? Which reply is better and why?

Personal Best Plan the perfect party. Who would you invite and what would you do?

11 and 12 REVIEW and PRACTICE

Grammar

1 Cross out (**X**) the sentence that is NOT correct.

1. a I have to get up early every morning. ____
   b I have got up early yesterday. ____
   c I got up early yesterday. ____

2. a You have to drive on the left in the UK. ____
   b I drove on the left when I was in the UK. ____
   c You haven't to drive on the left in the UK. ____

3. a What do you going to do next weekend? ____
   b Are you going surfing next weekend? ____
   c What are you going to do next weekend? ____

4. a How's she going to get there? ____
   b Who's she going to go with? ____
   c How long she's going to stay? ____

5. a Have you ever drove a Rolls Royce? ____
   b I've never driven a Rolls Royce. ____
   c I drove a Rolls Royce ten years ago. ____

6. a When have you see her? ____
   b Have you seen a famous person? ____
   c When did you see her? ____

7. a I went to Poland last year. ____
   b I've been to Poland twice. ____
   c I never gone to Poland. ____

8. a She wrote some famous poems. ____
   b She has wrote some famous poems. ____
   c She has written some famous poems. ____

2 Rewrite the sentences with the words in parentheses.

1. It's necessary for me to get up early. (have to)
   _____

2. You can choose to come or not. (have to)
   _____

3. I don't plan to get a new job next year. (not / going to)
   _____

4. I'm not hungry, so I don't want dinner. (not / going to)
   _____

5. The train always stops at the next station. (going to)
   _____

6. I went to Paris in 2010 and 2012. (have / twice)
   _____

7. I always go on vacation in my own country. (never / abroad)
   _____

8. She buys lottery tickets and isn't successful. (have / never)
   _____

3 Choose the correct options to complete the text.

Part-time teacher, part-time magician

Alan Jordan has two jobs. From Monday to Friday, he teaches in an elementary school where he [1]*has to / have to* teach seven-year-olds how to read, write, and count. In the evenings and on the weekends, he becomes Ali Giordano and performs magic tricks for his audience. I asked him about the two jobs.

Q Which job do you prefer?

A I like both jobs. In both, I [2]*have to / have* stand up in front of a large group of people and tell them stories. They [3]*don't have to / have to* listen carefully to me, and I [4]*have to / has to* be careful with my words.

Q [5]*Have you ever used / Did you ever used* magic with your students?

A Of course. Last week, [6]*I have taught / I taught* a complete math class using playing cards. They [7]*learned / have learned* arithmetic and saw magic at the same time.

Q Have you used magic in other lessons?

A Yes. For example, two weeks ago [8]*I taught / I've taught* my class some vocabulary. I put words on cards, and the children had to find the objects. Some of them [9]*have appeared / appeared* by magic in surprising places!

Vocabulary

1 Circle the word that is different. Explain your answer.

1	match	opera	actor	concert
2	boat	bike	ballet	bus
3	boring	stupid	awful	amazing
4	pool	campsite	hotel	apartment
5	hiking	exciting	surfing	sightseeing
6	beach	mountains	museum	artist
7	strange	interesting	fantastic	great
8	train	taxi	ferry	car

110

2 Match definitions 1–8 with words a–h.

1	really fantastic	a	ballet
2	tourists like doing this	b	relax
3	a form of classical dancing	c	campsite
4	you can do this on the beach	d	sightseeing
5	you can stay here on vacation	e	amazing
6	really bad	f	boring
7	this transports passengers by sea	g	terrible
8	the opposite of interesting	h	ferry

3 Put the words in the correct column.

opera   subway   great   plane
bus   play   amazing   ballet
game   exciting   truck   cool

Positive adjectives	Forms of transportation	Types of entertainment

4 Choose the correct options to complete the sentences.

Jack How was your weekend?
Victoria It was ¹*great / boring / terrible*. We went to Miami, saw a movie, and then had a nice meal.
Jack What was the movie like?
Victoria It was ²*boring / all right / exciting* with a fabulous car chase! Unfortunately, the ending was ³*interesting / stupid / amazing*.
Jack Really? That's too bad. And how was the meal?
Victoria We went to a ⁴*boring / cool / scary* restaurant. It's very fashionable, so it was expensive, but the food was good.
Jack Sounds great.
Victoria It certainly wasn't ⁵*strange / boring / stupid*. It was very crowded with fabulous music. What about your weekend?
Jack It was ⁶*all right / amazing / sad*. Nothing special. We went to a concert on Saturday.
Victoria How was it?
Jack ⁷*Great / Terrible / Exciting*! I don't really like classical music, and it lasted over three hours. It wasn't even a good orchestra. Luckily, we went to this ⁸*strange / boring / amazing* club afterwards.

REVIEW and PRACTICE 11 and 12

Personal Best

Lesson 11A — List five forms of transportation.

Lesson 12A — Think of four places you can go to for entertainment.

Lesson 11A — Write a sentence with *I don't have to*.

Lesson 12A — Write a question with *ever*.

Lesson 11B — Write two sentences, one with *definitely* and one with *possibly*.

Lesson 12A — Write a sentence with *never* in the present perfect.

Lesson 11C — Name six vacation activities.

Lesson 12C — Think of three irregular past participles and their simple past forms.

Lesson 11C — Write a sentence about a place you plan to go to this year.

Lesson 12D — Think of two expressions for inviting someone to something.

Lesson 11D — Give three expressions for checking information.

Lesson 12D — Think of two expressions for accepting an invitation.

111

GRAMMAR PRACTICE

1A The verb *be*

We use the verb *be* to say who people are and to give other information about them (for example, where they are from, what job they do, where they are, how they are).

I'm Juan. I'm Mexican.
This is Michel. He's from France.
My sister is a teacher. She's in the classroom.
How are you? I'm fine.

We also use the verb *be* to talk about ages.

I'm 25.

We add *not* after the verb *be* to make the negative: *'m not*, *'re not*, and *'s not*. We can also use the forms *aren't* for *'re not*, and *isn't* for *'s not*. We form questions by putting the verb before the subject.

The full forms of the verb *be* are *am*, *is*, and *are*. We don't use contractions in short answers.

▶ 1.4	I	he / she / it	you / we / they
+	I'm Spanish.	Tom's from Chicago.	You're Japanese.
−	I'm not Portuguese.	Maria's not / isn't Australian.	We're not / aren't from Vietnam.
?	Am I from Canada?	Is she from New York?	Are you from Turkey?
Y/N	Yes, I am. / No, I'm not.	Yes, she is. / No, she's not / isn't.	Yes, we are. / No, we're not / aren't.

We use the contraction *'s* with third person singular nouns, names, and pronouns.

My sister's here.
Sabine's here.
She's here.

We use the contraction *'re* with *you*, *we*, and *they*.

You're my friend.
We're Colombian.
They're from Brazil.

But we use *are* with plural nouns and names.

My friends are from Brazil.
Gina and Laura are German.

We use the contractions *'s not* or *isn't* with *he*, *she*, and *it*, and *'re not* or *aren't* with *you*, *we*, and *they*.

He's not/He isn't here.
They're not/They aren't here.

We usually use *aren't* with plural nouns and names.

Gina and Laura aren't Brazilian.

1 Complete the sentences with the correct affirmative form of the verb *be*.

1 She _____ Brazilian.
2 They _____ from Argentina.
3 Pedro _____ in the classroom.
4 Fabio and Daniele _____ here.
5 I _____ 27.
6 My name _____ Yara.
7 We _____ students.
8 My teachers _____ American.

2 Read the information. Complete the questions and write the short answers (e.g. *Yes, she is*).

Fiona Murray is a student in Montreal, Canada. She's 22 years old. She's from Boston, in the state of Massachusetts. Her parents are Irish.

1 _____ her name Fiona?
  _____
2 _____ she 23 years old?
  _____
3 _____ she a student?
  _____
4 _____ she from Montreal?
  _____
5 _____ her parents Canadian?
  _____
6 _____ her parents from Ireland?
  _____

3 Complete the conversation. Use contractions where possible.

A Nice to meet you. My name ¹_____ Carla.
B Nice to meet you, too. I ²_____ William.
A Where ³_____ you from?
B I ⁴_____ from China. ⁵_____ you from Italy?
A No, I ⁶_____ from Italy. I ⁷_____ from Argentina.
B ⁸_____ you here with your family?
A No, I ⁹_____. They ¹⁰_____ at home.

◀ Go back to page 5

GRAMMAR PRACTICE

1C Possessive adjectives and 's for possession

Possessive adjectives

We use possessive adjectives before nouns to say that something belongs to someone.

It's my wallet.
This is your book.
This is her phone.
Where is his bag?
Is this our umbrella?
This is their car.

▶ 1.12

Subject pronoun	Possessive adjective	
I	my	I'm Spanish. **My** name is Raúl.
you	your	Are **you** ready? **Your** taxi's here.
he	his	**He**'s a great teacher. **His** students are young.
she	her	**She**'s at work, but **her** handbag is at home.
it	its	**It**'s a great city. I like the city for **its** beaches.
we	our	**We**'re from the U.S., but **our** son is British.
they	their	**They**'re not here. **Their** train is late.

We use the same possessive adjective for singular and plural nouns.

It's my pen. They're my pens.
This is their car. These are their cars.

's for possession

We add *'s* to a singular name or noun to say that something belongs to someone.

Tom's book is here.
Where are Lisa's bags?
This is the teacher's desk.

We don't usually use *'s* to say that something belongs to a thing. We use *of*.

The front of the bus.
The end of the vacation.

With regular plural nouns that end in *-s*, we use an apostrophe (') after the *-s* to talk about possession.

These are the students' books.
My friends' names are Lucy and Samir.

With irregular plural nouns, we use *'s* to talk about possession.

The children's books are in the classroom.
The women's soccer team are the champions.
Where are the men's bags?

1 Choose the correct words to complete the sentences.

1 *She / Her* is 48.
2 *They / Their* names are Maria and Lucy.
3 *Her / She* keys are in the car.
4 I'm *you / your* teacher for today.
5 *We / Our* tickets are in his wallet.
6 *He / His* is from Vietnam.
7 *I / My* last name is Moszkowski.
8 Is *his / he* umbrella black?

2 Complete the sentences with possessive adjectives.

1 Marie and Sylvain are French. _____ family is from Paris.
2 This is _____ wallet. Look, here's your identity card.
3 I am Chinese. _____ family is from Beijing.
4 Italy is famous for _____ food.
5 _____ classmates are from all over the world. We have interesting discussions in class.
6 She's the mom in my host family. _____ name is Tamara.
7 He's my Spanish friend. _____ name is Marcos.
8 What's _____ last name, Megan?

3 Correct and write the statements and questions. Use *'s* or an apostrophe (') to indicate possession.

1 Are these your sister glasses?

_____

2 Benedict is Millie boyfriend.

_____

3 My mothers books are in my bag.

_____

4 Our teacher name is Susanna.

_____

5 My parents new car is an Audi.

_____

6 Our children favorite TV show is *The Simpsons*.

_____

◀ Go back to pages 8–9

113

GRAMMAR PRACTICE

2A Simple present: affirmative and negative

We use the simple present to talk about:

- facts.

I'm Italian.
We live in New York.
He doesn't work at a restaurant.

- regular routines.

I work every day.
We go to the movies on the weekend.
They get up at 10 on Sundays.

We form negatives with *don't/doesn't* + the base form of the verb.

▶ 2.3	I / you / we / they	he / she / it
+	We **work** in a hospital.	Laura **works** in an office.
	I **teach** English.	He **teaches** Japanese.
	They **have** a new car.	She **has** a beautiful apartment.
	You **make** great coffee.	Simon **makes** good tea.
–	We **don't work** in a school.	Paul **doesn't work** in a store.
	I **don't teach** French.	He **doesn't teach** in a school.
	They **don't have** a yard.	She **doesn't have** a dog.
	You **don't love** your job.	Damian **doesn't love** his girlfriend.

We usually add -s to the verb to make the third person singular (*he/she/it*) form.

He serves food in the restaurant.
She loves her job.
Ivan sings at festivals.
Camilla helps her parents on the weekend.

Spelling rules for third person singular (he/she/it)

We usually add -s to the base form.
work ⇨ works

When the verb ends in a consonant + **y**, we change the **y** to **i** and then we add -**es**.
study ⇨ studies

When the verb ends in -**sh**, -**ch**, -**x** or -**s**, we add -**es**.
finish ⇨ finishes   watch ⇨ watches

Some verbs are irregular.
go ⇨ goes   do ⇨ does   have ⇨ has

1 Choose the correct words to complete the sentences.
   1 Adam *have / has* a job in a garage.
   2 Dean likes Mexico, but he *don't / doesn't* like Mexico City.
   3 Tyler *speak / speaks* French, but he doesn't speak German.
   4 Carla works in the evening, but she doesn't *work / works* on the weekend.
   5 Barbara and Fatima *teach / teaches* Spanish at a college.
   6 We *doesn't have / don't have* an office in New York.

2 Complete the sentences with the correct affirmative form of the verbs in the box.

| watch   serve   start   cut   help   finish   work |
| go   live |

   1 I _____ in an apartment in Rio de Janeiro.
   2 He's a waiter. He _____ the food.
   3 My sister is a hairdresser. She _____ people's hair.
   4 They _____ for a bank in the city.
   5 Elena _____ tourists. She gives them information.
   6 We _____ to work every morning by bus.
   7 Karl _____ TV every evening.
   8 Sara _____ work at 9 a.m. and she _____ at 5 p.m.

3 Look at the information and complete the affirmative and negative sentences about Emma.

   work: ~~in a hospital~~   in a store
   go to work: ~~by bus~~   by car
   finish work: ~~at 4 p.m.~~   at 5:30 p.m.
   help: ~~tourists~~   customers

   1 Emma _____ in a hospital.
     She _____ in a store.
   2 She _____ by bus.
     She _____ by car.
   3 She _____ at 4 p.m.
     She _____ at 5:30 p.m.
   4 She _____ tourists.
     She _____ customers.

◀ Go back to page 13

2C Simple present: questions

We use questions in the simple present to ask about things that are facts, or regular routines. We form questions in the simple present with *do/does* + subject + base form.

Do you like soccer?
Does she live in a big apartment?
Does he work on the weekend?
Do they go out a lot?

We form short answers with *Yes/No*, + subject + *do/does/don't/doesn't*.

Yes, I do.
No, I don't.
Yes, she does.
No, she doesn't

▶ 2.12	I / you / we / they	he / she / it
?	**Do** they **live** in the city?	**Does** he **live** with you?
	Do we **have** more time?	**Does** it **have** a yard?
	Do you **work** at a café?	**Does** she **work** at a hotel?
Y/N	Yes, I **do**. / No, I **don't**.	Yes, she **does**. / No, she **doesn't**.

If we want more information, we put a question word (*what*, *where*, *when*, *why*, *who*, *how*, etc.) before *do/does* at the start of the question.

Where do you live?
Who do you live with?
What does he do on the weekend?
How do you get to work?
When does the class start?
Why do you like soccer?

1 Put the words in the correct order to make questions.
 1 like / you / do / Spanish / food / ?
 _____
 2 in / Santiago / does / Sandra / live / ?
 _____
 3 they / do / Hong Kong / work / in / ?
 _____
 4 Eric / does / drive / a car / ?
 _____
 5 finish / do / we / at / 5 p.m. / ?
 _____
 6 do / teach / English / you / ?
 _____

2 Look at the short answers to the questions in exercise 1. Correct the mistakes.
 1 Yes, I like. _____
 2 Yes, she do. _____
 3 No, they not. _____
 4 No, he don't. _____
 5 Yes, we does. _____
 6 Yes, I teach. _____

3 Write questions.

 1 you / come from Australia
 _____
 2 your apartment / have / a TV
 _____
 3 you / like movies
 _____
 4 when / you / go to work
 _____
 5 where / your best friend / live
 _____
 6 what / she / do
 _____

◀ Go back to page 17

GRAMMAR PRACTICE

3A Frequency adverbs and expressions

We use frequency adverbs with the simple present to talk about routines and how often we do things.

```
100%
always      I always watch TV on the weekend.
usually     I usually read the newspaper on the weekend.
often       I often go for a walk on the weekend.
sometimes   I sometimes study English on the weekend.
hardly ever I hardly ever drink coffee.
never       I never watch soccer on the weekend.
0%
```

We usually put frequency adverbs before the main verb.
I always listen to the radio in the car. NOT ~~Always I listen to the radio in the car~~, or ~~I listen always to the radio in the car~~.

But we usually put frequency adverbs after the verb *be*.
They're never late. NOT ~~They never are late~~.

We use *How often ... ?* to ask about how frequently actions happen.
How often do you go out for dinner?

We also use frequency expressions with the simple present to talk about regular habits and routines.
I visit my parents every day.
I visit my grandparents twice a week.
I visit my cousins once a year.

▶ 3.5

I go to the movies	every once a twice a three times a four times a	day. week. month. year.

Once means "one time" and *twice* means "two times."

We usually use frequency expressions at the end of a sentence. We sometimes use them at the start of a sentence.
I visit my cousins once a year.
Once a year, I visit my cousins.
NOT ~~I once a year visit my cousins~~.

1 Rewrite the sentences. Put the frequency adverbs in the correct places.
  1 My father reads the newspaper. (always)
    _____
  2 My aunt has lunch with friends. (often)
    _____
  3 My cousin is at home in the evening. (usually)
    _____
  4 They work on the weekend. (sometimes)
    _____
  5 I go to the movies. (never)
    _____
  6 I'm very busy. (often)
    _____

2 Complete the sentences. Put one word in each sentence.

  1 I go to the gym _____ day.
  2 We go on vacation three times a _____ – in March, May, and October.
  3 I see my grandparents twice _____ week.
  4 I usually have a cup of coffee _____ a day – with breakfast and after lunch.
  5 My dad plays golf three _____ a week.
  6 My brother visits me twice a week, but my sister only visits me _____ a week.

3 Correct the sentences.
  1 Never Sam listens to music.
    _____
  2 Always the apartments here are nice.
    _____
  3 We eat out hardly ever on Saturdays.
    _____
  4 Lidia drives to work every days.
    _____
  5 We see our cousins four or five times year.
    _____
  6 I go to the theater once time a month.
    _____

◀ Go back to page 23

GRAMMAR PRACTICE

3C love, like, hate, enjoy, don't mind + noun/-ing form

We use *love*, *like*, *hate*, *enjoy*, and *don't mind* to say if we feel positively or negatively about something.

The verbs *love*, *like*, and *enjoy* have a positive meaning.

I love tennis. ☺☺
I like basketball. ☺
I enjoy swimming. ☺

The verb *don't mind* has a neutral meaning.

I don't mind working on the weekend. 😐
Soraya doesn't mind cats. 😐

The verbs *don't like/don't enjoy* and *hate* have a negative meaning.

I don't like going to the gym. ☹
Emil hates watching soccer. ☹☹

We use a noun or the *-ing* form of a verb after these verbs. (We can also use the infinitive after *love*, *like*, and *hate*.)

▶ 3.9

I love	tennis. / playing tennis.
I enjoy	museums. / visiting museums.
I like	dogs. / walking my dog.
I don't mind	rock music. / listening to rock music.
I don't like	Indian food. / eating Indian food.
I hate	soccer. / watching soccer.

Spelling rules for the *-ing* form

We usually add *-ing* to the base form of the verb.

play ⇨ *playing*   *talk* ⇨ *talking*

When a verb ends in consonant + *e*, we usually remove the *e* and then add *-ing*.

take ⇨ *taking*   *live* ⇨ *living*
BUT *be* ⇨ *being*

When a one-syllable verb ends in a vowel + a consonant, we double the consonant and then add *-ing*.

sit ⇨ *sitting*   *plan* ⇨ *planning*

When a one-syllable verb ends in a vowel + a consonant, we double the consonant and then add *-ing*.

sit ⇨ *sitting*   *plan* ⇨ *planning*

1 Complete the sentences with the *-ing* form of the verb in parentheses.

 1 They like _____ new places. (visit)
 2 I like _____ time with my family. (spend)
 3 He doesn't like _____. (swim)
 4 She hates _____ dinner. (make)
 5 Does Freya like _____? (drive)
 6 I love _____ on the beach. (run)
 7 Do you like _____ a student? (be)
 8 My parents love _____ photos. (take)

2 Complete the sentences with *love*, *like*, *don't mind*, *don't like*, *hate*, and the *-ing* form of the verbs in the box.

| work   go   meet   play   make   cook   learn   listen |

 1 They ☺ _____ Japanese food.
 2 Sadiq ☺ _____ in a bank.
 3 I ☹ _____ French.
 4 Tania ☺☺ _____ clothes.
 5 I ☺ _____ my friends in town.
 6 We ☹☹ _____ golf.
 7 Liam 😐 _____ shopping.
 8 I ☺ _____ to the radio.

3 Read the sentences. Check (✓) the ones that are correct. Rewrite the incorrect ones.

 1 I love American movies. ☐
 _____
 2 Do you like cook? ☐
 _____
 3 Pedro doesn't like basketball. ☐
 _____
 4 I hate be late. ☐
 _____
 5 Tomiko enjoys to play soccer. ☐
 _____
 6 I love talking to my friends. ☐
 _____

◀ Go back to page 27

117

GRAMMAR PRACTICE

4A Prepositions of time

We use different prepositions to make common time expressions.

▶ 4.2

Preposition	We use this with ...	Example
in	*the* + parts of the day	in the morning(s) in the afternoon(s) in the evening(s)
	the + seasons	in the winter in the spring in the summer in the fall
	months of the year	in January in September
on	days of the week	on Monday(s) on Tuesday(s)
	days and parts of the day	on Thursday morning(s) on Saturday night(s) on Friday evening(s) on New Year's Day
	the weekend	on the weekend / on weekends
at	times	at 6 o'clock at 11:30
	midnight/noon/night	at midnight at noon / noon at night
	festivals	at Thanksgiving at New Year's
from ... to	days	from Wednesday to Sunday
	months	from January to June
	times	from 6:30 to 9:00
	years	from 2000 to 2006

Look! *at night* NOT ~~*in night*~~ BUT *on Friday night*

We use these time expressions at the start or at the end of a sentence. We use a comma after them if they are at the start.

I usually get up at 7:30.
At 7:30, I usually get up.
I have an Italian class on Wednesday evening.
On Wednesday evening, I have an Italian class.

We can use plurals for days, parts of the day, and *weekend* if we talk about things that we do regularly.

I don't work on the weekend / on weekends.
In the morning / In the mornings, I often go running before work.

1 Complete the sentences with *in*, *on*, *at*, or *from ... to*.

1 I usually take a shower _____ the evening.
2 Charles does his homework _____ night.
3 I'm at work _____ 8:30 _____ 6:30 every day.
4 They visit their cousins _____ New Year's Day.
5 We always go out _____ Friday nights.
6 Is it hot here _____ August?
7 The days are short _____ the winter.
8 What do you like doing _____ the weekend?

2 Read the text and <u>underline</u> eight mistakes. Write the correct prepositions below the text.

Every day, from Monday in Friday, I get up at 6:30. I leave the house at 7:30, and I start work on 8:15. I don't work on Friday afternoons. I finish work in noon.

On July and August, it's very hot. I usually go to the swimming pool with my children in the afternoons, and in night, we go for a walk.

In the weekend, I don't get up early. At Saturday mornings, I go running on 11, and then my wife and I make lunch. On Sundays, we usually take the children to visit my parents or my wife's parents.

1 _____   4 _____   7 _____
2 _____   5 _____   8 _____
3 _____   6 _____

3 Write sentences. Add prepositions.

1 I visit my grandparents / the weekend

_____

2 February / we usually go skiing

_____

3 I usually stop for a cup of coffee / noon

_____

4 Wednesday evenings / my sister does yoga

_____

5 Carlos works / Monday / Saturday

_____

6 My daughter's birthday is / the spring

_____

◀ Go back to page 31

4C Present continuous

We use the present continuous to talk about:
- things that are happening now.

I'm taking a shower.
It's raining.
What are you reading?

- things that are temporary.

We're staying at a hotel.
I'm not working this week.

We form the present continuous with the verb *be* + the *-ing* form of the main verb.

▶ 4.9	I	he / she / it	you / we / they
+	I'm getting dressed.	He's getting dressed.	We're getting dressed.
−	I'm not watching TV.	She's not watching TV.	We're not watching TV.
?	Am I sleeping?	Is she sleeping?	Are they sleeping?
Y/N	Yes, I am. / No, I'm not.	Yes, she is. / No, she's not/isn't.	Yes, they are. / No, they're not/aren't.

Spelling rules for the *-ing* form

We usually add *-ing* to the base form of the verb.

play ⇨ playing   talk ⇨ talking

When a verb ends in consonant + *e*, we usually remove the *e* and then add *-ing*.

take ⇨ taking   live ⇨ living

BUT be ⇨ being

When a one-syllable verb ends in a vowel + a consonant, we double the consonant and then add *-ing*.

sit ⇨ sitting   plan ⇨ planning

Look! We often use the present continuous with time expressions such as (*right*) *now*, *today* and *this week/month/year*.
I'm having breakfast right now.
I'm studying a lot this month.

GRAMMAR PRACTICE

1 Put the words in the correct order to make sentences.

1 using / the computer / Ella / is / ?
_____
2 parents / I / visiting / am / my
_____
3 reading / Matt / the newspaper / is
_____
4 isn't / my / working / phone
_____
5 staying / we / are / at a hotel / this weekend
_____
6 you / going / where / are / ?
_____

2 Complete the sentences with the correct present continuous forms of the verbs in parentheses.

1 I _____ dinner right now. (have)
2 We _____ to the beach now. (go)
3 The Internet _____ today. (not work)
4 _____ Tim _____ a shower? (take)
5 She _____ a coat today. (not wear)
6 What _____ you _____? (do)
7 I _____ today because it's Saturday. (not study)
8 _____ I _____ in the right place? (sit)

3 Look at the picture. Use the words to make questions and write true short answers.

1 they / talk
_____
2 they / have / a good time
_____
3 it / snow
_____
4 it / rain
_____
5 she / carry / an umbrella
_____
6 he / wear / glasses
_____

◀ Go back to page 35

119

GRAMMAR PRACTICE

5A Simple present and present continuous

We use the simple present to talk about facts and things that happen regularly.

Sam lives in Australia.
We wear a uniform at work.
I usually wake up at six o'clock.

We use the present continuous to talk about things that are happening now, or are temporary.

I'm wearing blue pants today.
I'm going to work by car today.
My friend is living in New York right now.

We often use the simple present and present continuous together to contrast the usual situation with what is happening now, or is temporary.

▶ **5.2 Present simple and present continuous**

It **usually doesn't** rain in the summer,	but it**'s raining** today.
I **usually wear** jeans to work,	but today I**'m wearing** a suit.
I **often don't** cook,	but I**'m cooking** every evening this week.

There are some verbs that describe a state, not an action. We normally don't use these verbs in the present continuous.

I prefer this music. NOT *I'm preferring this music.*
Sorry, I don't understand. NOT *Sorry, I'm not understanding.*
I have some new sandals. NOT *I'm having some new sandals.*

Look! Here are some common state verbs:
Feelings: *like, love, hate, want, prefer, need*
Thoughts and opinions: *know, believe, remember, forget, understand, think*
States: *be, belong, have* (when we talk about relationships or possessions)

1 Choose the correct words to complete the sentences and questions.
1 What *do you do / are you doing* right now?
2 *Is he going / Does he go* there often?
3 They*'re working / work* late tonight.
4 I *never read / 'm never reading* books.
5 I*'m studying / study* in my bedroom now.
6 Most people *finish / are finishing* school at eighteen or nineteen years old.

2 Complete the sentences with the simple present or present continuous form of the verbs in parentheses.
1 I _____ right now. (read)
2 He _____ to New York three times a year. (go)
3 They _____ us every summer. (visit)
4 How _____ Erica _____ to work today? (get)
5 I _____ coffee very often. (not drink)
6 We _____ a really good TV series right now. (watch)
7 I usually _____ juice for breakfast. (have)
8 Please be quiet – the baby _____. (sleep)

3 Read the information. Then complete the text about James.

James usually [1]_____ tea and toast for breakfast. He [2]_____ a suit. He [3]_____ all day. This week, James is on vacation. He [4]_____ coffee and croissants for breakfast. He [5]_____ shorts and a T-shirt. He [6]_____ a great time!

◀ Go back to page 41

GRAMMAR PRACTICE

5C can and can't

We use *can* and *can't* to talk about:

- ability.

I can swim.
My brother can play the guitar.
I can't speak Italian.
My sister can't cook.

- possibility.

You can make money from your hobby.
It can snow here in the winter.
You can't get there by bus.

- permission.

You can take my umbrella.
We can sit here.
We can't park on this street.
You can't use this gym if you're not a member.

To make questions with *can*, we put *can* before the subject. We use the same form for all people.

▶ 5.8   I / you / he / she / it / we / they

+	I **can play** the piano.
	They **can go** to the city by bus.
	We **can finish** work early today.
–	She **can't speak** Japanese.
	They **can't work** at night.
	You **can't walk** on the grass.
?	**Can** she **play** the guitar?
	Can you **come** to my party?
	Can we **park** the car here?
Y/N	Yes, we **can**. / No, we **can't**.

Look! The full form of *can't* is *cannot*. We don't often use *cannot*; *can't* is the usual negative form.
I can't meet you tonight. NOT ~~I cannot meet you tonight~~.

1 Look at the chart and complete the sentences with *can* or *can't*.

	Craig	Helen	Manuel	Silvia
cook	✔	✔	✘	✔
play tennis	✔	✘	✔	✘
drive	✔	✔	✔	✘
speak French	✘	✘	✘	✔

1 Craig _____ cook, but he _____ speak French.
2 Helen _____ play tennis, but she _____ drive.
3 Craig, Helen, and Manuel _____ speak French.
4 Manuel _____ cook, but he _____ drive.
5 Silvia _____ cook and speak French.
6 Craig, Helen, and Manuel _____ drive.

2 Write short answers to the questions about the people in exercise 1.

1 Can Silvia drive? _____
2 Can Craig play tennis? _____
3 Can Helen cook? _____
4 Can Manuel speak French? _____
5 Can Helen and Silvia play tennis? _____
6 Can Craig and Manuel drive? _____

3 Complete the sentences about the pictures. Use *can* or *can't* and the phrases in the box.

walk on the grass   ride a bike on this street
pay with a credit card   park here for one hour

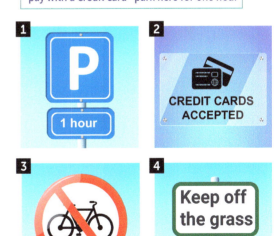

1 You _____
2 You _____
3 You _____
4 You _____

◀ Go back to page 45

121

GRAMMAR PRACTICE

6A there is/there are, some/any/no, prepositions of place

We use *there is* to say that something singular exists.

There's a sofa in the living room.
There's a small balcony in my apartment.

We use *there are* for the plural form.

There are five people in my family.
There are three bedrooms in her apartment.

We use *some* and *any* with plural nouns. We use *some* in affirmative sentences when more than one thing or person exists, but we don't say exactly how many.

There are some chairs in the classroom.
There are some new students in our class.
I have some books in my bag.

We use *any* in negative sentences and questions with plural nouns. We use *no* after an affirmative verb and with a singular or plural noun.

There are no tables. / There aren't any tables.
I have no brothers or sisters. / I don't have any brothers or sisters.
Are there any shelves in the bedroom?

▶ 6.3	Singular nouns	Plural nouns
+	**There's** a shelf in my bedroom.	**There are some** shelves in the kitchen.
–	**There's no** chair in my bedroom.	**There are no / There aren't any** chairs in the kitchen.
?	**Is there** a cabinet in your bedroom?	**Are there any** cabinets in the kitchen?
Y/N	Yes, **there is**. / No, **there's not/ there isn't**.	Yes, **there are**. / No, **there aren't**.

Prepositions of place

▶ 6.7 We use prepositions of place to describe location.
The window is across from the door.

in front of   under   next to   in
on   between   behind   across from

1 Read the advertisement and then complete the sentences with *there's a/there are* and *there's/there are no*.

> Third-floor two-bedroom apartment in a popular area near stores and a park. Five-minute walk to subway station. Living room with big windows. Kitchen, bathroom (shower only, no bathtub). Empty – ready to move in!

1 _____ two bedrooms.
2 _____ a bathroom.
3 _____ backyard, but _____ a park near the apartment.
4 _____ some big windows in the living room.
5 _____ bathtub in the bathroom.
6 _____ people in the apartment right now.
7 _____ some stores near the apartment.
8 _____ a subway station near the apartment.

2 Complete the questions and answers about an apartment.

1 _____ garage in your apartment building?
No, _____.
2 _____ shelves in the living room?
Yes, _____.
3 _____ basement that you can use?
Yes, _____.
4 _____ sofa in the living room?
Yes, _____.
5 _____ good restaurants in the area?
No, _____.
6 _____ schools for the children?
Yes, _____.

3 Look at the floor plan of a house. Complete the sentences with prepositions of place.

1 The kitchen is _____ the bathroom.
2 The bathroom is _____ the two bedrooms.
3 The dining room is _____ the kitchen.
4 There is a small yard _____ the house.
5 There is a large yard _____ the house.
6 There are some trees _____ the large yard.

◀ Go back to page 49

122

6C Modifiers

We use modifiers with adjectives to make them stronger or weaker.

It's really/very big.

It's pretty big.

It's not very big.

It's not big at all.

We use *really* and *very* to make an adjective stronger.
The city is really big.
The market is very busy on Saturdays.

We use *pretty* and *not very* to make an adjective weaker. If we use *pretty*, the adjective has the same meaning, but is weaker. If we use *not very*, the adjective has the opposite meaning.
The bridge is pretty old.
The apartment's not very old. = The apartment is pretty new.

We use *not* + adjective + *at all* to give a strong opposite meaning to an adjective.
The beach isn't crowded at all. = The beach is very empty.
The restaurant's not expensive at all. = The restaurant is very cheap.

▶ 6.12

modifier + adjective	modifier + adjective + (singular) noun
The house is **really/very beautiful**.	It's a **really/very beautiful** house.
The house is **pretty beautiful**.	It's a **pretty beautiful** house.
The house is**n't very beautiful**.	It's **not** a **very beautiful** house.
The house is**n't beautiful at all**.	It's **not** a **beautiful** house **at all**.

GRAMMAR PRACTICE

1 Rewrite the sentences. Put the modifier in parentheses in the correct place.
1 The beach is busy today. (very)
_____
2 The stadium is full at the moment. (not very)
_____
3 You can buy beautiful presents at the market. (really)
_____
4 This is an old apartment building. (pretty)
_____
5 This café is expensive. (not … at all)
_____
6 I'm reading an interesting book right now. (pretty)
_____

2 Put the words in the correct order to make sentences.
1 a / bathroom / there / large / is / pretty
_____
2 a / skyscraper / I / in / very / tall / work
_____
3 I / street / on / a / live / quiet / pretty
_____
4 clothes / are / these / very / expensive
_____
5 sister / at / isn't / my / busy / all
_____
6 food / good / the / isn't / very
_____

3 Look at Andy's review of his vacation. Complete the sentences about it using modifiers and the adjectives in parentheses.

The old town is ¹ __really beautiful__ (beautiful), but it's ² _____ (busy). The restaurants are ³ _____ (expensive), and the food is ⁴ _____ (good). The beaches are ⁵ _____ (crowded), but they're ⁶ _____ (clean). It's ⁷ _____ (good) place for families because it's ⁸ _____ (cheap) place to stay.

◀ Go back to page 53

123

GRAMMAR PRACTICE

7A Countable and uncountable nouns + some/any

Countable nouns are things that we can count.

I have a brother.
There are two glasses on the table.
There are fourteen students in the class.

Countable nouns have a singular and a plural form. We can use *a/an* with the singular form.

Do you want a banana?
I like bananas.
We need an egg for this recipe.
We need three eggs for this recipe.

Uncountable nouns are things that we can't count. They usually don't have a plural form, and we can't use *a/an* with them.

I don't like cheese.
Do you like lemonade?
There's a lot of sugar in this cake.
We're having pasta for dinner.

some/any

We use *some* in affirmative statements with uncountable nouns and plural countable nouns. We use it when we don't say exactly how much or how many.

There's some juice in the fridge.
There are some apples in the bowl.

We use *any* in negative statements and questions with uncountable nouns and plural countable nouns.

There isn't any milk.
We don't have any oranges.
Do you have any money?
Are there any strawberries?

▶ 7.4

	Countable nouns		Uncountable nouns
	Singular	Plural	
+	There's **a** banana.	There are **some** bananas.	There's **some** water.
−	There's **no** lemon.	There aren't **any** lemons.	There isn't **any** coffee.
?	Is there **an** onion?	Are there **any** onions?	Is there **any** tea?

Look! We usually use *some* in questions when we offer something to someone.

Do you want some soup?
Would you like some carrots?

---

1 Look at the picture. Write *a*, *an*, or *some*.

1 _____ meat
2 _____ chocolate
3 _____ melon
4 _____ apple
5 _____ bread
6 _____ orange
7 _____ potatoes
8 _____ tomatoes

2 Complete the conversation with *a*, *an*, *some*, or *any*.

A What's for lunch? Is there [1]_____ pasta?
B No, there isn't [2]_____ pasta. But there's [3]_____ rice in the cupboard.
A Good. And do we have [4]_____ meat or fish?
B Yes, we have [5]_____ chicken and [6]_____ fish. There's [7]_____ green pepper and [8]_____ onion, too, but there isn't [9]_____ salad.
A No problem. We can buy [10]_____ salad at the market.

3 Make sentences. Add *a*, *an*, *some*, or *any*.

1 there / not / cheese / on this pizza
_____
2 you / have / tomatoes / ?
_____
3 there / milk / in the fridge
_____
4 we / not have / yogurt
_____
5 there / mushrooms / in the shopping bag
_____
6 there / water?
_____

◀ Go back to page 59

GRAMMAR PRACTICE

7C Quantifiers: (how) much, (how) many, a lot of, a few, a little

We use *how much* and *how many* to ask about quantity. We use *how much* with uncountable nouns and *how many* with countable nouns.

How much fish do you eat every week?
How many students are there in your class?

We use *a lot of* or *lots of* with countable and uncountable nouns to talk about large quantities. We can use them in affirmative sentences, negative sentences, and questions.

I eat a lot of fruit.
I don't eat a lot of apples.
Do you eat a lot of potato chips?

We use *a lot of* and *many* to ask about quantities. We use *a lot of* with uncountable nouns and *many* with countable nouns.

Do you drink a lot of juice?
Are there many/a lot of students in your class?

We use *not much* and *not many* in negative sentences to talk about small quantities. We use *not much* with uncountable nouns and *not many* with countable nouns.

There isn't much sugar in this cake.
I don't eat many potato chips.

We use *a few* and *a little* in affirmative sentences and questions to talk about small quantities. We use *a little* with uncountable nouns and *a few* with countable nouns.

I'd like a little milk in my coffee.
Would you like a little sugar in your coffee?
I eat a few pieces of fruit every day.
Are there a few eggs in the fridge?

▶ 7.8	Countable nouns	Uncountable nouns
Large quantities	There are **a lot of/lots of** crackers. Are there **many** crackers? Are there **a lot of/lots of** crackers?	There's **a lot of/lots of** cheese. Is there **a lot of/lots of** cheese?
Small quantities	There are **a few** crackers. There aren't **many** crackers. There aren't **a lot of** crackers. Are there **a few** crackers?	There's **a little** cheese. There's not **much** cheese. There's not **a lot of** cheese. Is there **a little** cheese?

Look! With *a lot of / lots of*, we don't say *of* if we don't say the noun.
Do you have any milk?   Yes, we have a lot. NOT ~~Yes, we have a lot of.~~

1 Complete the questions with *How much* or *How many*.
   1 _____ cups of coffee do you drink every day?
   2 _____ sugar do you put in your coffee?
   3 _____ time do you spend online every day?
   4 _____ e-mails do you send every day?
   5 _____ rooms are there in your home?
   6 _____ water do you drink every day?
   7 _____ brothers and sisters do you have?
   8 _____ jewelry do you wear?

2 Choose the correct words to complete the sentences.
   1 There isn't *much / a lot* cheese in the fridge.
   2 I drink *a lot / a little* of tea every day.
   3 My friends don't send me *much / many* messages.
   4 I don't take *much / a little* sugar in my tea.
   5 It's good to eat *a lot / a little* fish every week.
   6 I have *much / lots of* cousins.
   7 Do your children eat *a few / a lot of* fruit?
   8 I drink *a little / a few* glasses of milk every day.

3 Look at the picture and complete the sentences with quantifiers.

   1 There are _____ cups.
   2 There isn't _____ cake.
   3 There are _____ bottles of water.
   4 There's _____ pizza.
   5 There aren't _____ potato chips.
   6 There's _____ salad.

◀ Go back to page 63

125

GRAMMAR PRACTICE

8A Past of *be*, *there was/there were*, and simple past: irregular verbs

We use the past of *be* and the simple past to talk about completed actions and situations in the past.

The past forms of the verb *be* are *was* and *were*.

Life was difficult in the 1930s.
Our house wasn't very big.
We were very happy.
We weren't rich.

▶ 8.2	I / he / she / it	you / we / they
+	I **was** busy last week.	We **were** busy last week.
–	He **wasn't** busy yesterday.	They **weren't** busy yesterday.

there was/there were

We use *there was/there were* to say that something existed in the past.

There was a TV in our living room.
There were two rooms in our apartment.

▶ 8.3	Singular	Plural
+	**There was** a fridge in our kitchen.	**There were** a lot of books in my bedroom.
–	**There was** no/**There wasn't** any freezer.	**There weren't** any CDs.

Simple past: irregular verbs

The verb *be* is irregular in the past. A lot of common verbs have an irregular simple past form, too.

We made a cake yesterday.
I had an English class last week.

We make the negative simple past form of all verbs with *didn't* + the base form of the verb.

We didn't make bread yesterday.
I didn't have a French class last week.

▶ 8.5	I / you / he / she / it / we / they
+	I **bought** a lot of books in the 1990s.
–	I **didn't buy** expensive clothes.

For a full list of irregular verbs, see page 176.

1 Complete the sentences with *was*, *wasn't*, *were*, or *weren't*.
 1 I _____ born in the U.S. I'm Canadian.
 2 Chris _____ at my house yesterday. He was at home.
 3 It _____ Friday yesterday. Today is Saturday.
 4 We _____ at the movies last night. We left at 10.00 p.m.
 5 The stores _____ open, so we didn't buy anything.
 6 There _____ any tickets, so we didn't go to the concert.
 7 Lucia _____ born in Uruguay in 1978.
 8 The market _____ busy this morning. It was so crowded.

2 Write the sentences in the negative.
 1 I had breakfast this morning.
    _____
 2 We read the newspapers yesterday.
    _____
 3 My dad made dinner last night.
    _____
 4 We bought a color TV in the 1970s.
    _____
 5 I was at home on Saturday.
    _____
 6 My parents were on vacation last week.
    _____

3 Complete the text with the past of *be* or the simple past of the verbs in parentheses.

In the 19th century, life [1]_____ (be) difficult for a lot of people. Usually homes [2]_____ (be) pretty small. There usually [3]_____ (not be) a bathroom in the house. People [4]_____ (not have) modern inventions like TVs or radios. They [5]_____ (not buy) many things, and there [6]_____ (not be) any computers. But people [7]_____ (read) books and children [8]_____ (have) toys.

◀ Go back to page 67

126

8C Simple past: regular verbs and past time expressions

We use the simple past to talk about completed actions and situations in the past.

With regular verbs, we usually add -ed to the base form of the verb.

My brother worked as a waiter in London for two years.
In the past, children played with traditional toys.
My brother wanted a bike for his birthday.
I finished my exams last month.

Spelling rules for regular affirmative simple past -ed endings

We usually add **-ed** to the verb.
work ⇨ worked   watch ⇨ watched

When a verb ends in **e**, we add **-d**.
dance ⇨ danced   live ⇨ lived

When a verb ends in consonant + **y**, we change the **y** to **i** and then we add **-ed**.
study ⇨ studied   try ⇨ tried

When a verb ends in vowel + **y**, we add **-ed**.
play ⇨ played   enjoy ⇨ enjoyed

When a verb ends in consonant + vowel + consonant, we usually double the final consonant and add **-ed**.
stop ⇨ stopped   plan ⇨ planned

We make the negative form of regular verbs with *didn't* + base form.

▶ 8.12   I / you / he / she / it / we / they

I **enjoyed** the meal.
I **didn't enjoy** the movie last night.
We **watched** the movie together.
We **didn't watch** TV.

Past time expressions

We often use past time expressions with the simple past to say when an action or situation happened.

I played tennis last week.
I played tennis yesterday morning.
I moved to Spain seven years ago.
In the 1920s, clothes were very different from now.

last	evening/night/week/month/year/spring/summer/fall/winter
yesterday	morning/afternoon/evening
two days three weeks five years	ago
in	1990/the 1930s/the 18th century

Look! We can say either "yesterday evening" or "last evening."

GRAMMAR PRACTICE

1 Complete the sentences with the verbs in the box. Use affirmative simple past forms.

| enjoy   live   play   work   listen   watch |
| study   want |

1 In his last job, Tony _____ at a bank.
2 We _____ to the news on the radio.
3 She _____ in Berlin in a great apartment.
4 Lena _____ to go out, but her friends were busy.
5 They _____ tennis in the park yesterday.
6 My parents _____ a movie online last night.
7 I _____ reading my new book on the weekend.
8 I _____ Spanish in Mexico a few years ago.

2 Complete the sentences with *yesterday*, *last*, *ago*, or *in*.

1 Emma called me _____ morning.
2 Cameron stayed with us _____ night.
3 I read four books on vacation _____ summer.
4 We moved to Chicago eight years _____.
5 My dad opened a restaurant _____ the 1980s.
6 We watched a terrible movie on TV _____ afternoon.
7 _____ 1969, a person walked on the moon for the first time.
8 Carmen finished college four months _____.

3 Write sentences. Use the simple past and complete the time expressions.

1 I / visit / China / 2013

2 my family / live / in Australia / 1970s

3 Lucas / not finish / his homework / night

4 Sam and Ellie / celebrate / Sam's birthday / at a restaurant / two days

5 the 1990s / a lot of people / listen to / dance music

6 my brother / not want / to go to the movies / night

◀ Go back to page 71

GRAMMAR PRACTICE

9A Past: questions

For the past of *be*, we form questions with *was/were* + subject.

Were you a good student?
Was your school near your home?
Were the exams very difficult?
Was English your favorite subject?

For the simple past, we form questions with *did* + subject + base form of the verb.

Did you study Spanish in school?
Did your parents go to college?
Did you have toast for breakfast today?

▶ 9.4		I / he / she / it	you / we / they
Verb *be*	?	**Was** the class interesting?	**Were** Tom and Mía in class yesterday?
	Y/N	Yes, it **was**. / No, it **wasn't**.	Yes, they **were**. / No, they **weren't**.
Other verbs	?	**Did** you **have** an English class last week?	
	Y/N	Yes, I **did**. / No, I **didn't**.	

We can put question words at the start of the question to ask for more information.

What was your favorite subject?
Where did you study?
Who was your favorite teacher?
Why did you study history?
When did you finish college?
How was your vacation?
How many students were there in your class?
How much did your dictionary cost?
How long did you stay?
How far did you go?

1 Complete the past questions with the words in parentheses.

1 _____ (be/it) sunny yesterday?
2 _____ (you/play) golf with Laura?
3 _____ (they/enjoy) the game?
4 _____ (be/Paul) good at golf?
5 _____ (you/like) the golf course?
6 _____ (be/it) busy?
7 _____ (be/your shoes) comfortable?
8 _____ (Paul/stay) with you on the weekend?

2 Write short answers to the questions in exercise 1.

1 Yes, _____.
2 Yes, _____.
3 Yes, _____.
4 No, _____.
5 Yes, _____.
6 No, _____.
7 No, _____.
8 No, _____.

3 Put the words in the correct order to make questions.

1 you / a / did / vacation / good / have / ?
_____
2 go / did / where / you / ?
_____
3 on the tour / how many / were / people / ?
_____
4 the / hotels / nice / were / ?
_____
5 have / did / what time / you / dinner in the hotel / ?
_____
6 food / like / the / you / did / ?
_____
7 stay / did / long / how / you / ?
_____

◀ Go back to page 77

GRAMMAR PRACTICE

9C Verb patterns: verb + infinitive

When we use two verbs together, we need to use the right form for the second verb.

We use an infinitive after some verbs. These verbs often (but not always) refer to plans for the future.

 9.8

We **want**		**go** to the movies tonight.
I **hope**		**see** you tomorrow.
We**'re planning**	to	**move** next year.
She**'d like**		**visit** the U.S.
My parents **need**		**buy** a new car.
I **intend**		**join** a gym.

Other verbs that are followed by an infinitive are: *begin, choose, continue, agree, decide, learn, prefer, offer, start.*

Look! *The verbs* begin *and* start *can be followed by an infinitive or the* -ing *form. The meaning is the same.*
I began learning English when I was five. / I began to learn English when I was five.
The bus didn't come, so we started walking home. / The bus didn't come, so we started to walk home.

The full form of *'d like* is *would like*. It means the same as *want*, but it is more polite.
I'd like to see your house.
Would you like to come on vacation with me?

We can also say *'d love/would love* + infinitive.
I'd love to go to Australia one day.
Would you like to go to the beach today? Yes, I'd love to!

Look! We use both an infinitive and the *-ing* form after *like* and *love*. The meaning is different from *'d like / 'd love*.
We like to travel/traveling. We'd like to go to Australia next year.
I love to play/playing soccer. I'd love to play for Real Madrid one day.

1 Complete the sentences with the infinitive of the verbs in the box.

check get start run lose make pass talk

1 I'm learning _____ jewelry.
2 She's planning _____ classes this fall.
3 Did he agree _____ to you about it?
4 Emilio wants _____ weight.
5 I need _____ my e-mails.
6 Lisa is planning _____ in shape this summer.
7 They decided _____ a marathon.
8 I hope _____ my exams this term.

2 Choose one or both options to complete the sentences.
1 He really doesn't like *to cook / cooking*.
2 I'd like *to change / changing* my diet.
3 Do you like *to play / playing* sports?
4 She'd love *to spend / spending* more time with her grandchildren.
5 I like *to earn / earning* lots of money.
6 Would you like *to make / making* some new friends?
7 He'd love *to go / going* to college.

3 Look at Gemma's New Year resolutions. Then write sentences using the verbs in parentheses.

1 She is planning to _____
2 _____
3 _____
4 _____
5 _____
6 _____
7 _____
8 _____

◀ Go back to page 81

129

GRAMMAR PRACTICE

10A Comparative adjectives

We use a comparative adjective + *than* to compare two things or people.

The park is nicer than the bus station.
Los Angeles is bigger than San Francisco.
The lasagna here is better than the chicken.

▶ 10.2   comparative adj + *than*

Adam is	**older than**	me.
Julie is	**friendlier than**	Laura.
Skiing is	**more dangerous than**	walking.

Spelling rules for comparative adjectives

When an adjective is one syllable, we add *-er*.
fast ⇨ faster   old ⇨ older

When a one-syllable adjective ends in *-e*, we add *-r*.
nice ⇨ nicer   safe ⇨ safer

When a one-syllable adjective ends in a consonant + vowel + consonant, we double the final consonant and add *-er*.
hot ⇨ hotter   big ⇨ bigger

When an adjective ends in consonant + *y*, we usually change the *y* to *i* and then we add *-er*.
easy ⇨ easier   friendly ⇨ friendlier   happy ⇨ happier
BUT shy ⇨ shyer   dry ⇨ dryer

When an adjective is two or more syllables, we usually use *more* + adjective.
dangerous ⇨ more dangerous   crowded ⇨ more crowded
modern ⇨ more modern

Some comparatives are irregular.
good ⇨ better   bad ⇨ worse   far ⇨ further/farther

Look! With some two-syllable adjectives, we usually use *-er*, not *more*.
quiet ⇨ quieter   narrow ⇨ narrower

We can also use *less* + adjective + *than* to compare things.

I'm less stressed on the weekend than during the week. = I'm more relaxed on the weekend than during the week.

We can add *much* and *a lot* before comparatives to show there is a big difference. We can add *a little* or *a bit* before comparatives to show the difference is small.

much, a lot, a little, a bit

big difference:

New York is	**much**	bigger than Boston.
Skiing is	**a lot**	more dangerous than walking.

small difference:

Today is	**a little**	hotter than yesterday.
The café is	**a bit**	more crowded than the restaurant.

1 Complete the sentences with the comparatives of the adjectives in parentheses.
 1 Do you think a walk on the beach is _____ than going to a bowling alley? (romantic)
 2 The second date is usually _____ than the first! (easy)
 3 Playing video games is _____ than watching TV. (exciting)
 4 The apartments here are _____ than those downtown. (large)
 5 Sneakers are _____ than sandals for long walks up mountains. (good)
 6 It's usually _____ here in the spring than in the summer. (wet)
 7 The movies are _____ than the theater. (cheap)
 8 Calling someone the wrong name on a date is _____ than being a few minutes late. (bad)

2 Look at the pictures. Choose the correct words and include comparative adjectives to complete the sentences.

 1 My hair was *a lot* / *a bit* _____ when I was younger.

 2 Joe's suitcase is *much* / *a little* _____ than Chris's.

 3 Mexico City is *much* / *a little* _____ from London than Seoul.

◀ Go back to page 85

GRAMMAR PRACTICE

10C Superlative adjectives

We use a superlative adjective to say that something is more than all the others in a group.

New York is the biggest city in the U.S.
The park is the nicest place in my town.
The lasagna is the best thing on the menu.

We use *the* with superlative adjectives.
New York is the biggest city in the U.S. NOT ~~*New York is biggest city in the U.S.*~~

▶ 10.11   *the* + superlative adj

Adam is	**the** oldest person	in our class.
Julie is	**the** friendliest person	that I know.
Skiing is	**the** most dangerous	sport.

Spelling rules for superlative adjectives

When an adjective is one syllable, we add *-est*.
fast ⇨ fastest   old ⇨ oldest

When a one-syllable adjective ends in *-e*, we add *-st*.
nice ⇨ nicest   safe ⇨ safest

When a one-syllable adjective ends in consonant + vowel + consonant, we double the final consonant and add *-est*.
hot ⇨ hottest   big ⇨ biggest

When an adjective ends in consonant + *y*, we usually change the *y* to *i* and then we add *-est*.
easy ⇨ easiest   friendly ⇨ friendliest   happy ⇨ happiest
BUT shy ⇨ shyest   dry ⇨ dryest

When an adjective is two or more syllables, we use *most* + adjective.
dangerous ⇨ most dangerous   crowded ⇨ most crowded
modern ⇨ most modern

For some two-syllable adjectives we don't use *most*.
clever ⇨ cleverest   quiet ⇨ quietest   narrow ⇨ narrowest

Some superlatives are irregular.
good ⇨ best   bad ⇨ worst   far ⇨ furthest/farthest

> **Look!** If we use a possessive adjective directly before the superlative, we don't include *the*.
> *Emily is my best friend.*
> *What's your most expensive possession?*

1 Complete the sentences with the superlatives of the adjectives in parentheses.
   1 She's _____ girl that I know. (pretty)
   2 My friend Sam was _____ person in my class. (popular)
   3 My son's _____ child in the world! (beautiful)
   4 _____ month of the year here is February. (hot)
   5 Singing in a band is _____ thing that I do. (exciting)
   6 When was _____ day of your life? (happy)

2 Complete the sentences with the superlatives of the adjectives in the box.

romantic   smart   nice   kind   expensive   noisy

   1 _____ piece of jewelry is this necklace. It cost more than 100 dollars.
   2 You're _____ person that I know. You understand things very quickly.
   3 My sister is _____ person in my family. She helps older people with their shopping.
   4 _____ place at school was the cafeteria. Everybody talked there!
   5 Mr. and Mrs. Brown are _____ neighbors. They're really lovely people and friendly, too.
   6 Sam often gives his girlfriend Katia flowers. He's _____ of all my friends.

3 Look at the pictures and complete the sentences with comparative or superlative adjectives.

big   small

700 students	500 students	1000 students
Anna	**Jodie**	**Fumiko**

   1 Anna's school is _____ than Jodie's.
   2 Jodie's school is _____.
   3 Fumiko's school is _____.

good   bad

Michael	Jack	Matt

   4 Matt got _____ grades than Jack on his exams.
   5 Michael got _____ grades.
   6 Jack got _____ grades.

◀ Go back to page 89

131

GRAMMAR PRACTICE

11A *have to/don't have to*

We use *have to* + the base form of the verb to say that something is necessary.

We have to wear a uniform in school.
I have to go to work by bus.
My brother has to get up at 5:30 every morning.
Donna has to call her parents every night.

We use *don't have to* + base form to say that something isn't necessary.

I don't have to work on Mondays.
They don't have to study today. It's Sunday.
Carlotta doesn't have to buy a new computer. She got one for her birthday.
Simon doesn't have to cook dinner tonight. He's at a restaurant.

We use *have to/don't have to* for situations in the present and in the future.

I have to wear a uniform at work. (present situation)

I don't have to get up early tomorrow. (future situation)

▶ 11.2	I / you / we / they	he / she / it
+	I **have to work** tomorrow.	Jack **has to take** the train to work.
−	I **don't have to work** on Sunday.	He **doesn't have to start** work at 7:30.
?	Do you **have to take** the train today?	Does he **have to wear** a uniform?
Y/N	Yes, I **do**. / No, I **don't**.	Yes, he **does**. / No, he **doesn't**.

> **Look!** We use *had to/didn't have to* to say that something wasn't necessary in the past.
> *I had to visit my aunt every weekend.*
> *We didn't have to play sports after school.*

1 Choose the correct words to complete the sentences.

1 I *have to / don't have to* drive to work because there are no buses or trains near my house.
2 We bought our train tickets online so we *have to / don't have to* buy them at the station.
3 Visitors to our office *have to / don't have to* sign the visitors' book. They can't go into the building if they don't sign it.
4 Elena is a waitress and she usually *has to / doesn't have to* work on the weekend because it's a busy time at the restaurant.
5 You *have to / don't have to* wash those cups. Put them in the dishwasher!
6 We *have to / don't have to* walk the dog twice a day because he needs the exercise.
7 My brother *has to / doesn't have to* go far to work. His office is only about a kilometer from his home.
8 My parents *have to / don't have to* teach me to drive, but they're giving me a lot of lessons at the moment!

2 Complete the sentences with the correct form of *have to* or *don't have to*.

1 I'm sorry. I can't talk now. I _____ go!
2 "_____ you _____ get up early to go to work?" "Yes. I get up at five."
3 Matt _____ get in shape. He already swims, runs, and plays soccer every week.
4 You _____ make dinner. I can do it.
5 _____ children _____ go to school when they're five?
6 My sister _____ teach in a school as part of her degree in education.
7 We _____ stay at home. Do you want to go for a walk?
8 What train _____ Paul _____ catch in the morning?

3 Look at the job information. Complete the sentences with *have to* or *don't have to* and the verbs from the box.

a uniform ✘	clothes from the store ✔
clothes at full price ✘	customers ✔
after 6 p.m. ✘	on the weekend ✔
a degree ✘	18+ ✔

buy   have   work (x2)   wear (x2)   be   serve

1 You _____ a uniform.
2 You _____ clothes from the store, but you _____ our clothes at full price. You get 50% off.
3 You _____ customers.
4 You _____ on the weekend, but you _____ after 6 p.m.
5 You _____ over 18, but you _____ a degree.

◀ Go back to page 95

GRAMMAR PRACTICE

11C *be going to* and future time expressions

We use *be going to* + the base form to talk about future plans.

I'm going to visit friends in Mexico this year.
He's going to have pizza for dinner tonight.
We're not going to stay at a hotel.
What are you going to do this summer?

▶ 11.7

	I	he / she / it	you / we / they
+	I'm going to relax by the pool.	She's going to stay at a campsite.	We're going to visit a museum.
−	I'm not going to study this weekend.	She's not/She isn't going to stay at an apartment.	My friends aren't going to visit me next year.
?	Am I going to meet your friends later?	Is she going to stay at a hostel?	Are they going to eat out tonight?
Y/N	Yes, I am. / No, I'm not.	Yes, she is. / No, she's not/she isn't.	Yes, they are. / No, they're not/ they aren't.

Look! When the main verb is *go*, we do not normally use *to go* after *going*.
Are you going surfing tomorrow?
Camille is going abroad next year.
But it is also correct to use *to go*.
Are you going to go surfing tomorrow?
Camille is going to go abroad next year.

Future time expressions

We often use the following future time expressions with *be going to*:

this	morning / afternoon / evening / week / weekend / month / year / spring / summer / fall / winter / January, etc.
tomorrow	morning / afternoon / evening / night
next	week / month / year / spring / summer / fall / winter / January, etc.
in	the morning / afternoon / evening / spring / summer / fall / winter / January, etc.

Look! We say *tonight*, NOT *this night*.

Today is Monday, January 1st.

Monday	January 1st	this week	this morning	tonight
Tuesday	January 2nd		tomorrow morning	tomorrow night
Wednesday	January 3rd			
Thursday	January 4th			
Friday	January 5th			
Saturday	January 6th	this weekend		
Sunday	January 7th			
Monday	January 8th		next Monday	next Monday night

1 Write sentences. Use *be going to*.

1 Mark / play / guitar / this evening
_____

2 my parents / go / vacation / tomorrow
_____

3 my sister / not run / a marathon / this summer
_____

4 I / cook / dinner / tonight
_____

5 you / go / swimming / this afternoon?
_____

6 we / not use / our car / this year
_____

2 Jamie, Fran, Paola, and Alfredo are on vacation together. Complete the conversation with the correct form of *be going to* and a verb from the box.

| read | visit | play | relax | not do | take (x2) | do | go (x2) |

Jamie What ¹_____ you and Alfredo _____ tomorrow?
Paola In the morning, we ²_____ sightseeing in the city. We ³_____ the castle and go shopping. What about you?
Jamie We ⁴_____ running, and then we ⁵_____ by the pool. In the afternoon, Fran ⁶_____ a surfing class, and I ⁷_____ my book on the beach.
Paola ⁸_____ Fran _____ a surfing class every day?
Jamie Yes, she is. She really wants to learn.
Paola Don't you want to?
Jamie No, I just want to relax. I ⁹_____ much this week. Just a bit of running and swimming.
Paola What about volleyball? Alfredo ¹⁰_____ volleyball this evening. Are you interested?
Jamie Yeah! Thanks!

3 Today is Monday, March 10th. Write the time expressions for the days and times.

1 the morning of March 11th _____
2 March 17–23rd _____
3 March 10–16th _____
4 the evening of March 10th _____
5 April _____
6 Saturday, March 15th and Sunday, March 16th _____

◀ Go back to page 99

133

GRAMMAR PRACTICE

12A Present perfect with *ever* and *never*

We use the present perfect to talk about experiences in our lives.

I've visited China.
He hasn't been to Australia.
Have you worked in a restaurant?

We often use *ever* in a question with the present perfect. It emphasizes that we are talking about "our whole lives up to now."

Have you ever listened to classical music?
Have your parents ever been to a festival?

We often use *never* to make a negative sentence with the present perfect. It emphasizes that we are talking about "our whole lives up to now."

I've never tried Russian food.
He's never been to Scotland.

We form the present perfect with the verb *have* and the past participle of the main verb.

▶ 12.2	I / you / we / they	he / she / it
+	I**'ve visited** a lot of castles.	He**'s been** to Vietnam.
–	They **haven't studied** Italian.	She **hasn't played** badminton.
?	**Have** you **stayed** in this hotel?	**Has** he **worked** in London?
Y/N	Yes, I **have**. / No, I **haven't**.	Yes, he **has**. / No, he **hasn't**.

For regular verbs, the past participle form is the same as the past simple form. It ends in *-ed*. See page 127 for the spelling rules for simple past forms ending in *-ed*.

> **Look!** In the present perfect, we use the past participle *-ed* form for negative sentences and questions, as well as affirmative sentences. This is different from the simple past, where we only use the simple past *-ed* form for affirmative sentences. Compare:
> *Did you visit the National Gallery yesterday?*
> *Have you visited the National Gallery?* NOT ~~Have you visit the National Gallery?~~
> *I didn't visit the National Gallery yesterday.*
> *I haven't visited the National Gallery.* NOT ~~I haven't visit the National Gallery.~~

Like the simple past, a lot of common verbs have an irregular past participle. For a full list of irregular verbs, see page 176.

> **Look!** When we talk about experiences, we sometimes use *been to* instead of *gone to* to say that someone went somewhere and returned.
> *She's been to London three times.* = (She went and returned.)

1 Choose the correct words to complete the sentences.
 1 Lev *has / have* worked as a professional dancer.
 2 I've *never / ever* been to an opera.
 3 I *has / have* acted in a few plays.
 4 *Have you ever / Have ever you* listened to jazz?
 5 Tom doesn't work here. He's *been / moved* to a different company.
 6 We've *ever / never* visited the museum in my town.

2 Complete the sentences with the past participles of the verbs in parentheses.
 1 I've never _____ a foreign language. (study)
 2 I've _____ in a restaurant, but I've never _____ in a store. (work)
 3 Have you ever _____ volleyball? (play)
 4 Has your mother-in-law ever _____ with you? (stay)
 5 I've never _____ to a classical concert. (be)
 6 We've never _____ a famous person. (see)
 7 We've never _____ together. (act)
 8 My sisters haven't _____ me in New York. (visit)
 9 I've _____ a lot of Indian food. (cook)

3 Write short conversations. Use the present perfect.

1
A you / ever / go / to Peru?
_____
B no / I / never / go / to South America
_____
2
A your mom / ever / study / English?
_____
B yes / and / she / study / German, too
_____
3
A Charlie and Kate / ever / play / rock music?
_____
B no / but / they / play / classical music
_____

◀ Go back to page 103

12C Present perfect and simple past

We use the present perfect to talk about an experience in our lives. We use the present perfect to introduce a topic and say that it happened.

I've met Jennifer Lawrence.
I've been to New York.
My sister has started a new job.

When we give details about the experience (for example, when something happened, what exactly happened, who you were with, or how you felt), we use the simple past.

I've met Jennifer Lawrence. I met her in a hotel in London.
I've been to New York. I went there in 2005.
My sister has seen a shark. She was really scared.

When we ask for more details about past events, we usually use the simple past, not the present perfect.

Where did you meet Jennifer Lawrence? NOT *Where have you met Jennifer Lawrence?*
When did you go to New York? NOT *When have you been to New York?*
How did your sister feel? NOT *How has your sister felt?*

We often start a conversation with the present perfect. When we give details about the experience, or ask for them, we change to the simple past.

▶ 12.11

Situation	Form	Example
Question about an experience	Present perfect	**Have** you ever **been** to Spain?
Answer	Present perfect	Yes, I **have**.
Details	Simple past	I **went** there two years ago.
Question asking for details	Simple past	**Did** you **go** to Madrid?
Answer	Simple past	No, I **didn't**. But I **went** to Valencia and Málaga.

For a full list of irregular verbs, see page 176.

GRAMMAR PRACTICE

1 Choose the correct words to complete the conversation.
   A ¹*Have you ever been / Did you ever go* to Peru?
   B Yes, I have. ²*I've been / I went* with some friends from college last year.
   A Where ³*have you been / did you go*?
   B To Machu Picchu. ⁴*It's been / It was* fantastic.
   A I'd love to go there! ⁵*I've been / I went* to Lima in 2010, but not Machu Picchu.
   B Machu Picchu is amazing! ⁶*We've had / We had* a great time.
   A What ⁷*have you done / did you do* there?
   B ⁸*We've been / We went* on some incredible hikes.

2 Complete the conversation with the words in parentheses using the present perfect or the simple past.
   A ¹_____ (you / ever / see) the movie *Selma*?
   B Yes. I ²_____ (see) it in 2015.
   A ³_____ (you / like) it?
   B Yes, it ⁴_____ (be) great. David Oyelowo ⁵_____ (play) Martin Luther King Jr. very well.
   A ⁶_____ (he / win) any awards?
   B Yes, he ⁷_____ (win) some awards.
   A ⁸_____ (he / be) in other movies?
   B Yes. He ⁹_____ (be) in *Lincoln*. I ¹⁰_____ (love) that movie!

3 Write the conversation. Use the present perfect and the simple past.

   A you / ever / do / karate?
   _____
   B yes / I / try / it / two years ago
   _____
   A what / you / think / of it?
   _____
   B I / really / like / it
   _____
   A where / you / learn?
   _____
   B I / take / classes at the sports center
   _____

◀ Go back to page 107

VOCABULARY PRACTICE

1A Countries and nationalities

1 ▶ 1.2 Complete the chart with the nationalities in the box. Listen and check.

| Portuguese | British | Mexican | French | Argentinian |
| Polish | Chinese | Italian | Brazilian | Spanish |

Country		Nationality
¹ China		_____
² Japan		Japanese
³ Portugal		_____
⁴ Vietnam		Vietnamese
⁵ England		English
⁶ Ireland		Irish
⁷ Poland		_____
⁸ Scotland		Scottish
⁹ Spain		_____
¹⁰ Turkey		Turkish
¹¹ the UK		_____
¹² Germany		German
¹³ Mexico		_____
¹⁴ the U.S.		American
¹⁵ Argentina		_____
¹⁶ Australia		Australian
¹⁷ Brazil		_____
¹⁸ Canada		Canadian
¹⁹ Colombia		Colombian
²⁰ Egypt		Egyptian
²¹ Peru		Peruvian
²² Italy		_____
²³ Russia		Russian
²⁴ France		_____

2 Complete the sentences about the people.
   1 Diego is Peruvian. He's from _____.
   2 Natasha is Russian. She's from _____.
   3 Troy is American. He's from _____.
   4 Mesut is Turkish. He's from _____.
   5 Dominique and Ellie are Canadian. They're from _____.
   6 Ana is Colombian. She's from _____.
   7 Maciek and Janusz are Polish. They're from _____.
   8 Hong is Vietnamese. She's from _____.
   9 Oscar and Ana are Brazilian. They're from _____.
   10 José Carlos is Mexican. He's from _____.

◀ Go back to page 4

1A Numbers 1–1,000

1 ▶ 1.7 Write the missing numbers. Listen and check.

0 zero/oh	21 twenty-one
1 one	22 twenty-two
2 two	23 _____
3 three	30 thirty
4 four	31 _____
5 five	32 thirty-two
6 six	40 forty
7 seven	50 _____
8 eight	60 sixty
9 nine	70 seventy
10 ten	80 eighty
11 _____	90 ninety
12 twelve	100 a hundred/one hundred
13 thirteen	101 a hundred and one
14 fourteen	102 _____
15 _____	200 two hundred
16 sixteen	210 two hundred and ten
17 seventeen	322 _____
18 eighteen	468 four hundred and sixty-eight
19 nineteen	713 _____
20 _____	1,000 a thousand/one thousand

We often pronounce zero "oh" when we say numbers one at a time: "I'm in room four-oh-three."(=403)

2 Look at the pictures and complete the numbers in words.

1 It's Lucy's birthday. She's _____.

5 A normal year has _____ days.

2 The Jones family live on _____, Main Street.

6 It's _____ kilometers to Paris.

3 The population of Newtown is _____.

7 Our hotel room is number _____.

4 The bike is _____ dollars.

8 The watch is _____ euros.

◀ Go back to page 5

VOCABULARY PRACTICE

1C Personal objects

1 ▶ 1.9 Match the words in the box with pictures 1–20. Listen and check.

| key   sunglasses   mirror   gloves   chewing gum   flashlight   tissues   photo   stamps   glasses |
| identity card   watch   umbrella   hairbrush   wallet   candy   change purse   comb   tablet   cell phone |

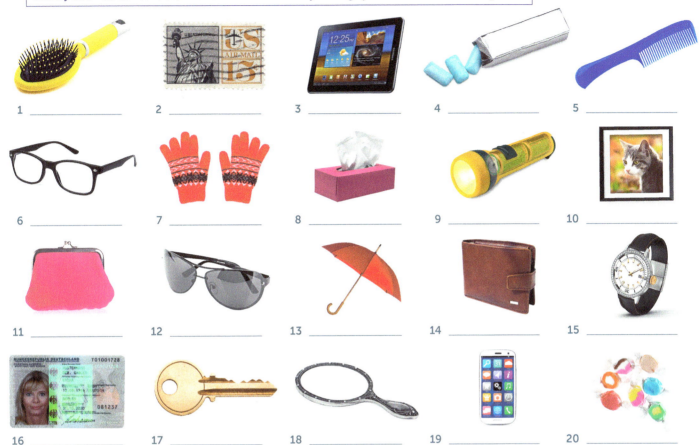

2 Read the information about plurals. Write plurals for the words.

> **Look!** We make most plurals by adding *-s* or *-es*. We add *-es* if a word ends in *-ch*, *-sh*, *-s*, *-x*, or *-z*:
> *stamp* ⇨ *stamps*, *watch* ⇨ *watches*.

1 comb _____
2 hairbrush _____
3 card _____
4 key _____
5 mirror _____
6 cell phone _____
7 photo _____
8 change purse _____
9 tablet _____
10 flashlight _____
11 umbrella _____
12 wallet _____

4 ▶ 1.10 Now read about the pronunciation of plurals ending in *-s* and *-es*. Put the plurals from exercise 2 into the chart. Listen and check.

/s/	/z/	/ɪz/
when the final sound in the word is /t/, /k/, /p/, /f/, or /θ/	when the final sound in the word is /b/, /d/, /g/, /l/, /m/, /n/, /v/, /ð/, or a vowel sound	when the final sound in the word is /tʃ/, /dʒ/, /ʒ/, /ʃ/, /s/, /ks/, or /z/
	combs	

3 Choose the correct words to complete the sentences.
1 Is that rain? Where's my *umbrella / hairbrush*?
2 Look at this *photo / mirror* of my boyfriend.
3 Do you have a *tablet / stamp*? I want to send a letter.
4 What time is it? I don't have my *wallet / watch*.
5 It's very cold today. Take some *mirrors / gloves* with you.
6 I always wear *combs / glasses* when I read.
7 Where's my car *key / card*?
8 I have twenty dollars in my *change purse / flashlight*.
9 It's very sunny. Where are my *tablets / sunglasses*?
10 *Chewing gum / Candy* is bad for your teeth.

◀ Go back to page 8

137

VOCABULARY PRACTICE

2A Jobs and job verbs

1 ▶ 2.1 Match the jobs in the box with pictures 1–20. Listen and check.

| hairdresser   tour guide   police officer   doctor   electrician   teacher   taxi driver   dentist   flight attendant   singer   mechanic |
| nurse   lawyer   waiter/waitress   receptionist   businessperson   accountant   construction worker   chef   salesclerk |

1 _____

2 _____

3 _____

4 _____

5 _____

6 _____

7 _____

8 _____

9 _____

10 _____

11 _____

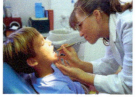
12 _____

13 _____

14 _____

15 _____

16 _____

17 _____

18 _____

19 _____

20 _____

2 ▶ 2.2 Match the two parts to make sentences. Listen and check.

1 He cooks
2 He drives
3 He fixes
4 They make
5 She serves
6 He wears
7 They start
8 She teaches
9 He finishes
10 He cuts
11 She helps
12 She sells

a a taxi.
b food in a restaurant.
c English in a school.
d work at 9 a.m.
e people's hair.
f food to customers.
g people at a tourist office.
h cars in a garage.
i computers in a store.
j a suit at work.
k clothes in a factory.
l work at 6 p.m.

3 Complete the sentences with job verbs and jobs.

1 Mario works in a garage. He _____ cars. He's a _____.
2 Samantha works in a high school. She _____ French and Spanish. She's a _____.
3 Hitoshi and Kazuo work in the kitchen of a restaurant. They _____ the food for the customers. They are _____.
4 Tomiko also works in the restaurant. She _____ the customers in the restaurant. She's a _____.
5 Maya is a _____. She _____ people's hair.
6 Terry works at night. He _____ a taxi in different places in New York. He's a _____.
7 Raul works in a clothing store. He _____ clothes. He's a _____.
8 Ola, Piotr, and Marta are in a pop group. Marta plays the drums, Piotr plays the guitar, and Ola _____. She's the group's _____.
9 Mark works on airplanes. He _____ a uniform. He _____ food and drink to the passengers. He's a _____.
10 Clara works in a hospital. She _____ work at 7 p.m., and she _____ late, at 8:30 p.m. She's not a doctor. She's a _____.

◀ Go back to page 13

VOCABULARY PRACTICE

2B Activities (1)

1 ▶ 2.7 Look at pictures 1–20 and complete the phrases with the words in the box. Listen and check.

> study   book   (my) friends   read   time   walk   guitar   movie   TV
> dinner   watch   play   radio   listen   running   coffee   movies   relax

1 go to the _____   2 go out for _____   3 go out for _____   4 go for a _____   5 go _____   6 _____ to music

    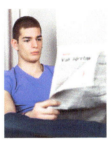 

7 listen to the _____   8 spend _____ with my family   9 _____ tennis   10 play the _____   11 _____ the newspaper   12 read a _____

13 _____   14 see a _____   15 _____   16 meet _____   17 _____ soccer   18 watch _____

2 Complete the sentences with phrases from exercise 1. Use the correct form.
   1 My sister _____ in a band. She's really good.
   2 My dad always _____ at breakfast. He likes reading the sports section.
   3 We _____ on Saturday evenings. We go to a very good Chinese restaurant.
   4 I want to get some exercise. Do you want to _____ with me in the park?
   5 I _____ all the time. I'm a Barcelona fan.
   6 I _____ in the car. I play my favorite songs.
   7 After work on Fridays, I _____ in town, and we go to a café to talk.
   8 On the weekend, Rosie _____ : her parents, her brother, and her two sisters.
   9 My sister and I _____ on Saturdays. I usually have a cappuccino, and she has a latte.
   10 I _____ in the library after class.

3 Correct the mistakes in the sentences. Rewrite the sentences.
   1 My friend Tara plays a guitar in a rock group.
   _____
   2 Do you want to watch movie tonight?
   _____
   3 I always listen music on the train.
   _____
   4 I usually meet the friends after work.
   _____
   5 I want to go the movies this weekend.
   _____
   6 My parents play the tennis with their friends.
   _____

◀ Go back to page 14

139

VOCABULARY PRACTICE

3A Family

1 ▶ 3.2 Complete Jack's family tree with the words in the box. Listen and check.

| wife father-in-law sister-in-law daughter brother sister nephew niece father aunt cousin (×2) grandmother |

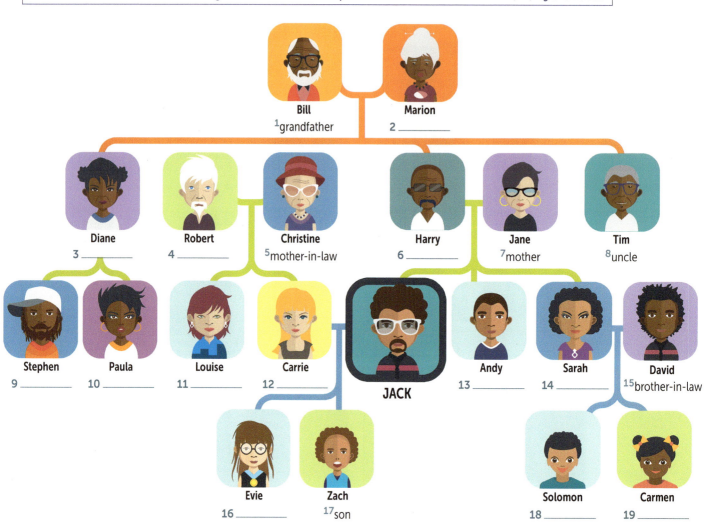

2 ▶ 3.3 Complete the sentences with the correct names.
1 _____ and _____ are Jack's parents.
2 _____ and _____ are Jack's in-laws (mother- and father-in-law).
3 _____ and _____ are Jack's grandparents.
4 _____ and _____ are Jack's children.
5 _____, _____, _____ and _____ are Harry and Jane's grandchildren.
6 Jack is _____ and _____'s son-in-law.
7 Carrie is _____ and _____'s daughter-in-law.
8 Jack is _____'s husband.
9 _____, _____ and _____ are Bill and Marion's grandsons.
10 _____ is Robert and Christine's granddaughter.

3 Complete the chart with the family words from exercises 1 and 2.

male	female	male and female

4 Find three false definitions. Write the correct definitions.
1 My nephew is my brother's son. _____
2 My mother-in-law is my wife's sister. _____
3 My daughter is my son's sister. _____
4 My granddaughter is my daughter's daughter. _____
5 My niece is my cousin's daughter. _____
6 My father-in-law is my husband's father. _____
7 My grandparents are my nephew's parents. _____
8 My cousins are my aunt's children. _____

◀ Go back to page 23

140

VOCABULARY PRACTICE

3C Activities (2)

1 ▶ 3.7 Match the phrases below with pictures a–p. Listen and check.

a

b

c

d

e

f

g

h

i

j

k

l

m

n

o

p

do	play	go	have	visit
1 karate ____	4 golf ____	7 bowling ____	12 a barbecue ____	14 a gallery ____
2 yoga ____	5 volleyball ____	8 bike riding ____	13 a picnic ____	15 a museum ____
walk	6 the violin ____	9 dancing ____		16 relatives ____
3 the dog ____		10 shopping ____		
		11 swimming ____		

2 Complete the sentences with the verbs in the correct form.
1 They _____ a barbecue every time it's hot and sunny.
2 We always _____ a picnic for my birthday.
3 I _____ yoga on Friday mornings.
4 We _____ volleyball on the beach.
5 I sometimes _____ galleries.
6 I always _____ dancing with my family on Saturday evenings.
7 My son _____ the violin in his school orchestra.
8 I don't go to the gym, but I _____ dancing on weekends.
9 My best friend _____ bike riding every Sunday afternoon.
10 My children often _____ bowling with their friends.

3 Write the phrases from exercise 1 that match the sentences.
1 If you're interested in very old things, you can do this.
   _____
2 This is when you go to see your cousins, grandparents, etc.
   _____
3 Lots of people do this Japanese sport.
   _____
4 Lots of people do this sport on the beach in the summer.
   _____
5 You can do this in the sea or at a pool.
   _____
6 This is when you cook a meal outside.
   _____
7 You need a bicycle for this.
   _____
8 You need a very large open green space if you want to do this sport.
   _____

◀ Go back to page 26

VOCABULARY PRACTICE

4A Daily routine verbs

1 ▶ 4.1 Match pictures a–o with activities 1–15. Listen and check.

1 have lunch _____
2 have dinner _____
3 go to school _____
4 get dressed _____
5 wake up _____
6 take a shower _____
7 get up _____
8 go to work _____
9 take a bath _____
10 go to bed _____
11 go to sleep _____
12 finish school _____
13 get home _____
14 finish work _____
15 have breakfast _____

◀ Go back to page 30

4B The weather and the seasons

1 ▶ 4.5 Look at the pictures and complete the sentences with the cities. Listen and check.

22° BARCELONA | -11° ST PETERSBURG | 14° SHANGHAI | 36° MUMBAI | 12° SAN FRANCISCO | 10° LIVERPOOL | 1° STOCKHOLM

1 It's raining/rainy in _____.
2 It's snowing/snowy in _____.
3 It's hot in _____.
4 It's warm in _____.
5 It's very cold in _____.
6 It's wet in _____.
7 It's sunny in _____.
8 It's foggy in _____.
9 It's windy in _____.
10 It's cloudy in _____.
11 It's icy in _____.
12 It's cold in _____.

2 Label the pictures with the seasons. Then write a word from exercise 1 to describe the weather in each season.

summer   fall   spring   winter

_____ , _____   _____ , _____   _____ , _____   _____ , _____

◀ Go back to page 32

VOCABULARY PRACTICE

5A Clothes

1 ▶ 5.1 Label the clothes and jewelry in the pictures with the words in the box. Listen and check.

| belt tie necklace bracelet pants T-shirt earrings boots coat jacket jeans sandals blouse |
| sneakers scarf jewelry dress gloves hat shirt shoes shorts skirt socks suit sweater |

2 Choose the correct words to complete the sentences.

1 My pants are too big. I need a *necklace* / *belt*.
2 Jim hates wearing a suit and *tie* / *scarf*. He prefers jeans and a T-shirt.
3 When Anna goes running, she wears *boots* / *sneakers*.
4 I like wearing jewelry, especially *sandals* / *earrings*.
5 It's cold outside. Wear a scarf and *gloves* / *shorts*.
6 My daughter likes climbing trees, so she wears *pants* / *a skirt*.
7 Sally's going to a party, so she's wearing a *T-shirt* / *dress*.
8 In the summer, I like wearing *shorts* / *shoes* and sandals.
9 Should I wear my red *blouse* / *socks* or my blue shirt with my jeans?
10 You need to wear a *coat* / *suit* when you go to a job interview.

◀ Go back to page 40

5A Ordinal numbers

1 ▶ 5.4 Write the ordinal numbers. Listen and check.

1 first
2 _____
3 third
4 _____
5 _____
6 sixth
7 seventh
8 _____
9 _____
10 tenth
11 _____
12 _____
13 thirteenth
14 fourteenth
15 _____
20 twentieth
21 _____
22 twenty-second
30 thirtieth
40 _____
50 fiftieth

2 Complete the sentences with the ordinal numbers in parentheses. Write them in words.

1 Kazakhstan is the _____ biggest country in the world. (9)
2 December is the _____ month of the year. (12)
3 Barack Obama was the _____ president of the U.S. (44)
4 International Women's Day is March _____. (8)
5 Valentine's Day is on February _____. (14)
6 Veterans Day is November _____. (11)

◀ Go back to page 41

143

VOCABULARY PRACTICE

5C Hobbies

1 ▶ 5.7 Match the verbs in the box with pictures 1–15. You need some verbs more than once. Listen and check.

| collect play make sew knit sing dance take write paint draw bake |

1 _____

2 _____

3 _____ online games

4 _____

5 _____ photos

6 _____ a blog

7 _____ the drums

8 _____ jewelry

9 _____

10 _____ chess

11 _____

12 _____

13 _____ stamps

14 _____

15 _____ coins

2 Match the hobbies with the descriptions.
1 These hobbies are connected to music.
_____
2 People often do these hobbies in beautiful places.
_____
3 This hobby is connected to food.
_____
4 You study and collect objects for this hobby.
_____
5 You need another person to do this hobby.
_____
6 These hobbies are connected to clothes.
_____
7 You need to use the Internet for this hobby.
_____

3 Choose the correct words to complete the sentences.
1 Right now, I'm *drawing* / *knitting* a sweater. I want to finish it before the winter.
2 I collect *stamps* / *coins*. My favorite one is made of gold.
3 Everyone can *sew* / *take photos* on their smartphones, but some people can do it really well.
4 My friend Emily *makes* / *sews* jewelry. She's making me a necklace for my birthday.
5 We need someone who *plays the drums* / *bakes* for our band. Do you know anyone?
6 My cousin is traveling in Africa at the moment, and she *makes* / *writes* a blog every day. I like reading it to find out what she's doing.
7 My wife loves *painting* / *baking,* and I love eating her cakes and cookies. We're a perfect match!
8 My friend Matt is learning to *dance* / *sing*. Right now, he's learning the tango.

144 ◀ Go back to page 44

VOCABULARY PRACTICE

6A Rooms and furniture

1 ▶ 6.1 Label the picture with the rooms and places in the box. Listen and check.

| yard | balcony | kitchen | bedroom | living room | bathroom (x2) | dining room | study | garage | hall | attic | basement | stairs |

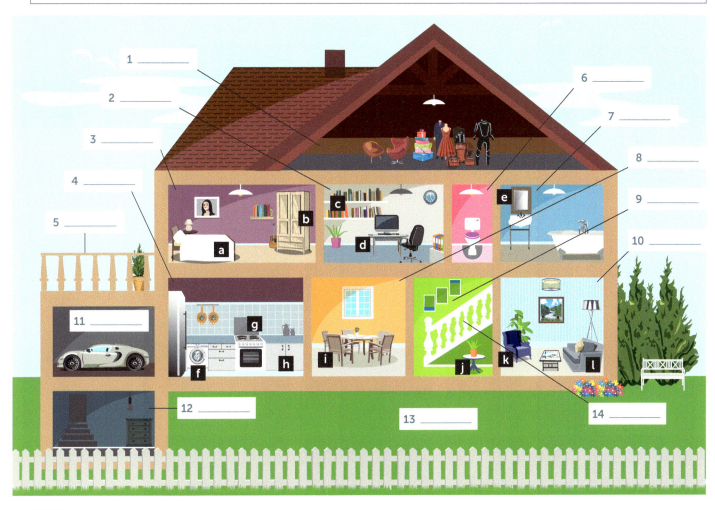

2 ▶ 6.2 Find the furniture items in the picture. Write the letters a–l. Listen and check.

1 armchair ____   4 stove ____   7 shelves ____   9 table ____   11 washing machine ____
2 bed ____   5 cabinets ____   8 sofa ____   10 closet ____   12 mirror ____
3 chairs ____   6 desk ____

◀ Go back to page 48

6B Common adjectives

1 ▶ 6.8 Match the adjectives with their opposites. Listen and check.

1 expensive   a wide
2 clean   b uncomfortable
3 narrow   c light
4 noisy   d cheap
5 comfortable   e traditional
6 heavy   f dirty
7 modern   g quiet

2 Complete the sentences with opposite adjectives.

1 I don't like _____ restaurants. I like _____ places where you can talk with friends.
2 My girlfriend usually buys _____ clothes. I'm different – I buy _____ clothes and have some money for other things.
3 We have two sofas. One is old, but very _____ – it's perfect for watching a movie. The other one is new, but it's _____.
4 My husband wants to buy some _____ furniture, but I don't. I want some _____ things because our apartment is very new.
5 Your T-shirt is really _____! Go and find a _____ blouse.
6 My bike is very _____, but Carl's is really _____. I can carry his bike with one hand.
7 I only have a double bed and a small closet in my bedroom. The room's _____ and the bed's _____, so I have no space.

◀ Go back to page 50

145

VOCABULARY PRACTICE

6C Places in a city

1 ▶ 6.15 Match the places in the box with pictures 1–14. Listen and check.

| apartment building bridge cathedral concert hall library market monument |
| mosque office building park skyscraper square stadium theater |

1 _____ 2 _____ 3 _____ 4 _____ 5 _____

6 _____ 7 _____ 8 _____ 9 _____ 10 _____

11 _____ 12 _____ 13 _____ 14 _____

2 Match the places in a city with the definitions. Some places go with more than one definition.
1 People live here. _____
2 You go here for entertainment. _____, _____, _____
3 This is a religious building. _____, _____
4 This is usually a tall building. _____, _____, _____
5 This can be outdoors or indoors. _____
6 It is very quiet in this building. _____
7 You often find this in the center of a square. _____
8 You can sometimes find restaurants here. _____

3 Complete the sentences with places in a city.
1 This famous _____ is for Abraham Lincoln.
2 Let's go to the _____ and buy some food for a picnic.
3 We live on the ninth floor of this _____.
4 You can see the _____ from about 20 km. away. It's very tall.
5 I work in a small _____ downtown. It has four floors.
6 At the _____, you leave your shoes at the door before you go in.
7 There are concerts and soccer games at this _____.
8 You can walk or ride a bike over this _____, but you can't drive over it.
9 There are concerts in our city's _____ every winter.
10 The central _____ in Wroclaw is really beautiful. There are colorful houses on all four sides.
11 I often go to the _____ to study.

◀ Go back to page 53

VOCABULARY PRACTICE

7A Food and drink

1 🎧 7.1 Complete the food groups with the words in the box. Listen and check.

| cabbage | cereal | cookies | eggs | fish | grapes | juice | melon |
| mushrooms | onion | orange | peas | potato chips | rice | tea | yogurt |

fruit 
1 pear 2 apple 3 banana 4 lemon 5 strawberry 6 _____ 7 _____ 8 _____

vegetables 
9 pepper 10 carrot 11 beans 12 tomato 13 cucumber 14 potato 15 _____ 16 _____ 17 _____ 18 _____

grains 
19 pasta 20 bread 21 _____ 22 _____

protein and dairy 
23 meat 24 beef 25 cheese 26 ice cream 27 milk 28 _____ 29 _____ 30 _____

snacks and others 
31 cake 32 salad 33 French fries 34 soup 35 _____ 36 _____

drinks 
37 coffee 38 cola 39 _____ 40 _____

2 Read the definitions and write the words.

1 A small yellow fruit. _____
2 Food for breakfast. We usually eat it with milk. _____
3 A white vegetable. We often cook with it. _____
4 A cold brown drink. _____
5 Very small green vegetables. _____
6 The meat from a cow. _____
7 An orange vegetable. _____
8 A small green or purple fruit. _____
9 A large green vegetable. _____
10 A large green or yellow fruit. _____

◀ Go back to page 58

147

VOCABULARY PRACTICE

7C Containers and portions

1 ▶ 7.6 Match the phrases in the box with pictures 1–15. Listen and check.

| a bar of | a bag of | a bottle of | a bowl of | a box of | a can of (x2) | a carton of |
| a cup of | a glass of | a jar of | a packet of | a piece of | a slice of | a spoonful of |

 1 _____ tea

 2 _____ bread

 3 _____ juice

 4 _____ tomatoes

 5 _____ cookies

 6 _____ cereal

 7 _____ cheese

 8 _____ pasta

 9 _____ olive oil

 10 _____ honey

 11 _____ carrots

 12 _____ chocolate

 13 _____ water

 14 _____ cola

 15 _____ sugar

2 Choose the food or drink that <u>isn't</u> possible.
1 a bowl of *soup / ice cream / cola*
2 a jar of *olives / jam / meat*
3 a bag of *cookies / apple juice / potato chips*
4 a slice of *yogurt / cake / apple*
5 a can of *peas / tomatoes / sugar*
6 a carton of *cereal / juice / milk*
7 a piece of *cheese / meat / tea*
8 a cup of *coffee / potato / water*
9 a can of *honey / cola / lemonade*
10 a spoonful of *oil / honey / cheese*

3 Complete the sentences with the correct words.
1 I have two or three _____ of coffee every day.
2 How many _____ of bread do you want?
3 There are two _____ of lemonade in the fridge.
4 We need a big _____ of apple juice.
5 I have a _____ of cereal in the cabinet, but I don't want it.
6 We love olives, so we always have a few _____ in the cabinet.
7 It's very hot. I need a _____ of water.
8 If I want a snack, I buy a _____ of chocolate.
9 There's a _____ of strawberry jam, if you want some on your toast.
10 I sometimes buy a _____ of potato chips for my daughter.

◀ Go back to page 63

VOCABULARY PRACTICE

8A Inventions

1 ▶ 8.1 Match the words in the box with pictures 1–18. Listen and check.

| freezer | color TV | smartphone | fridge | digital camera | cassette player | dishwasher | (clothes) dryer | DVD player |
| black-and-white TV | laptop | GPS | toaster | video player | microwave | CD player | vacuum cleaner | washing machine |

1 _____ 2 _____ 3 _____ 4 _____

5 _____ 6 _____ 7 _____

8 _____ 9 _____ 10 _____ 11 _____

12 _____ 13 _____ 14 _____

15 _____ 16 _____ 17 _____ 18 _____

2 Match the words from exercise 1 with the descriptions below.

1 You use this to watch a show. _____, _____, _____
2 You keep food in this. _____, _____
3 You use this to cook food. _____, _____
4 You use this after you wash clothes. _____
5 You use this to listen to music. _____, _____, _____, _____
6 You can use this to help you find a place. _____, _____
7 You can use this if you want to watch a movie. _____, _____, _____
8 You can use the Internet on this. _____, _____
9 You can take photos with this, but you can't use the Internet. _____
10 You can use this to wash plates and cups. _____.

◀ Go back to page 66

149

VOCABULARY PRACTICE

8B Life stages

1 ▶ 8.7 Match the words and phrases in the box with pictures 1–12. Listen and check.

be-born   meet someone   get divorced   finish school   go to college   retire
have a baby/family   start school   get married   get a job   get a degree   die

1 *be born*   3 _____   5 _____   7 _____   9 _____   11 _____

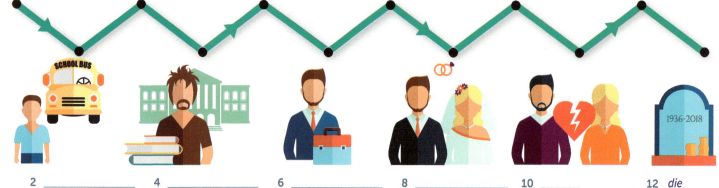

2 _____   4 _____   6 _____   8 _____   10 _____   12 *die*

2 Complete the sentences with phrases in the correct form.
  1 My dad _____ last year. But he's still really busy all the time!
  2 My sister and my brother-in-law want to buy a big house with lots of bedrooms before they _____.
  3 In the U.S., children _____ when they are five years old.
  4 These days, a lot of people use the Internet to try to _____ special.
  5 Dani doesn't want to _____ after he finishes school. He wants to start working, instead.
  6 Jenny is in college. She wants to _____ in French and Russian.
  7 My friends Emily and Martyn _____ last year on a beach in the Caribbean! It was beautiful!
  8 Most women have babies in the hospital, but my dad _____ at home.

◀ Go back to page 68

8B Irregular verbs

1 ▶ 8.9 Match the irregular simple past forms in the box with the verbs. Listen and check.

spoke   heard   said   began   had   ate   drank   left
thought   gave   drove   did   saw   got   came   took
went   met   wrote   knew

1 begin _____   11 say _____
2 come _____   12 see _____
3 do _____   13 leave _____
4 drink _____   14 speak _____
5 drive _____   15 get _____
6 eat _____   16 take _____
7 go _____   17 think _____
8 give _____   18 write _____
9 hear _____   19 meet _____
10 know _____   20 have _____

2 Complete the text with the simple past forms of the verbs in the box.

have   drive   leave   come   do   get (x2)   know   take   meet

This is my family, and I'm Australian, but my dad is British. He ¹_____ the UK, and ²_____ here in 1985. He ³_____ a job in Sydney because he ⁴_____ some people there. He ⁵_____ my mom. They ⁶_____ married and ⁷_____ two children – my brother and me. They ⁸_____ a lot of things with us and ⁹_____ us to lots of beautiful places. We ¹⁰_____ from Sydney to Melbourne once, and another time from Sydney to Brisbane, in our old car!

150

◀ Go back to page 69

VOCABULARY PRACTICE

9A School subjects and education

1 ▶9.1 Match the school subjects in the box with pictures 1–15. Listen and check.

art   biology   chemistry   geography   history   IT (information technology)   literature   math (mathematics)
foreign languages   music   PE (physical education)   physics   science   social studies   technology

2 ▶9.2 Match the parts of the phrases. There are usually two or more possible matches. Listen and check.

1 pass
2 take
3 go to
4 do
5 get into
6 fail

a nursery school
b kindergarten
c elementary school
d middle school
e high school
f college
g an exam
h a test
i homework

3 Complete the definitions with words from exercises 1 and 2.
1 Very young children go to learn in these places. _____, _____
2 In this subject, you learn about the past. _____
3 In this subject, you read books and plays. _____
4 In this subject, you play different kinds of sports. _____
5 This verb means "get a bad result." _____
6 This is where you can study after you finish high school. _____
7 This verb means "get a good result." _____
8 In this subject, you learn about different animals and plants. _____
9 In this subject, you learn how to communicate with people in different countries. _____
10 Children go to learn in these places between the ages of 12 and 18. _____, _____

◀ Go back to page 76

151

VOCABULARY PRACTICE

9C Resolutions

1 ▶ 9.6 Write the phrases under the headings. Listen and check.

1 be (more) organized
2 buy (a car)
3 get (more) exercise
4 earn (more) money
5 get a (new) job
6 get in shape
7 have an interview
8 improve your diet
9 improve your relationship
10 join a gym
11 lose weight
12 make (new) friends
13 meet someone new
14 run a marathon
15 save (more) money

health
_____
_____
_____

money
_____
_____
_____

work and study
_____
_____
_____

relationships
_____
_____
_____

2 Choose the correct verbs to complete the sentences.

1 I want to *get / go* in shape this year.
2 My brother *improved / saved* a lot of money last year and bought a new house.
3 I want to *get / make* a new job this year because I don't like my job.
4 My boyfriend and I don't *make / get* much exercise. We're lazy!
5 If you want to *join / lose* weight, you need to get some exercise.
6 Kelly *is / does* very organized. She has a to-do list.
7 Do you know a good way to *see / make* new friends?
8 I don't *earn / do* much money. I want a new job!

3 Match the sentences.

1 I want to improve my relationship with my girlfriend.
2 I want to join a gym.
3 Last year, I decided to improve my diet.
4 I want to meet someone new this year.
5 I really don't like having interviews.

a I play soccer and I want to get in shape for that.
b I didn't have a boyfriend last year.
c I don't like answering questions about myself.
d I started eating a lot more fresh vegetables.
e I didn't spend much time with her last year.

10A Adjectives to describe places

1 ▶ 10.1 Match the adjectives with the correct pictures. Listen and check.

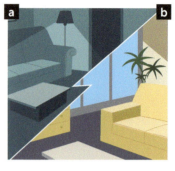

1 dark _____
2 light _____
3 empty _____
4 crowded _____

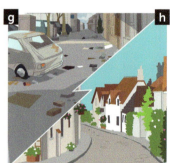

5 friendly _____
6 unfriendly _____
7 lovely _____
8 horrible _____

9 beautiful _____
10 ugly _____
11 safe _____
12 dangerous _____

2 Complete the sentences with adjectives from exercise 1.

1 Why is this restaurant _____? Perhaps the food's not good.
2 We love living in this area because it's _____ for the children to play outside.
3 People are _____ in small towns. They always say "hello."
4 I usually walk to work. There's a bus, but it's always _____ and you can't get a seat.
5 The outside of our apartment building is a bit _____, but it's not a problem. You can't see it when you're inside!
6 My bedroom is my favorite room. It has big windows, and it's really _____ all day.

◀ Go back to page 80

◀ Go back to page 84

VOCABULARY PRACTICE

10B Describing appearance

1 ▶ 10.6 Complete the diagrams with the words in the box. Listen and check.

| curly | earrings | elderly | light | gray | heavy | medium-length | mustache | slim | tall |

build
1 overweight/_____   2 thin/_____

height
3 short   4 _____

age
5 young   6 middle-aged   7 _____

hair color
8 blond/_____   9 black   10 dark   11 brown   12 red   13 white   14 _____

hair style
15 bald   16 straight   17 _____   18 wavy

hair on the face
19 beard   20 _____

hair length
21 long   22 short   23 _____

others
24 piercing   25 glasses   26 _____

2 Match pictures a–h with the descriptions.
1 This person is elderly. She has wavy gray hair. ____
2 This person has short brown hair. He doesn't have an earring. ____
3 This person is young. She has medium-length red hair. ____
4 This person has medium-length light hair. She wears glasses. ____
5 This person has short blond hair, a beard, and a moustache. He doesn't wear glasses. ____
6 This person is bald, with a white beard, and mustache. He wears glasses. ____
7 This person has black hair. She has black earrings. ____
8 This person is middle-aged. He has brown hair and an earring. ____

a    b    c    d

e    f    g    h

◀ Go back to page 86

VOCABULARY PRACTICE

10C Personality adjectives

1 ▶ 10.10 Match the adjectives in the box with pictures 1–12. Listen and check.

smart   confident   funny   generous   kind   popular   lazy   polite   brave   cheerful   shy   talkative

1 _____

2 _____

3 _____

4 _____

5 _____

6 _____

7 _____

8 _____

9 _____

10 _____

11 _____

12 _____

2 Choose the correct adjectives to complete the sentences.
1 My brother hates parties because he's really *generous / shy*.
2 Elvira is very *talkative / polite* in class. The teacher sometimes says, "Please be quiet for a moment, Elvira!"
3 Jürgen was really *smart / kind* to me after I failed my exam.
4 Sam is *confident / nice* when she speaks English. She always wants to practice.
5 I want to lose weight. I need to be a little less *lazy / brave* and get more exercise!
6 I think it's important to be *polite / funny*, so I always say "please" and "thank you."

3 Complete the sentences with words from exercise 1.
1 Alison is very _____. She always pays for my coffee.
2 Joe is so _____. He makes everyone laugh.
3 I wish I was _____ like my friend. He always gets good grades.
4 Most people are _____, although there are some horrible people.
5 You're so _____! Are you really going to do a bungee jump?
6 Belinda is always _____, even when things aren't going well for her.

◀ Go back to page 88

VOCABULARY PRACTICE

11A Travel and transportation

1 ▶ 11.1 Complete expressions 1–18 with the words in the box.

| bike boat bus (x2) car ferry foot helicopter motorcycle |
| plane scooter ship streetcar subway taxi train truck van |

 1 by _____
 2 by _____
 3 by _____
 4 by _____
 5 by _____
 6 by _____

 7 by _____
 8 on _____
 9 by _____
 10 by _____
 11 by _____
 12 by _____

 13 by _____
 14 by _____
 15 by _____
 16 by _____
 17 by _____
 18 by _____

2 Write the forms of transportation in the correct columns.

by water	by air	on land

3 Choose the correct phrases to complete the sentences.

1 I prefer to go to work *by bike* / *by bus*. The exercise wakes me up.
2 I'm scared of flying, so I wouldn't want to go *by helicopter* / *by motorcycle*.
3 I don't like to take the subway after midnight, so I usually go home *by ship* / *by taxi* if I'm out late.
4 A lot of people travel *by ferry* / *by motorcycle* in my city. It's quicker and easier than by car.
5 I love traveling *by car* / *by train*. You can walk around, if you want!
6 I go to college *by subway* / *by van*. I can't sightsee, but it's very quick.
7 I'm from France, but I live in Spain. I usually go home to visit my family *by bus* / *by truck*. It's sometimes slower, but it's cheaper than flying.
8 My town is next to a very wide river. There's no bridge, but you can go across the river *by streetcar* / *by ferry*.

◀ Go back to page 94

155

VOCABULARY PRACTICE

11C Vacation activities

1 ▶ 11.5 Match sentences 1–12 with pictures a–l.

1 They're going sightseeing. ____
2 She's going surfing. ____
3 They're going to the beach. ____
4 They're going to the mountains. ____
5 She's going hiking. ____
6 She's relaxing on the beach. ____
7 He's relaxing by the pool. ____
8 They're staying at a hotel. ____
9 She's staying at an apartment. ____
10 They're staying at a campsite. ____
11 She's staying with friends. ____
12 They're visiting a museum/an art gallery. ____

2 Read about the people. Then choose a vacation activity from the box for them.

a stay at an apartment	c go surfing	e stay at a campsite	g visit a museum/an art gallery
b go hiking	d relax by the pool	f go sightseeing	h stay at a hotel

1 Luís likes walking in different places, like mountains and forests. _____
2 Shelley and Phil like visiting cities, but they don't like staying at hotels. _____
3 Juan is very athletic, and he loves the ocean. _____
4 Hong likes art and history. _____
5 Maciek doesn't like doing housework like cooking and making the bed. He likes staying at very comfortable places. _____
6 Linus loves visiting cities. He always wants to see a lot of different places and take lots of photos. _____
7 Fabio has three new books to read. He loves hot weather, but he doesn't like the sea. _____
8 Mina and her family love the country. They like being outside, and they don't like hotels. _____

◀ Go back to page 98

VOCABULARY PRACTICE

12A Entertainment

1 ▶ 12.1 Match the people in the box with pictures 1–6 and the events with pictures 7–12. Listen and check.

| actor   artist   dancer   band/musician   opera singer   player |

| concert   game   opera   play   exhibit   ballet |

1 _____

2 _____

3 _____

7 _____

8 _____

9 _____

4 _____

5 _____

6 _____

10 _____

11 _____

12 _____

2 Complete the chart with words from exercise 1.

person/people	event
1 _____	exhibit
band	2 _____
3 _____	ballet
4 _____	game
actor	5 _____
opera singer	6 _____

3 Complete the sentences with words from exercise 1.
1 I love this _____'s work. She uses beautiful colors.
2 My friend's _____ are really good. They play rock music.
3 Do you like _____? Or do you prefer modern dance?
4 How many _____ are there on a soccer team?
5 What's your favorite Shakespeare _____?
6 There's an art _____ at City Hall.
7 Did you go to the jazz _____ on Friday night?
8 My cousin is an _____. He's been on TV a few times.

◀ Go back to page 102

12B Opinion adjectives

1 ▶ 12.6 Complete the chart with the adjectives in the box. Listen and check.

| awesome   awful   boring   amazing   exciting   interesting
all right   terrible   sad   strange   horrible   fun   fantastic
stupid   cool   great   scary |

Positive ☺	OK 😐	Negative ☹

2 Read the sentences and choose the adjective that's <u>not</u> possible.
1 This play is *terrible / cool / boring*. Can we go home now?
2 I don't like *sad / scary / exciting* movies. I prefer action movies.
3 I had an amazing time at the party last night. It was *all right / awesome / fun*.
4 New York is a really *interesting / exciting / scary* city. I'm going to go there again.
5 We had a nice vacation in Chile, but the weather was *awful / horrible / great*.
6 I don't think I like Pedro very much. He's a bit *fun / strange / scary*!
7 I went to hear a really *fantastic / awesome / terrible* singer on the weekend. She was amazing!
8 The movie was a bit *interesting / stupid / strange*. I didn't really like it.

◀ Go back to page 104

157

COMMUNICATION PRACTICE

1A Student A

1 You are Max. Listen and answer Student B's questions.

Name: Max Lundberg
Nationality: Canadian
Age: 41

2 This is Student B. Ask questions and complete the information.

What's your name? How do you spell it?
_____

Where are you from? _____

How old are you? _____

1C Student A

Look at the people and the possessions. Take turns asking and answering questions with Student B.
Find out who the following possessions belong to. You can only answer *Yes* or *No*.

Is it Eliza's pen? Are they the children's candies?

Sarah

the students

the children

Eliza

the Johnsons

Tom

Sadiq

the teacher

1D Student A

1 Look at the contacts. Ask Student B for the missing phone numbers and e-mail addresses. Ask for clarification if you don't understand.

   A *What's Emi's cell-phone number?*

2 Now listen and answer Student B's questions about the contacts.

Contact	Emi
Mobile	
Email	eesponisa_92@pbmail.com

Contact	Jeff
Mobile	1-917-555-6321
Email	

Contact	Liz
Mobile	
Email	liz.sharp87@pbmail.com

Contact	Ravi
Mobile	1-302-555-8930
Email	

COMMUNICATION PRACTICE

2A Student A

1 Listen to Student B and complete the descriptions.

Mark is a ¹_____. He ²_____ in a ³_____. He's from ⁴_____, but he ⁵_____ in Toronto. He ⁶_____ in the evening, and he ⁷_____ on the weekend.

Paula is a ⁸_____. She ⁹_____. She's from ¹⁰_____, but she ¹¹_____ in Manchester. She ¹²_____ in the evening, but she ¹³_____ on the weekend.

2 Now describe these people to your partner.

MAYER
Job: mechanic / fixes cars
Place of work: garage
From: Warsaw
Lives: Berlin
Works: evening ✘ weekend ✔

VIVIANA
Job: teacher / teaches English
Place of work: elementary school
From: Lisbon
Lives: Rio de Janeiro
Works: evening ✘ weekend ✘

2C Student A

1 You want a roommate who has a job, likes music, and cooks. Student B's friend, Jon, needs a room. Ask Student B questions. Is Jon a good roommate for you?

1 where / he / live?
2 what / he / do?
3 what / he / do / free time?
4 he / cook?
5 he / like / music?

2 Student B wants a roommate. Your friend, Helen, needs a room. Answer Student B's questions about Helen.

Helen lives with her mother. She works in an office. After work, she goes to the gym. She doesn't stay at home every night – she goes out a lot with her friends. She doesn't like cats.

bad   OK   good

3A Student A

1 How often does Flora do these things? Ask Student B.

A *How often does Flora go to the movies?*
B *She goes to the movies three times a month.*

2 Answer Student B's questions about Justin.

	Flora	Justin
1 go to the movies		never
2 cook in the evening		four times a week
3 play online games		every day
4 see his/her grandparents		often
5 go running		twice a week
6 listen to the radio		sometimes

3C Student A

Sophia and Sam are a couple. Ask Student B questions about Sam, and answer Student B's questions about Sophia. Find the following:

One thing that Sophia and Sam both love _____
One thing that Sophia and Sam both like _____
One thing that Sophia and Sam both hate _____

A *Does Sam like art?*   B *No. He hates it!*

Sophia

love ☺☺	like ☺	hate ☹☹
art	cook	jazz
walk the dog	soccer	go shopping
have a picnic	go out for dinner	watch TV
do yoga	read magazines	visit family

3D Student A

You want to meet Student B for coffee this weekend. You're free at the following times. Ask and answer questions to find a time when you're both free.

A *Would you like to go out for coffee at 10 o'clock on Saturday morning?*
B *I'm sorry, I can't.*

SATURDAY
Free time
10:00 a.m. – 11:30 a.m.
2:30 p.m. – 3:00 p.m.
6:30 p.m. – 8:30 p.m.
10:00 p.m. – 11:00 p.m.

SUNDAY
Free time
11:00 a.m. – 3:00 p.m.
4:45 p.m. – 6:00 p.m.

159

COMMUNICATION PRACTICE

4A Student A

1 Look at the pictures of Zak. Ask Student B questions about the missing information. Write the missing times or time expressions. Answer Student B's questions.

A *When does Zak wake up?*
B *He wakes up at ...*

1 _____

2 8:15

3 _____

4 noon

5 _____

6 midnight

7 _____

8 Friday nights

9 _____

10 weekend

11 _____

12 winter

2 Compare with Student B. Do you have the same times?

4C Student A

Take turns describing your picture to Student B and listen to Student B's description. Find six differences between your picture and Student B's picture. Say what the people are doing.

A *In my picture, Clare and John are eating.*

B *In my picture, they're not eating. They're ...*

COMMUNICATION PRACTICE

5A Student A

1 Look at the pictures. Describe Eric to Student B. Use the words in the boxes to help you.

| have   wear   go to work | by bike   toast   by bus   jeans and a shirt   a suit   eggs |

Eric usually … But today, he …

2 Listen to Student B's description. Complete the sentences about Emily.
   1 Emily usually has _____ for breakfast, but today she's having _____.
   2 She usually wears _____, but today she's wearing _____.
   3 She usually goes to work _____, but today she's going _____.

3 Check your pictures and sentences with Student B. Do the sentences describe the pictures correctly?

5C Student A

Ask Student B about Alisha and complete the chart. Answer Student B's questions about Artur.

   A *Can Alisha speak a foreign language?*
   B *Yes, she can. She can speak Italian.*

Can he/she …	Artur	Alisha
… speak a foreign language?	Yes (English and German)	
… dance?	No	
… play a musical instrument?	No	
… ride a horse?	No	
… take good photos?	Yes	
… cook?	Yes (Polish food)	
… fix things?	Yes (bikes)	

5D Student A

1 You are a customer in a department store. Student B is a salesclerk. Student B begins the conversation. Ask him/her these questions.

- Yes, please. Do you sell coats?
- How much is it?
- Do you have this coat in gray?
- Can I try it on?
- Can I pay with this credit card?
- Great. Thanks.

2 You are a salesclerk in a department store. Student B is a customer. Begin the conversation with him/her. Use these sentences.

- Do you need any help?
- Yes, we do. Here are some in a 28.
- We have them in black, blue, green, and gray.
- Yes, of course.
- They're near the shoes. I'll show you.
- I'm not sure. Let me ask someone. One moment. … They're 60 dollars.

COMMUNICATION PRACTICE

6A Student A

1 Look at the picture and the objects in the box. Ask Student B questions to find out where they are.

| mirror   pictures   books   ball |

A *Is there a mirror above the bed?*   B *No, there's not.*

2 Answer Student B's questions about his/her missing objects. You can only answer *yes* or *no*.

6C Student A

1 A Look at the information about three cities. Ask Student B for the missing information and write it in the chart.

A *Is the market in Blue City busy?*   B *Yes. It's very busy.*

B Answer Student B's questions.

Blue City	Yellowtown	Greenville
mosque – really beautiful ✔	beach – clean?	Old Town – really pretty ✔
market – busy?	restaurants – not very expensive ✘	cathedral – beautiful?
museum – really interesting ✔	local people – friendly?	Central Park – not very clean ✘
art gallery – good?	hotels – really nice ✔	river – clean?
food and drink – not expensive at all ✘	museum – interesting?	monuments – not very famous ✘

2 Decide which city you want to visit in pairs.

A *I want to go to Yellowtown because it has really nice hotels.*   B *Yes, but the beach isn't very clean.*

7A Student A

1 Look at the two recipes. Ask Student B if he/she has the food items. Which dish can you cook?

A *Do you have any eggs?*
B *Yes. I have six.*

Omelet
3 eggs
1 onion
potatoes
1 pepper
cheese

Stirfry
rice
2 peppers
2 carrots
2 onions
chicken

2 Look at the food in your kitchen. Answer Student B's questions.

B *Do you have any beef?*
A *Yes, I do.*

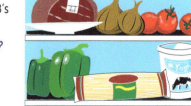

162

COMMUNICATION PRACTICE

7C Student A

1 Read about the Mediterranean diet. Ask Student B about the food items in the box and complete the sentences.

   A *Can you eat any cheese on the Mediterranean diet?*
   B *Yes, but you can't eat much.*

   | cheese | fish | lemons | onions | olive oil | pastries |
   | tomatoes | meat | eggs | oranges | candy | |

   ### THE MEDITERRANEAN DIET

   People who live near the Mediterranean Sea usually live for a long time and are healthy. If you want to try the Mediterranean diet, follow these rules:

   You can eat a lot of: _____.
   You can't eat much/many: _____.
   You can't eat any: _____.

2 Read about the Paleo diet. Look at the pictures and answer Student B's questions.

   B *Can you eat any bananas on the Paleo diet?*
   A *Yes, but you can't eat many.*

   ### THE PALEO DIET

   The Paleo diet is similar to what people ate 2.5 million years ago. You can only eat natural food. If you want to try the Paleo diet, follow these rules:

   You can eat a lot of:

   You can't eat much/many:

   You can't eat/drink any:

7D Student A

1 You are a waiter. Read each sentence to your partner and wait for his/her response. Read the next sentence. Sentences 1 and 2 are on the telephone.

   1 *Good afternoon, The Red Lion Restaurant. How can I help?*
   2 *For how many people?*
   3 *Hello. How can I help you?*
   4 *Are you ready to order?*
   5 *Would you like a starter?*
   6 *And what would you like for the main course?*
   7 *Would you like that with French fries or salad?*
   8 *Can I get you any drinks?*
   9 *Would you like anything for dessert?*

2 Now switch roles and repeat the activity. You are Student B. Go to page 172.

8A Student A

1 Read the facts for each decade to Student B. Don't say the decade! Ask him/her to guess the decade.

2 Now listen to Student B's facts. Try to guess the decade.

   Is it the nineteen eighties?
   Is it the two thousands?

GUESS THE DECADE!

In this decade ...
- people had black-and-white TVs.
- the Russians sent the first satellite into space.
- John Wayne, Frank Sinatra, and Marilyn Monroe were popular Hollywood stars.

Answer: the 1950s ("nineteen fifties")

In this decade ...
- the Summer Olympics were in China.
- some countries in Europe had a new type of money.
- a lot of people bought a GPS.

Answer: the 2000s ("two thousands")

8C Student A

1 Look at the information in the chart. Take turns telling Student B facts about the people, using the simple past. Listen and complete the chart with Student B's information.

   A *Paulo was born in Recife, in Brazil.*

2 Compare your information with Student B. Is it the same?

	Paulo	Emma	Daria
be born in	Recife, in Brazil		St. Petersburg, in Russia
want to be / when he/she / be / a child		a pilot	
study / in college	French		medicine
travel to		Peru in 2015	
cook / for dinner last night	lasagna		steak
play		chess on the weekend	

163

COMMUNICATION PRACTICE

9A Student A

Ask Student B simple past questions to complete the text about Fabia's elementary school. Answer Student B's questions.

A *Where was Fabia's school?*
B *It was one mile from her house.*

Finland has one of the best education systems in the world. Read about Fabia's time in elementary school.

I didn't go to nursery school or kindergarten. I started elementary school when I was seven years old. My school was ¹_____ (where?). I went to school by bus every day.
I ² _____ school (did / enjoy?)! Classes started at nine o'clock in the morning. There were fifteen students in my class, and I always sat next to
³ _____ (who?). My teacher's name was Johannes, and he was our teacher for six years. My favorite subjects were ⁴ _____ (what?), and I still love learning foreign languages now. I hated math, and I was bad at
⁵ _____ (what subjects?).

9C Student A

Take turns reading the sentences with Student B. Student B finishes your sentences and you finish Student B's sentences.

	Your sentences	Student B's sentences
1	Jenna is studying Spanish. She's planning …	… to save some money every month.
2	Saul wants to be a doctor. He needs …	… to spend some time in the U.S. to improve it.
3	Carlotta eats a lot of junk food. She wants …	… to improve their relationship.
4	Hans wants to lose weight. He'd like …	… to do a course in Asian cooking.
5	Brigit doesn't like her job. She's hoping …	… to learn to write computer programs.
6	Sasha moved to a new city recently. She'd like …	… to get in shape this year.

9D Student A

1 Read your problems to Student B. Listen to his/her suggestion(s) and respond.

A *I left my backpack on the bus this morning!*
B *How terrible! Can you call the Lost and Found?*
A *That's a good idea.*

- I left my backpack on the bus this morning!
- I have an exam tomorrow, but I don't know the subject very well.
- I can't study at home because it's always noisy.
- My roommate never cleans the kitchen.
- My laptop stopped working last night!

2 Listen to Student B's problems. Sound sympathetic and make suggestions to him/her from the list below.

B *My boss lives in New York, and she only visits us once a year.*
A *I'm sure it's difficult to be so far away from her. How about asking her to visit twice a year?*
B *I'm not sure I should. She's very busy.*

- take some time off work and visit her
- watch less television in the evening
- ask your boss to visit twice a year
- get more practice and take it again
- turn your phone off

COMMUNICATION PRACTICE

10A Student A

1 You want to reserve a hotel for your vacation. You have two young children. Ask Student B questions to find out about the two hotels. Which one is better?

A *Which hotel is nearer the beach?*
B *The Apex Hotel is nearer the beach.*

You're looking for a hotel that is:

	APEX HOTEL	SEA VIEW HOTEL
near the beach	☐	☐
quiet	☐	☐
small	☐	☐
friendly	☐	☐
clean	☐	☐
safe	☐	☐
less expensive	☐	☐

2 You are a travel agent. Answer Student B's questions about the two hotels.

	Sunset Hotel	Party Hotel
Price	$$$	$
Beach	100 meters	600 meters
Clubs	300 meters	10 meters
Stores	50 meters	1 kilometer
Number of rooms	60	200
Comments	modern hotel (2015) uncomfortable beds cheap food	old hotel (1970) comfortable beds expensive food

10C Student A

Take turns asking and answer the trivia questions with Student B. You have different questions. Complete the questions with the superlative of the adjectives in parentheses. Score 1 point for each correct answer. Who can score the most points? The correct answers are in **red**. Tell Student B the extra information about the correct answers.

A *What is the cleanest city in the world? a) Calgary in Canada, b) Tokyo in Japan, or c) Florence in Italy?*

GENERAL KNOWLEDGE TRIVIA

1 What is _____ (clean) city in the world?   **a)** **Calgary in Canada**   **b)** Tokyo in Japan   **c)** Florence in Italy
In a 2016 survey, Calgary in Canada was the winner of "The Cleanest City" award.

2 Who was _____ (popular) person on Facebook in 2016?   **a)** Daniel Radcliffe   **b)** **Cristiano Ronaldo**   **c)** Meryl Streep
In 2016, Cristiano Ronaldo had more than 107 million "Likes" on Facebook.

3 How long was _____ (long) pizza in the world?   **a)** 800 meters   **b)** **1.8 kilometers**   **c)** 80 meters
In 2016, 250 pizza chefs made a pizza that was 1.8 kilometers long in Naples, Italy. They used 2,000 kilograms of mozzarella cheese.

4 What soccer team has _____ (noisy) fans in the world?   **a)** Arsenal in England   **b)** Colo Colo in Chile   **c)** **Galatasaray in Turkey**
The noise of Galatasaray fans at their stadium in Istanbul can reach 130 decibels – that's louder than a jet airplane when it takes off!

5 What is _____ (high) capital city in the world?   **a)** **La Paz in Bolivia**   **b)** Addis Ababa in Ethiopia   **c)** Kathmandu in Nepal
La Paz in Bolivia is 3,640 meters above sea level. For tourists, it can be hard to breathe, walk, and sleep.

11A Student A

1 Ask Student B questions about John's job, using *have to*. Complete the chart with *yes* or *no*. Then guess what John's job is.

A *Does John have to wear a uniform at work?*
B *No, he doesn't.*

2 Now answer Student B's questions about Tiffany. You can only say *yes* or *no*.

	JOHN	TIFFANY
		Tiffany is a flight attendant.
1 wear a uniform?		Yes
2 drive at work?		No
3 work at night sometimes?		Yes
4 travel to other countries?		Yes
5 help people?		Yes
6 be in shape?		Yes
7 work alone?		No
8 speak to a lot of people?		Yes

165

COMMUNICATION PRACTICE

11C Student A

1 Ask Student B about his/her vacation plans and complete the chart. Use *be going to*.

A *Where are you going to go?*
B *I'm going to go to Lima in Peru.*

2 Now answer Student B's questions about your vacation plans. Use the information in the chart.

		You	Student B
1	Where / go?	Crete, Greece	
2	When / go?	June 10th	
3	Who / go with?	my family	
4	How / travel?	boat	
5	Where / stay?	apartment	
6	What / do?	relax by the pool go to the beach play tennis go surfing	
7	When / return?	June 24th	

11D Student A

1 You are Karol. You are checking in at the Sea View Hotel. Tell the receptionist about your reservation, answer his/her questions, and ask for the missing information. Check anything that you aren't sure about.

Your name	Karol Lisicki
Type of room	Deluxe room
Number of nights	2
Discount?	?
Breakfast included?	?
WiFi password	?
Room number and floor	?

B *Welcome to the Sea View Hotel. Checking in?*
A *Yes. I reserved a room in the name of ...*

2 You are the receptionist at the Castle Hotel. Greet the guest, ask for his/her reservation information, and give him/her the information he/she asks for.

Guest name	?
Type of room	?
Number of nights	?
Discount?	NO
Breakfast included?	YES
WiFi password	THECASTLE99
Room number and floor	357, third floor

12A Student A

1 Ask and answer questions with Student B about the people in the chart. Use the present perfect + *ever*.

A *Has Henry ever been to a music festival?*   B *Yes, he has.*

	Nadia	Henry	Elena	Oliver
go to a music festival	✗			✔
watch a basketball game		✗	✔	
see the Mona Lisa in Paris			✔	✗
travel to another continent	✔	✗		
climb a mountain		✗	✗	
study a foreign language	✗			✗
dance all night			✔	✗
sing in a band	✔	✗		

2 Now imagine that you work for a dating agency. Work with Student B. Which two of the four people have the most similar interests?

12C Student A

1 Ask Student B questions with the prompts. Use the present perfect + *ever* for question "a," and the simple past for question "b." Then decide if you think his/her answer is true.

A *Have you ever met a famous person?*
B *Yes, I have.*
A *Who did you meet?*
B *I met Penélope Cruz.*
A *I think that's true.*
B *No, it's not true!*

a you / meet a famous person?
a you / win / a competition?
a you / buy / flowers for someone?
a you / be / the U.S.?
a you / see / the same movie several times?
a you / eat / sushi?

b Who / you / meet?
b What / you / win?
b Who / you / buy them for?
b Which cities / you / visit?
b Which movie / be / it?
b What / you think of it?

2 Now answer Student B's questions. For question "a," answer *Yes, I have*. Invent information for each question "b," if necessary.

COMMUNICATION PRACTICE

1A Student B

1 This is Student A. Ask questions and complete the information.

What's your name? How do you spell it?
_____

Where are you from? _____

How old are you? _____

2 You are Li. Listen and answer Student A's questions.

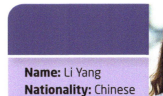

Name: Li Yang
Nationality: Chinese
Age: 24

1C Student B

Look at the people and the possessions. Take turns asking and answering questions with Student A.
Find out who the following possessions belong to. You can only answer *Yes* or *No*.

Is it Tom's phone? Is it the Johnsons' umbrella?

Sarah

the students

the children

Eliza

the Johnsons

Tom

Sadiq

the teacher

1D Student B

1 Look at the contacts. Listen and answer Student A's questions.

2 Now ask Student A for the missing phone numbers and e-mail addresses. Ask for clarification if you don't understand.

   B *What's Emi's e-mail address?*

Contact	Emi
Mobile	0034666063267
Email	

Contact	Jeff
Mobile	
Email	jeffreyjones@pbmail.com

Contact	Liz
Mobile	1-310-555-8274
Email	

Contact	Ravi
Mobile	
Email	r.d.g.freelance@pbmail.com

COMMUNICATION PRACTICE

2A Student B

1 Describe these people to your partner.

MARK
Job: nurse / in a hospital
From: Chicago
Lives: Toronto
Works: evening ✔ weekend ✔

PAULA
Job: chef / cooks Japanese food
From: Sydney
Lives: Manchester
Works: evening ✘ weekend ✔

2 Now listen to Student A and complete the descriptions.

Mayer is a ¹_____. He ²_____ in a ³_____. He's from ⁴_____, but he ⁵_____ in Berlin. He ⁶_____ in the evening, but he ⁷_____ on the weekend.

Viviana is a ⁸_____. She ⁹_____ in a ¹⁰_____. She's from ¹¹_____, but she ¹²_____ in Rio de Janeiro. She ¹³_____ in the evening, and she ¹⁴_____ on the weekend.

2C Student B

1 Student A wants a roommate. Your friend, Jon, needs a room. Answer Student A's questions about Jon.

> Jon lives with his parents. He's a student. In his free time, he plays the guitar. He doesn't cook. He has a girlfriend. He loves music.

2 You want a roommate who has a job, doesn't stay home every night, and likes cats (you have one). Student A's friend, Helen, needs a room. Ask Student A questions. Is Helen a good roommate for you?

1 where / she / live ?
2 what / she / do ?
3 what / she / do / after work ?
4 she / stay home / every night ?
5 she / like / cats ?

bad   OK   good

3A Student B

1 Answer Student A's questions about Flora.

A *How often does Flora go to the movies?*
B *She goes to the movies three times a month.*

2 How often does Justin do these things? Ask Student A.

		Flora	Justin
1	go to the movies	three times a month	
2	cook in the evening	rarely	
3	play online games	never	
4	see his/her grandparents	every day	
5	go running	once a week	
6	listen to the radio	often	

3C Student B

Sophia and Sam are a couple. Ask Student A questions about Sophia, and answer Student A's questions about Sam. Find the following:

One thing that Sophia and Sam both love _____
One thing that Sophia and Sam both like _____
One thing that Sophia and Sam both hate _____

B *Does Sophia like doing yoga?*
A *Yes. She loves it!*

Sam

love ☺☺	like ☺	hate ☹
jazz	soccer	cook
go out for dinner	have a picnic	go shopping
walk the dog	watch TV	art
visit family	do yoga	read magazines

3D Student B

You want to meet Student A to go running this weekend. You're free at the following times. Ask and answer questions to find a time when you're both free.

B *Would you like to go running at 8:45 on Saturday morning?*
A *I'm sorry, I can't.*

SATURDAY
Free time
8:30 a.m. – 10:00 a.m.
1:30 p.m. – 2:30 p.m.
5:30 p.m. – 6:30 p.m.

SUNDAY
Free time
12:00 p.m. – 4:00 p.m.
7:30 p.m. – 9:30 p.m.

COMMUNICATION PRACTICE

4A Student B

1 Look at the pictures of Zak. Ask Student A questions about the missing information. Write the missing times or time expressions. Answer Student A's questions.

B *When does Zak walk the dog?*
A *He walks the dog at ...*

1 7:25

2 _____

3 9:00 – 5:30

4 _____

5 22:00 – 23:45

6 _____

7 Wednesday evenings

8 _____

9 Saturday mornings

10 _____

11 summer

12 _____

2 Compare with Student A. Do you have the same times?

4C Student B

1 Take turns describing your picture to Student A and listen to Student A's description. Find six differences between your picture and Student A's picture. Say what the people are doing.

A *In my picture, Clare and John are eating.*
B *In my picture, they're not eating. They're ...*

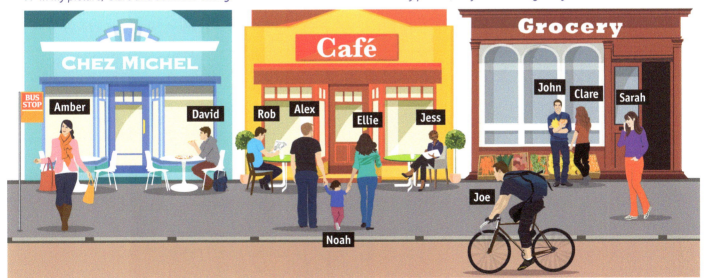

169

COMMUNICATION PRACTICE

5A Student B

1 Listen to Student A's description. Complete the sentences about Eric.
   1 Eric usually has _____ for breakfast, but today he's having _____.
   2 He usually wears _____, but today he's wearing _____.
   3 He usually goes to work _____, but today he's going _____.

2 Look at the pictures. Describe Emily to Student A. Use the words in the boxes to help you.

| have   wear   go to work | pants and a sweater   coffee   a skirt and a blouse   by subway   by car   tea |

Emily usually ...   But today, she ...

3 Check your pictures and sentences with Student A. Do the sentences describe the pictures correctly?

5C Student B

1 Ask Student A about Artur and complete the chart. Answer Student A's questions about Alisha.

   B *Can Artur play a musical instrument?*
   A *No, he can't.*

Can he/she ...	Artur	Alisha
... speak a foreign language?		Yes (Italian)
... dance?		Yes (the Tango)
... play a musical instrument?		Yes (the drums)
... ride a horse?		No
... take good photos?		No
... cook?		Yes (Italian food)
... fix things?		Yes (computers)

5D Student B

1 You are a salesclerk in a department store. Student A is a customer. Begin the conversation with him/her. Use these sentences.

- Yes, we do. I'll show you where they are.
- It's 75 dollars.
- Just a moment, I'll check. Yes. Here you are.
- Yes, we take all credit cards.
- Hello. Can I help you?
- Yes, of course. The dressing rooms are over there.

2 You are a customer in a department store. Student A is a salesclerk. Student A begins the conversation. Ask him/her these questions.

- And what colors are there?
- Great. Thanks.
- Yes, please. Do you have these pants in a size 28?
- Thanks. Can I try them on?
- Thanks. How much are they?
- Where are the dressing rooms?

COMMUNICATION PRACTICE

6A Student B

1 Look at the picture and answer Student A's questions about his/her missing objects. You can only answer *yes* or *no*.

A *Is there a mirror above the bed?*   B *No, there's not.*

2 Look at the objects in the box. Ask Student A questions to find out where they are.

shoes   clock   shelves   lamp

6C Student B

1 A Look at the information about three cities. Answer Student A's questions..

B Ask Student A for the missing information and write it in the chart.

B *Is the mosque in Blue City beautiful?*   A *Yes. It's really beautiful.*

Blue City	Yellowtown	Greenville
mosque – beautiful?	beach – not very clean ✗	Old Town – pretty?
market – very busy ✓	restaurants – expensive?	cathedral – really beautiful ✓
museum – interesting?	local people – really friendly ✓	Central Park – clean?
art gallery – not very good ✗	hotels – nice?	river – really clean ✓
food and drinks – expensive?	museum – not interesting at all ✗	monuments – famous?

2 Decide which city you want to visit in pairs.

A *I want to go to Yellowtown because it has really nice hotels.*   B *Yes, but the beach isn't very clean.*

7A Student B

1 Look at the food in your kitchen. Answer Student A's questions.

A *Do you have any eggs?*
B *Yes. I have six.*

2 Look at the two recipes. Ask Student A if he/she has the food items. Which dish can you cook?

B *Do you have any beef?*
A *Yes, I do.*

Kebab
beef
1 onion
bread
yogurt
2 peppers

Spaghetti Bolognese
beef
1 onion
3 tomatoes
spaghetti
1 pepper

171

COMMUNICATION PRACTICE

7C Student B

1 Read about the Mediterranean diet. Look at the pictures and answer Student A's questions.

A *Can you eat any cheese on the Mediterranean diet?*
B *Yes, but you can't eat much.*

THE MEDITERRANEAN DIET

People who live near the Mediterranean Sea usually live for a long time and are healthy. If you want to try the Mediterranean diet, follow these rules:

You can eat a lot of:

You can't eat much/many:

You can't eat any:

2 Read about the Paleo diet. Ask Student A about the food items in the box and complete the sentences.

B *Can you eat any bananas on the Paleo diet?*
A *Yes, but you can't eat many.*

| bananas apples milk nuts fish meat |
| bread eggs potatoes coffee cheese |

THE PALEO DIET

The Paleo diet is similar to what people ate 2.5 million years ago. You can only eat natural food. If you want to try the Paleo diet, follow these rules:

You can eat/drink a lot of: _____.

You can't eat/drink much/many: _____.

You can't eat/drink any: _____.

7D Student B

1 You are a restaurant customer. Listen to your partner. Choose a sentence and answer.

1 It's for six people.
2 Yes. Can I have the chicken soup, please?
3 Yes. Could I have some seltzer, please?
4 With French fries, please.
5 I'd like to reserve a table for Wednesday evening, please.
6 Hello. We have a table reserved in the name of Cox.
7 I'd like the steak, please.
8 No, thank you. Could we have the check, please?
9 Yes, we are.

2 Now switch roles and repeat the activity. You are Student A. Go to page 163.

8A Student B

1 Listen to Student A's facts. Try to guess the decade.

Is it the nineteen sixties?
Is it the nineteen thirties?

2 Now read the facts for each decade to Student A. Don't say the decade! Ask him/her to guess the decade.

GUESS THE DECADE!

In this decade ...
- Space Invaders and Pac-Man were popular video games.
- people first bought cell phones in stores.
- the UK had its first female Prime Minister.

Answer: the 1980s ("nineteen eighties")

In this decade ...
- the first Winter Olympics were in France.
- jazz music was popular.
- there was a new country – the USSR.

Answer: the 1920s ("nineteen twenties")

8C Student B

1 Look at the information in the chart. Take turns telling Student A facts about the people, using the simple past. Listen and complete the chart with Student A's information.

B *Emma was born in Austin, in the U.S.*

2 Compare your information with Student A. Is it the same?

	Paulo	Emma	Daria
be born in		Austin, in the U.S.	
want to be / when he/she / be / a child	a chef		a doctor
study / in college		history	
travel to	China in 2007		Canada in 1998
cook / for dinner last night		spaghetti	
play	golf on the weekend		volleyball yesterday afternoon

172

COMMUNICATION PRACTICE

9A Student B

Ask Student A simple past questions to complete the text about Fabia's elementary school. Answer Student A's questions.

B *Did Fabia go to nursery school and kindergarten?*
A *No, she didn't.*

Finland has one of the best education systems in the world. Read about Fabia's time in elementary school.

I ¹_____ (did / go?) to nursery school or kindergarten. I started elementary school when I was seven years old. My school was one mile from my house. I went to school ²_____ (how?) every day. I really enjoyed school! Classes started at ³_____ (what time?). There were fifteen students in my class, and I always sat next to my best friend, Emma. My teacher's name was ⁴_____ (what?), and he was our teacher for six years. My favorite subjects were English and Swedish, and I still love learning foreign languages now. I hated ⁵_____ (what subject?), and I was bad at art and music.

9C Student B

Take turns reading the sentences with Student A. Student A finishes your sentences and you finish Student A's sentences.

	Your sentences	Student A's sentences
1	Kyle and his girlfriend argue a lot. They need ...	... to improve her diet.
2	Christa is joining a gym. She's hoping ...	... to travel through South America.
3	Mahmood is interested in IT. He'd like ...	... to start running.
4	Eleni's English isn't very good. She's planning ...	... to make some new friends.
5	Nathan loves Thai food. He wants ...	... to get a new job soon.
6	Claire wants to buy a new car. She's hoping ...	... to get a place to study medicine in college.

9D Student B

1 Listen to Student A's problems. Sound sympathetic and make suggestions for him/her from the list below.

A *I left my backpack on the bus this morning!*
B *How terrible! Can you call the Lost and Found?*
A *That's a good idea.*

- go to the library
- take it to the repair shop
- call the Lost and Found
- watch some online videos about your subject
- talk to him/her about it

2 Read your problems to Student A. Listen to his/her suggestion(s) and respond.

B *My boss lives in New York, and she only visits us once a year.*
A *I'm sure it's difficult to be so far away from her. How about asking her to visit twice a year?*
B *I'm not sure I should. She's very busy.*

- My boss lives in New York, and she only visits us once a year.
- I failed my driving test yesterday.
- My mother's in the hospital, but I'm very busy at work.
- My friends call me in the evening when I want to study.
- I often don't have time to do my homework in the evening.

173

COMMUNICATION PRACTICE

10A Student B

1 You are a travel agent. Answer Student A's questions about the two hotels.

  A *Which hotel is nearer the beach?*
  B *The Apex Hotel is nearer the beach.*

	Apex Hotel	Sea View Hotel
Price	$$	$$$
Beach	200 meters	500 meters
Clubs	30 meters	1 kilometer
Stores	100 meters	2 kilometers
Number of rooms	80	20
Comments	friendly staff dirty rooms on a busy street	unfriendly staff clean rooms safe, quiet location

2 You want to reserve a hotel for your vacation. You're going on vacation with a big group of friends. Ask Student A questions to find out about the two hotels. Which one is better?

You're looking for a hotel that is:

	SUNSET HOTEL	PARTY HOTEL
near the beach	☐	☐
near the clubs	☐	☐
good for shopping	☐	☐
big	☐	☐
modern	☐	☐
comfortable	☐	☐
cheap	☐	☐

10C Student B

Take turns asking and answering the trivia questions with Student A. You both have different questions. Complete the questions with the superlative of the adjectives in parentheses. Score 1 point for each correct answer. Who can score the most points? The correct answers are in **red**. Tell Student A the extra information about the correct answers.

  A *What is the happiest country in the world? a) Brazil, b) Australia or c) Denmark?*

GENERAL KNOWLEDGE TRIVIA

1 According to a UN report, what is _____ (happy) country in the world?   **a)** Brazil   **b)** Australia   **c)** *Denmark*
  With a population of 5.6 million, Denmark reached Number 1 in the "World Happiness Report" in 2016.

2 Which was _____ (expensive) film of these three?   **a)** *Pirates of the Caribbean 4*   **b)** *Titanic*   **c)** *Jurassic World*
  Pirates of the Caribbean 4 cost $378.5 million in 2011. It didn't get good reviews, but it earned more than $1 billion.

3 How big is _____ (big) spider in the world?   **a)** *30 centimeters wide*   **b)** 1 meter wide   **c)** 10 centimeters wide
  The Goliath Birdeater tarantula lives in the rainforests of South America and is the size of a dinner plate!

4 Which is _____ (cheap) car in the world?   **a)** Lamborghini Aventador   **b)** *Tata Nano*   **c)** Volkswagen Golf
  The Tata Nano is made in India. It cost $2,000 in 2009.

5 How tall was _____ (tall) man in the world?   **a)** 3.24 meters   **b)** 2.43 meters   **c)** *2.72 meters*
  Robert Wadlow was born in 1918 in the U.S. In 1940, he was 2.72 meters tall.

11A Student B

1 Answer Student A's questions about John's job. You can only say *yes* or *no*.

  A *Does John have to wear a uniform at work?*
  B *No, he doesn't.*

2 Now ask Student A questions about Tiffany's job, using *have to*. Complete the chart with *yes* or *no*. Then guess what Tiffany's job is.

	JOHN	TIFFANY
	John is a truck driver.	
1 wear a uniform?	No	
2 drive at work?	Yes	
3 work at night sometimes?	Yes	
4 travel to other countries?	Yes	
5 help people?	No	
6 be in shape?	No	
7 work alone?	Yes	
8 speak to a lot of people?	No	

COMMUNICATION PRACTICE

11C Student B

1 Answer Student A's questions about your vacation plans. Use the information in the chart.

  A *Where are you going to go?*
  B *I'm going to go to Lima in Peru.*

2 Now ask Student A about his/her vacation plans and complete the chart. Use *be going to*.

		Student A	You
1	Where / go?		Lima, Peru
2	When / go?		January 16th
3	Who / go with?		my partner
4	How / travel?		plane
5	Where / stay?		hotel
6	What / do?		try local food
			visit the museums
			go shopping
			watch a soccer game
7	When / return?		January 30th

11D Student B

1 You are the receptionist at the Sea View Hotel. Greet the guest, ask for his/her reservation information, and give him/her the information he/she asks for.

Guest name	?
Type of room	?
Number of nights	?
Discount?	YES
Breakfast included?	NO
WiFi password	seaviewhotel2000
Room number and floor	105, first floor

  B *Welcome to the Sea View Hotel. Checking in?*
  A *Yes. I reserved a room in the name of ...*

2 You are Wendy. You are checking in at the Castle Hotel. Tell the receptionist about your reservation, answer his/her questions, and ask for the missing information. Check anything that you're not sure about.

Your name	Wendy Zhao
Type of room	Standard room
Number of nights	3
Discount?	?
Breakfast included?	?
WiFi password	?
Room number and floor	?

12A Student B

1 Ask and answer questions with Student A about the people in the chart. Use the present perfect + *ever*.

  B *Has Nadia ever been to a music festival?* A *No, she hasn't.*

	Nadia	Henry	Elena	Oliver
go to a music festival		✔	✘	
watch a basketball game	✔			✔
see the Mona Lisa in Paris	✘	✔		
travel to another continent			✘	✔
climb a mountain	✔			✔
study a foreign language		✔	✔	
dance all night	✔	✔		
sing in a band			✘	✔

2 Now imagine that you work for a dating agency. Work with Student A. Which two of the four people have the most similar interests?

12C Student B

1 Answer Student A's questions. For question "**a**," answer *Yes, I have*. Invent information for each question "**b**" if necessary.

2 Now ask Student A questions with the prompts. Use the present perfect + *ever* for question "**a**," and the simple past for question "**b**." Then decide if you think his/her answer is true.

  A *Have you ever lost something important?*
  B *Yes, I have.*
  A *What did you lose?*
  B *I lost my credit card.*
  A *I think that's true.*
  B *No, it's not true!*

  a you / lost something important? b What / you / lose?
  a you / fly / in a helicopter? b Where / you / go?
  a you / see / a lion? b Where / you / see it?
  a you / go / the UK? b Which cities / you / visit?
  a you / read / the same book several times? b Which book / be / it?
  a you / eat / curry? b What / you think of it?

175

IRREGULAR VERBS

Infinitive	Past simple	Past participle	Infinitive	Past simple	Past participle
be	was, were	been	meet	met	met
become	became	become	pay	paid	paid
begin	began	begun	put	put	put
bite	bit	bitten	read (/riːd/)	read (/red/)	read (/red/)
break	broke	broken	ride	rode	ridden
bring	brought	brought	ring	rang	rung
build	built	built	rise	rose	risen
buy	bought	bought	run	ran	run
choose	chose	chosen	say	said	said
come	came	come	see	saw	seen
cost	cost	cost	sell	sold	sold
do	did	done	send	sent	sent
forbid	forbade	forbidden	sleep	slept	slept
forget	forgot	forgotten	speak	spoke	spoken
forgive	forgave	forgiven	spend	spent	spent
get	got	gotten	stand	stood	stood
give	gave	given	steal	stole	stolen
go	went	gone	stick	stuck	stuck
grow	grew	grown	swim	swam	swum
have	had	had	take	took	taken
hear	heard	heard	teach	taught	taught
hide	hid	hidden	tell	told	told
hold	held	held	think	thought	thought
keep	kept	kept	throw	threw	thrown
know	knew	known	understand	understood	understood
leave	left	left	wake	woke	woken
let	let	let	wear	wore	worn
lose	lost	lost	win	won	won
make	made	made	write	wrote	written